SOURCEBOOK
FOR
RESEARCH
IN
MUSIC

SOURCEBOOK
FOR
RESEARCH
IN
MUSIC

PHILLIP D. CRABTREE
AND
DONALD H. FOSTER

INDIANA UNIVERSITY PRESS
BLOOMINGTON & INDIANAPOLIS

The paper used in this publication meets the minimum requirements of American National Standard for Information Sciences—Permanence of Paper for Printed Library Materials, ANSI Z39.48-1984.

⊚ ™

Manufactured in the United States of America

Library of Congress Cataloging-in-Publication Data

Crabtree, Phillip.
    Sourcebook for research in music / Phillip D. Crabtree and Donald H. Foster.
       p. cm.
    Includes indexes.
    ISBN 0-253-31476-3 (cloth : alk. paper)
    1. Music—Bibliography. 2. Music—History and criticism—Bibliography 3. Bibliography—Bibliography—Music. I. Foster, Donald H. II. Title. III. Title: Source book for research in music.
  ML113.C68   1993
  016.7—dc20   92-32038

1 2 3 4 5 97 96 95 94 93

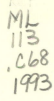

ML
113
.C68
1993

Contents

Preface

This book is intended as an introductory reference source of varied information, largely bibliographical, pertaining to research in the field of music. It has come largely out of the authors' years of experience in teaching Introduction to Graduate Study and Senior Research, two courses in music bibliography, research, and writing at the College-Conservatory of Music, University of Cincinnati, and it may function as a text in such courses, as well as in any music research class or seminar, graduate or upper-class undergraduate. If so used, it is not necessarily meant to be followed page by page from beginning to end, but adapted in accordance with the needs and emphases of different instructors and schools or individuals using the book. Its use is by no means limited to the classroom; it may also serve as a guide to current important sources in music for music researchers, faculty members, librarians, performing and teaching musicians, and musical amateurs.

The *Sourcebook for Research in Music* consists of seven chapters of bibliographies, each of a different type of source, preceded by a chapter of introductory materials regarding research in music. The bibliographies are usually divided into subcategories in order to avoid the confusion of long, undifferentiated lists of variously related items. The organization of the book is evident in the detailed table of contents, with all of the subheadings included, which should facilitate fairly rapid access to particular categories or types of sources. Furthermore, there are collective annotations throughout the book that introduce and identify specific items within the bibliographies they precede, often singling out sources of particular importance or distinguishing between different ones; where appropriate, cross references are made to items appearing elsewhere in the book. Finally, there are two indexes: the first of authors, editors, compilers, and translators; the second of titles of books, articles, and series.

The past decade or so has witnessed an extraordinary expansion of the materials of music, and the field is growing ever more rapidly. It has become a herculean task to try to keep up with the many effort-saving sources that are constantly becoming available. Thus, in the interest of practicality and usefulness, emphasis has been placed on the more recent and up-to-date ones rather than on those of more purely historical or musicological interest, and on English-language sources rather than on those in foreign languages. Certain major early sources have occasionally been included, usually under the heading "Of Historical Interest," and some of the bibliographies include more recent sources in other languages as well, chiefly German and French, when considered to be of particular importance. (Brief lists of bibliographical terms in these languages have been provided in chapter 1 to assist further in confronting such sources.) Some of the bibliographies—in particular the "Basic Bibliographical Tools for Research in Music" in chapter 2—are meant to provide the means of direct access to materials of research; others emphasize the basic or current representative sources of significance. In other words, in the bibliographies and other materials that follow, the guiding principle, to one extent or another, is selectivity rather than comprehensiveness, as detailed in the chapter introductions and collective annotations throughout.

We have not tried to cover every conceivable area in which research might be conducted in music. For exhaustive lists of sources in areas such as, for example, the literature of specific instruments and performing ensembles, the music of individual countries throughout the world, popular music, and folk music, the reader should consult Vincent H. Duckles and Michael A. Keller, *Music Reference and Research Materials: An Annotated Bibliography*, 4th ed., rev.; and Guy A. Marco, ed., *Information on Music: A Handbook of Reference Sources in European Languages* (both listed on p. 32 below).

Three sources, *The New Grove Dictionary of Music and Musicians*, *The New Harvard Dictionary of Music*, and, to a lesser extent, *Die Musik in Geschichte und Gegenwart*, are cited fairly often throughout these pages, so they are given in abbreviated form whenever they occur (full citations appear in chapter 4 below on pp. 93, 97, and 92 respectively).

The stylistic and bibliographical format followed throughout is the one specified in Kate L. Turabian's *A Manual for Writers of Term Papers, Theses, and Dissertations*, 5th ed. (listed on p. 192 below). We have made a few adaptations, the most important of which are: (1) In the case of sources in second or later editions, or of translations of sources published earlier, the date of the original edition is also given (e.g., "First published in 1963"). (2) In the interest of simplicity, information about reprint and microform editions is usually omitted, the main exceptions being those instances in which something new has been added in the reprint, such as a list of corrections or a new preface. (3) Normally, when more than one city and/ or publishing firm is listed in a source, only one of each is cited here, the city usually being the one where the principal headquarters is located. (4) Ordinarily, complicated or frequently changing publication information in serial publications, e.g., in the case of sets and monuments of music, has been abbreviated. For complete publication data related to music editions, see Hill and Stephens' recent *Collected Editions, Historical Series and Sets, and Monuments of Music: A Bibliography* (listed on p. 41 below).

We wish to extend our thanks to the following persons whose expertise and assistance have helped in various ways in the preparation of this book: Charles Benner, J. Bunker Clark, Carl Dahlgren, Karen Faaborg, Warren George, Lewis B. Hilton, Roland Jackson, David Lasocki, Michael Luebbe, bruce d. mcclung, Severine Neff, Bruno Nettl, Edward Nowacki, Karin Pendle, Lewis Peterman, Jennifer Stasack, Jennifer Thomas, J. Randall Wheaton, Lizabeth Wing, and Robert Zierolf; and to Robert Johnson and his staff at the Gorno Memorial Music Library of the University of Cincinnati: Paul Cauthen, Sharon Downing, Ollie Meyer, Mark Palkovic, and Rebecca Willingham. Finally, we are grateful to E. Eugene Helm, Jon Piersol, and Ruth Watanabe for their initial encouragement in this project.

University of Cincinnati

June 1992

SOURCEBOOK
FOR
RESEARCH
IN
MUSIC

CHAPTER ONE

Introductory Materials

As a preliminary to the bibliographies that constitute the main body of this volume, this chapter presents some general information pertaining to research in music. First there is a list of standard English terms that relate to the scholarly study of music or to general bibliography and library research, with definitions. Next follow lists of such terms in the two other most important languages of research in music, German and French, together with English equivalents. The final list is a general outline of the music classification numbers in the most standard research library cataloguing system in North America, that of the Library of Congress.

COMMON BIBLIOGRAPHICAL TERMS

The terms that follow have been brought together because of their application to scholarship in general and the scholarly study of music in particular. Some (e.g., *abstract, anthology, catalog, discography*) will be quite familiar and are generally known, while others might be confusing (*congress report, journal, magazine, periodical*). Many, even most, are likely to be less familiar because they are new (*CD-ROM; online catalog, database*), or relate to the study of books (*codex, foliation, incunabula, siglum, watermark*), manuscripts (*autograph, choirbook, holograph*), printing (*colophon, facsimile, frontispiece*), research libraries (*archive, carrel, microforms, serial, stacks*), or scholarship (*collate, historical set, iconography, Urtext*). Some are technical or specialized enough so that they are not to be found in most dictionaries. For further information and other terms, see Elizabeth H. Thompson, *A.L.A. Glossary of Library Terms* (Chicago: American Library Association, 1943); and Mary C. Turner, *The Bookman's Glossary*, 4th ed., rev. and enl. (New York: R. R. Bowker, 1961).

abstract—a summary of a book, article, etc.; also called **précis** (e.g., *Dissertation Abstracts, RILM Abstracts*).

anthology—a representative collection of selected musical or literary works or excerpts.

archive—a place in which public or institutional records are systematically preserved, or a repository of any documents or other materials, especially those of historical value.

arrangement—a reworking of a musical composition so that the performing forces, the musical content, or the form are substantially different from the original (compare **edition,** definition c, and **transcription**).

autograph—a document (music manuscript, letter, etc.) written or signed in a person's own hand; thus, a primary source (see **sources, primary and secondary;** compare **holograph, manuscript**).

carrel—an alcove or desk in a library—often in the **stacks**— comprising a table and shelves for private study, to which books in a library's collection may be charged for research use.

catalog, catalogue—(a) a list of the contents of a library, book collection, or group of libraries (see **union catalog**); (b) a list or index of compositions, usually by a single composer rather than of a collection or a repertory of music (see **thematic catalog**).

CD-ROM ("compact disk read-only memory")—any information, such as a database, stored on compact disks and readable on the screen of a computer designed for this purpose, or one equipped with a CD-ROM drive (see **online catalog, database**).

choirbook—a music manuscript in a large enough **format** and with the separate voice parts of the compositions contained in it written large enough on the same or on facing pages so that an entire choir could sing from it (in use especially in the fifteenth and early sixteenth centuries). (See also **partbook, manuscript.**)

codex (pl.: codices)—an ancient book or unbound sheets in **manuscript** (e.g., Squarcialupi Codex, Trent Codices; see *The New Harvard Dictionary of Music,* "Sources [pre-1500]").

collate—to compare minutely in order to determine whether two or more books or manuscripts are identical copies or variants.

collected works, complete edition—the publication of the entire compositional output of a single composer in a scholarly edition (compare **edition,** definition c, **historical set, monument**).

colophon—(a) an inscription usually placed at the end of a book or manuscript and containing facts relative to its production; (b) an identifying mark, emblem, or device sometimes used by a printer or publisher on the title page, cover, spine, or jacket, i.e., a logotype (commonly called "logo") (compare **imprint**).

congress report—a publication containing the texts of the papers read at a congress or conference, either a one-time event on a particular topic, such as an individual composer, or the regular meeting of a society; in the first instance, the report would normally be an independent publication, and in the second, it could be one of a series of such volumes (see **proceedings**) or published in the association's **journal**.

copyright (©)—the "right to copy"; the exclusive, legally secured right to reproduce, publish, record, and sell the matter and form of a literary, musical, or artistic work for a period in the United States of fifty years beyond the death of the writer, with no right of renewal (Copyright Act of 1976); different rules apply for works copyrighted before January 1, 1978, when the new law went into effect.

discography—a listing of phonograph records, compact disks, video tapes, and/or tape recordings.

edition—(a) all the impressions of a literary work printed at any time or times from one setting-up of type (excluding a **facsimile** reproduction, which constitutes a different edition); (b) one of the successive forms—e.g., second, revised, enlarged, corrected, etc.—in which a work is published, either by the author or a subsequent editor (see also **reprint edition, revised edition**); (c) the presentation of an older musical composition in a version that makes it accessible to modern performers (compare **arrangement, transcription**).

engraving—the process of incising a design, musical composition, etc., on a metal plate, or the resulting print made from it when the incised lines are inked.

facsimile—an exact reproduction (but not necessarily the original color or size) of a **manuscript** or printed source (compare **reprint edition**).

fair copy—a neat copy of a corrected document.

fascicle—one of the temporary divisions of a work which is issued in small installments intended to be bound together permanently at a later time.

Festschrift—a publication on the occasion of a celebration, or in honor of someone (e.g., on the occasion of a renowned scholar's sixtieth birthday), usually consisting of articles bypracticing scholars in the field of the one honored, e.g., colleagues, former students, or other professionals.

foliation—the consecutive numbering of the leaves (i.e., the sheets of paper with a page on each side) of a book or manuscript, as opposed to the numbering of the pages (see also **recto, verso**).

folio (f., fo., fol.)—(a) a leaf of a **manuscript** or book (see **recto, verso**); (b) formed of sheets each folded once into two leaves or four pages ("in folio"); (c) a page size more than 15 inches/38 centimeters high; (d) a volume of this size.

format—the general makeup of a book as to size and other features (see also **folio, oblong, octavo, quarto**).

frontispiece—an illustration preceding and facing the title page of a book.

historical set—a set of volumes of music of historical significance (compare **anthology, monument;** see chapter 7 of this book).

holograph—a document (music manuscript, letter, etc.) *wholly* in the handwriting of its author (from the Greek word *holos*, "whole" or "complete"; thus, a primary source (see **sources, primary and secondary;** compare **autograph, manuscript**).

iconography—the study of the representation of objects by means of images or statues, reliefs, mosaics, paintings, etc.

imprint—the publisher's name, often with address and date of publication, placed at the foot of the title page or elsewhere in a book (compare **colophon**).

incipit—the first few notes or words of text used to identify a musical composition.

incunabula (pl.)—Latin, "cradle"; books printed from movable type before 1500 (i.e., the cradle of printing).

ISBN, ISSN (International Standard Book Number; International Standard Serial Number)—code numbers in an international identification system first developed in the United Kingdom in 1967 and adopted in the U.S. in 1968; the identifying code is placed at the front of books and **serials** respectively (e.g., ISBN 0-697-03342-2, ISSN 1044-1608).

journal—(a) a generic term to refer to, or sometimes used in the title of, a scholarly periodical (e.g., *Journal of the American Musicological Society*); (b) a diary or daily record of occurrences, transactions, or reflections. (Compare **magazine, periodical, proceedings, review, yearbook;** see chapter 6 of this book.)

lexicon—a book containing an alphabetical or other systematic arrangement of words and their definitions; a dictionary.

magazine—a **periodical** containing articles, pictures, reviews, advertisements, etc., often of popular interest and sometimes focusing on a specific subject area.

manuscript (MS, ms)—(a) a book, document, musical composition, letter, etc., written by hand; (b) an author's written or typed copy of a work before it is printed; thus, a primary source (see **sources, primary and secondary;** compare **autograph, holograph**).

microforms—a general term for microfilm and other miniature processes of reproduction such as the following:

> **microcard**—a card on which numerous pages of a book are reproduced in greatly reduced size.

> **microfiche**—a card-like transparency on which appear multiple frames of microfilm.

> **microfilm**—a photographic reproduction in which the image is reduced to fit a frame of 35 mm or 16 mm film.

monograph—a scholarly study (book or article) treating a single subject or a limited aspect of a subject (see also **treatise**).

monument, musical—a scholarly edition of the music of one region or country (*Denkmal* [pl.: *Denkmäler*] is the German equivalent) (see **edition,** definition c; refer to chapter 7 of this book).

necrology—(a) a notice of the death of a person; obituary; (b) a list or record of people who have died within a certain period of time; in either sense there may or may not be biographical information included.

oblong (ob., obl.)—a book size wider than it is high (e.g., 4° obl., 8° obl.).

octavo (8°, 8vo)—the size of a piece of paper cut eight from a sheet, or a page size about 9 3/4 inches/25 centimeters high.

online catalog, database—a catalog of information (such as a library's holdings with information about each item) loaded into a computer, which may be called up by author, title, subject, keyword(s), type or set of composition(s), etc., on a computer terminal (see **catalog, catalogue,** definition a).

opus (pl. opera, opuses)—a creative work, usually a composition, to which a number is assigned by a composer or publisher to indicate its order in a composer's written and/or published output.

partbook—one of a set of printed or manuscript books, each containing the music for only one voice or instrument part in an ensemble (in use throughout the sixteenth century and into the seventeenth).

periodical—a publication ordinarily with a fixed interval between issues (compare **serial**).

précis—a summary of a book, article, etc.; also called **abstract.**

proceedings—a published report of a conference or meeting of a society or congress, frequently accompanied by abstracts or texts of the papers presented there (see also **congress report**).

pseudonym—pen name; nom de plume.

quarto (4°, 4to)—the size of a piece of paper cut four from a sheet, or a page size about 12 inches/30 centimeters high.

rastrology—the study of musical staves drawn by hand using a rastum (Latin, "rake"), a pen with five or more points used to draw one or more staves at a time; the comparison of differences and irregularities between the lines and staves thus drawn may lead to conclusions such as probable date, identity of the scribe, etc., of a manuscript.

recto (r)—the side of a **folio** that is to be read first, i.e., the right-hand page (e.g., "fol. 2r"; see also **verso**).

reprint edition—a later **edition** of a work that ordinarily is no longer in print, often issued by another publisher who specializes in these editions, such as Da Capo or Dover (compare **facsimile, revised edition**).

reprography—the process of copying documents by xerography, photography, etc.

review—(a) a writing which gives a critical assessment of something, such as a written work or musical performance; (b) a term often used in titles of scholarly periodicals (e.g., *Performance Practice Review, La revue musicale*).

revised edition—an edition of a work incorporating major revisions by the author or an editor and often supplementary matter designed to bring it up to date (compare **reprint edition**).

serial—any publication usually appearing at regular intervals, including **periodicals,** annuals (**yearbooks**), newspapers, **proceedings,** etc.

shelflist—a bibliographical record of a library collection in call-number order.

siglum (pl.: sigla)—a letter or letters with or without numbers used to identify a manuscript or printed source, library, or archive (see *The New Harvard Dictionary of Music*, "Sources [Pre-1500]").

sources, primary and secondary—a primary source is a composition, letter, or document by a composer, author, or some other person, or any document dating from the historical period in question that gives the words of the witnesses or recorders of an event; a secondary source is second- or third-hand information and may be based on primary sources.

stacks—a library term for the main area in a library where books are shelved. Stacks are either "open," if the general public is admitted to them, or "closed," if they are not.

stemmatics—from stemma (Latin, "garland, wreath"); the genealogical study of musical or literary manuscripts.

thematic catalog—a list or index of compositions, usually by a single composer rather than of a collection or repertory of music, in which each composition or movement is identified by an **incipit** (compare **catalog, catalogue,** definition b).

transcription—(a) the transliteration of an early work into modern musical notation; (b) the process or result of adapting a musical composition (usually instrumental) to a medium other than its original one, which may vary from little more than a transference from one medium to another to a modification of the original necessitated by the change of medium (compare **arrangement, edition**).

treatise—a learned, formal writing on a subject, usually in book form (see also **monograph**).

union catalog—a library catalog listing the holdings of a group of cooperating libraries (see **catalog, catalogue,** definition a).

Urtext—original text, often a prototype from which later variants (texts, compositions, etc.) are derived.

verso (v)—the side of a **folio** that is to be read second, i.e., the reverse side or left-hand page (e.g., "fol. 2v"; see also **recto**).

watermark—a manufacturer's identifying mark or design embedded in a sheet of paper, resulting from different thicknesses in the paper and visible when held up to light.

yearbook—a publication issued annually, such as the *Bach-Jahrbuch* or *"Recherches" sur la musique française classique*, that contains scholarly contributions and information in a given area.

GERMAN BIBLIOGRAPHICAL TERMS

The English equivalents given for the following German terms are those that concern bibliography and scholarship (e.g., *Folge* can also mean "sequel," "result," "inference," etc., as well as "series");· in particular, note terms that are not obvious cognates or are even misleading ones, sometimes called "false friends" (e.g., *Band, Brief, Kapitel, Register*). Abbreviations commonly used in scholarly German are given here, and other standard ones may be found listed in any good German-English dictionary. The abbreviations of musical terms have been taken largely from Richard Schaal's *Abkürzungen in der Musik-Terminologie* (see p. 97 below), which is devoted entirely to abbreviations in music; and from *Die Musik in Geschichte und Gegenwart* [*MGG*] (see p. 92 below), whose abbreviations are listed at the beginning of each volume.

Abbildung (Abb.)—illustration, figure
Abdruck (Abdr.)—impression, print, reproduction
Abhandlung (Abh.)—treatise
Abkürzung (Abk.)—abbreviation
Abschrift (Abschr.)—reprint, copy
Anhang (Anh.)—appendix, supplement (see also **Beilage, Beiheft**)
Anmerkung (Anm.)—footnote (see also **Fussnote**)
Anthologie (Anth.)—anthology
Archiv (Arch.)—record office, archive
Aufführungspraxis—performance practice
Auflage (Aufl.)—edition (see also **Ausgabe, Gesammelte Werke, Gesamtausgabe, Sammelwerk, Sämtliche Werke**)
Ausgabe (Ausg.)—edition (see also **Auflage, Gesammelte Werke, Gesamtausgabe, Sammelwerk, Sämtliche Werke**)
Ausgewählte Werke (AW)—selected works
Band (Bd.)—volume
Bearbeiter; Bearbeitung (Bearb.)—compiler, author, reviser; compilation, edition, arrangement
Beiheft (Beih.)—supplement (see also **Anhang, Beilage**)
Beilage (Beil.)—supplement, appendix (see also **Anhang, Beiheft**)
Beispiel (Beisp.)—example ("zum Beispiel" [z.B.]—for example, e.g.)
Beitrag (Beitr.)—contribution (i.e., to a journal)
Bemerkungen (Bem.)—remarks, annotations, commentary
Bericht (Ber.)—report, commentary (see also **Kritischer Bericht, Revisionsbericht**)

Besprechung—review, criticism, conference
beziehungsweise (bzw.)—respectively; or, or else; more
    specifically
Bibliothek (Bibl.)—library
Bildnis (Bildn.)—portrait, likeness
Bildtafel—plate in a book
Blatt (Bl.)—leaf, folio; newspaper
Brief—letter, epistle
Buchhändler; Buchhandlung (Buchh.)—bookseller; bookshop
das heisst (d.h.)—that is, i.e. (also "das ist")
Denkmäler (Dkm.) (pl.)—monuments
Doktorarbeit; Dissertation (Diss.)—doctoral dissertation
Druck (Dr.)—print, printing, impression
ebenda(selbst) (ebd.)—in the same place, ibidem
Einleitung (Einl.)—introduction
erscheinen (ersch.)—to be published
Festschrift (Fs.)—publication on the occasion of a celebration or
    in honor of someone
Folge (F.); Neue Folge (N.F.)—series, continuation, issue; new
    series or issue ("und folgende" [u.ff.]—and following)
Fussnote—footnote (see also **Anmerkung**)
geboren (geb.)—born
gedruckt (gedr.)—printed
Gegenwart (Gegenw.)—present time
Gesammelte Werke (GW)—complete works (see also **Auflage,
    Ausgabe, Gesamtausgabe, Sammelwerk, Sämtliche
    Werke**)
Gesamtausgabe (GA)—complete works (see also **Auflage,
    Ausgabe, Gesammelte Werke, Sammelwerk, Sämtliche
    Werke**)
Geschichte (Gesch.)—history
Gesellschaft (Ges.)—society, association, club (see also **Verein,
    Musikverein**)
gestorben (gest.)—died
getauft (get.)—baptized
Handbuch (Hdb.)—handbook, manual
Handschrift (Hs.)—manuscript (see also **Manuskript**)
Heft (H.)—number, part
Herausgeber (Hrsg.); herausgegeben (hg.)—editor (see also
    Redakteur); edited, published (see also **publiziert**)
in Vorbereitung (in Vorb.)—in preparation
Inhalt (Inh.)—table of contents
insbesondere (insb.)—especially, particularly
Jahr (J.)—year

Jahrbuch (Jb.)—yearbook
Jahreszahl (JZl.)—date, year
Jahrgang (Jg.)—the bound issues of a periodical for one year
Jahrhundert (Jh.)—century
Kapitel (Kap.)—chapter
Katalog (Kat.)—catalog
Komponist (Komp.)—composer
Kritischer Bericht (Krit. Ber.)—critical report or commentary (see
    also Revisionsbericht)
Kunst—art ("Tonkunst"—music [tonal art])
Lexikon (L)—dictionary (abb. used in combination with an
    author, e.g., RiemannL) (see also **Wörterbuch**)
Lieferung (Lfg.)—part of a work, fascicle
Literatur (Lit.)—literature, letters, bibliography
Manuskript (Ms.)—manuscript (see also **Handschrift**)
Mitarbeiter (Mitarb.)—collaborator
Mitteilung (Mitt.)—announcement, communication (see also
    Nachricht)
Mitwirkung (Mitw.)—cooperation
Monatsheft—monthly periodical
Musik Lexikon (M Lex.)—music lexicon, dictionary (see also
    Wörterbuch)
Musikforschung (Mf.)—music research (see also
    Musikwissenschaft)
Musikgeschichte (Mg.)—music history
Musikverein (MV)—musical society (see also **Gesellschaft**)
Musikwissenschaft (Mw.)—musicology (see also
    Musikforschung)
Nachricht (Nachr.)—communication, report, notice (see also
    Mitteilung)
Nachwort (Nachw.)—concluding remarks, epilogue
Neuausgabe, Neue Ausgabe (NA)—new edition
Neudruck (Neudr.)—reprint
ohne (o.)—without ("ohne Jahr" [o.J.]—no year [of publication];
    "ohne Ort" [o.O.]—no place [of publication], no opus
    [number])
Partitur (P., Part.)—musical score
publiziert (publ.)—published (see also **herausgegeben**)
Quelle—source
Redakteur; Redaktion (Red.)—editor (see also **Herausgeber**);
    editorial matter, editorial staff
Register—index
Reihe (R.)—series, set, tone row ("Neue Reihe" [N.R.]—new
    series)

revidiert (rev.)—revised

Revisionsbericht—critical commentary (see also **Kritischer Bericht**)

Sammelband (Sbd., Smlbd.)—volume containing a collection of essays

Sammelwerk (Sw., Swk.)—collected works (see also **Auflage, Ausgabe, Gesammelte Werke, Gesamtausgabe, Sämtliche Werke**)

Sammlung (Samlg., Samml., Slg., Slng.)—collection, compilation, set

Sämtliche Werke—complete works (see also **Auflage, Ausgabe, Gesammelte Werke, Gesamtausgabe, Sammelwerk**)

Schrift—writing, book, periodical, etc.

Schriftleiter; Schriftleitung (Schriftl.)—editor (see also **Herausgeber, Redakteur**); editorship, editorial staff (see also **Redaktion**)

Seite (S.)—page

siehe oben (s.o.)—see above, supra

siehe unten (s.u.)—see below, infra

Skizzen (SK)—sketches, outlines

Stimmbuch (Stb.)—part book

Tabelle (Tab.)—table, chart, graph (see also **Tafel**)

Tafel (Taf.)—table (see also **Tabelle**)

Teil (Tl.)—part, division ("zum Teil" [z.T.]—in part)

Titelblatt—title page

Überlieferung—tradition, inheritance, surviving original sources, etc.

Übertragung (Übtr.)—translation, transcription

und andere (u.a.)—and others, et al.

und so weiter (usw.)—and so forth, etc.

unter anderem (u.a.)—among others

Urtext—original text

Verein (Ver.)—association, society (see also **Gesellschaft**)

Verfasser (Verf.)—composer, writer

vergleich (vgl., vergl.)—compare

Verlag (Vlg.)—publishing house

Verzeichnis (Verz.)—catalogue

Vierteljahrsschrift (Vjs.)—quarterly periodical

Vorrede (Vorr.)—preface (see also **Vorwort**)

Vortrag (Vortr.)—lecture, discourse, report

Vorwort (Vorw.)—foreword (see also **Vorrede**)

Wochenblatt—weekly periodical

Wörterbuch (Wb.)—dictionary (see also **Lexikon**)

Zahl (Zl.)—number, numeral, figure

Zeitschrift (Zs., Ztschr.)—periodical
Zeitung (Ztg.)—newspaper
zugleich (zugl.)—at the same time, together, conjointly, with (see also **zusammen**)
zur Zeit (z.Z., z.Zt.)—now, at present
zusammen (zus.)—together, jointly (see also **zugleich**)

FRENCH BIBLIOGRAPHICAL TERMS

As in the preceding list of German terms, the English equivalents for the following French terms concern bibliography and scholarship only (e.g., besides "sheet of paper" or "folio," *feuille* can mean "leaf," "veneer," etc.), and similarly include "false friends" (e.g., *avertissement, dessin, libraire*).

abréger—to abbreviate
analyse—book review (see also **compte rendu**); analysis
annexe—appendix (to a book)
annuaire—yearbook
aperçu—literary sketch, outline, summary (see also **esquisse**)
augmenté(e)—enlarged ("édition augmentée")
auteur—author ("du même auteur"—by the same author) (see also **écrivain**)
avant-propos—preface, foreword; introduction (see also **avertissement, avis**)
avertissement—preface, foreword (see also **avant-propos, avis**)
avis—notice ("avis au lecteur"—preface, foreword) (see also **avant-propos, avertissement**)
beaux-arts—fine arts
bibliothèque—library
cahier—short book or magazine; copybook
catalogue raisonné—descriptive catalogue
chapitre—chapter
chez—at the (publishing) house of
collection—set or series of books (see also **fonds, recueil, série**)
compositeur—composer
compte rendu—book review or résumé (see also **analyse**)
corrigé(e)—corrected ("édition corrigée")
côte—call number
dépôt légal—registration of copyright
dessin—drawing, sketch
dictionnaire—dictionary (see also **lexique**)

dirigé(e)—directed ("collection dirigée par Jean Marin"—series of books under the general editorship of . . .)

écrit—writing, written work

écrivain—writer (see also **auteur**)

éditer—to publish, issue (usually not "to edit") (see also **publier**)

esquisse—literary or pictorial sketch, outline (see also **aperçu**)

étude—study (noun)

feuille, feuillet—sheet of paper, folio

fonds—collection in a library ("les fonds Dupont"—the Dupont collection) (see also **collection, recueil**)

gravure—engraving

hebdomadaire—weekly (see also **mensuel, trimestriel**)

impression—printing ("2e impression"—2nd printing) (see also **tirage**)

imprimer—to print

inédit—unpublished

journal—newpaper

lexique—lexicon, dictionary (see also **dictionnaire**)

libraire—bookseller (not "library")

librairie—bookshop (not "library")

livre—book

livret—libretto

mélange—miscellany (see also **recueil**)

mensuel(le)—monthly (see also **hebdomadaire, trimestriel**)

musicographe; musicographie—writer on music; works about music

oeuvre—work, output

oeuvres complètes (o.c.)—complete works

ouvrage—work of literature, art, etc.

page de titre—title page

partie—part of a book, etc.

partition—musical score

paru—published ("déjà paru"—already published)

périodique—periodical (see also **revue**)

planche—plate in a book ("planches hors texte"—plates not numbered with the pages of text)

précis—abstract

publier—edit, publish (see also **éditer**)

recueil—collection, selection, miscellany ("recueil choisi"—anthology) (see also **collection, fonds, mélange**)

rédacteur; rédaction—editor ("rédacteur en chef"—chief editor); editorial staff

rédiger—to edit (a newspaper), to draft or write (an article, etc.)

réimpression—reprinting

reliure—bookbinding
revu(e)—revised ("édition revue")
revue—magazine, periodical (see also **périodique**)
série—series (see also **collection**)
siècle—century
sommaire—short, brief ("bibliographie sommaire"); table of
    contents (see also **table des matières**)
table des matières—table of contents (see also **sommaire**)
tableau—table in a book (e.g., "tableau chronologique")
thèse—thesis, doctoral dissertation
tirage—printing (see also **impression**)
titre—title
tome (t.)—volume; division of a book
traduction—translation
traité—treatise
travail—work, piece of work
trimestriel(le)—quarterly (every three months) (see also
    hebdomadaire, mensuel)
voir (v.)—see (e.g., "v. Annexe 2"—see Appendix 2)

LIBRARY OF CONGRESS MUSIC
CLASSIFICATION

The holdings of most North American research and university libraries are arranged according to the Library of Congress classification system, although other systems, chiefly the Dewey Decimal, are sometimes used. Because of the wide application of the Library of Congress system, the portions that pertain to music and music literature are listed below in some detail. In a library that uses the system, these letter(s) and number(s) are followed by a decimal point and further letter(s) and number(s) (the so-called cutter or author number, e.g., ML 1255 .B23 1983, ML 410 .B4H92, etc.), which may or may not be the same as those in the Library of Congress's own complete call numbers. The initial letter-number combinations, however, are the same from one library to another (e.g., oratorios are always catalogued between M 2000 and M 2007, biographies of individual composers under ML 410, analytic guides between MT 90 and MT 145). This greatly facilitates searching or browsing in any LC-based library's stacks or shelflist. The following list is adapted from *Class M, Music and Books on Music: Library of Congress Classification Schedules Combined with Additions and Changes through 1986* (Detroit: Gale Research, 1987). For the complete alphabetical listing of subject headings, in music as well as in all other areas, consult *Library of Congress Subject Headings*, 15th ed., 4 vols. (Washington, D.C.: Cataloging Distribution Service, Library of Congress, 1992).

Music

1	Collections
1.A1–.A15	Music printed or copied in manuscript in the United States or the colonies before 1860
2–2.3	Collections of musical sources by two or more composers
3–3.1	Collected works of individual composers
3.3	First editions

Instrumental Music

5	Collections
6–175	Solo instruments
176	Instrumental music for motion pictures
176.5	Instrumental music for radio and television
177–990	Music for two or more solo instruments
1 80–298.5	Duets
300–386	Trios
400–486	Quartets
500–586	Quintets
600–686	Sextets
700–786	Septets
800–886	Octets
900–986	Nonets and larger combinations of purely chamber music
990	Chamber music for instruments of the 18th century and earlier
1000–1075	Orchestra
1100–1160	String orchestra
1200–1269	Band
1270	Fife (bugle) and drum music, field music, etc.
1350–1353	Reduced orchestra
1356–1356.2	Dance orchestra and instrumental ensembles
1360	Mandolin and similar orchestras of plectral instruments

1362	Accordion band
1365	Minstrel music
1366	Jazz ensembles
1375–1420	Instrumental music for children
1450	Dance music
1470	Chance compositions
1473	Electronic music
1480	Music with color apparatus, etc.
1490	Music, printed or copied in manuscript, before 1700

Vocal Music

1495	Collections
1497–1998	Secular vocal music
1500–1527.8	Dramatic music (opera, ballet, etc.)
1528–1529.5	Duets, trios, etc., for solo voices
1530–1546.5	Choruses with orchestra or other ensemble
1547–1600	Choruses, part–songs, etc., with accompaniment of keyboard or other solo instrument, or unaccompanied
1608	Choruses, etc., in tonic sol–fa notation
1609	Unison choruses with or without accompaniment of every kind
1610	Cantatas, choral symphonies, etc., for unaccompanied chorus (secular and sacred) with or without solo voices
1611–1624.8	Songs for one voice
1625–1626	Recitations, *gesprochene Lieder*, with accompaniment
1627–1853	National music
1900–1980	Songs (part and solo) of special character (society songs, etc.)
1985	Musical games
1990–1998	Secular music for children
1999–2199	Sacred vocal music
1999	Collections of music by two or more composers
2000–2007	Oratorios
2010–2017.7	Services by denomination
2018–2019.5	Duets, trios, etc., for solo voices
2020–2036	Choruses, cantatas, etc., for choral ensembles

2060–2101.5	Choruses, part–songs, etc., with accompaniment of keyboard or other solo instrument, or unaccompanied
2102–2114	Songs for one voice
2115–2146	Hymnals by denomination
2147–2188	Liturgy and ritual
2147–2155.6	Roman Catholic
2156–2160.87	Orthodox
2161–2183	Protestant
2184	Other Christian churches
2186–2187	Jewish
2188	Other non–Christian religions
2190–2196	Sacred vocal music for children
2198–2199	Gospel, revival, temperance, etc., songs
5000	Unidentified compositions

ML   Literature on Music

1–5	Periodicals
12–21	Directories, almanacs
25–28	Societies
29–33	Foundations and institutions
35–38	Festivals, Congresses
40–44	Programs
48–54.8	Librettos
55–60	Collected essays, etc., by several authors, including Festschriften
90	Writings of musicians (collections)
93–97	Manuscripts, autographs, etc. (paleography)
100–109	Dictionaries, encyclopedias
111–158	Bibliography
113–118	International
120	National
132	Graded lists, by medium
134	Catalogues of composers' works
135	Manuscripts
136–158	Catalogs
159–3797	History and criticism
	Special periods
162–169	Ancient
170–190	Medieval
193–197	1600 +

885–893	Studies and exercises
898–949	Techniques for children
950–960	Ballet, opera, music in theaters, and production

Some Nonmusical General Classifications
Relating to Research in Music

A	General Works	L	Education
B	Philosophy, Psychology	N	Arts
D	History	P	Languages, Literature
GV	Dance	Q, T	Science, Technology
K	Law	Z	Bibliography

CHAPTER TWO

Basic Bibliographical Tools for Research in Music

This chapter consists of lists of the most important current basic sources, to be used as the point of departure for researching virtually any topic in the field of music. The sources listed in the various categories should be consulted, as appropriate, along with related books on the subject in question—period or regional music histories, biographies, histories of genres or forms, general and specialized music dictionaries and encyclopedias, chief texts on the subject, etc.—for the preliminary compilation of a working bibliography. Sources may be found under subject headings in a particular library's card catalog or online catalog, and also by browsing in appropriate areas of its stacks, but these are just two of many initial steps that need to be taken, casual and unsystematic ones at that, and they rarely if ever uncover materials such as periodical articles, chapters in jointly authored publications or Festschriften, prefaces in volumes of collected sets and monuments, etc. One methodical way to begin to find materials of this sort is to consult the relevant bibliographical tools listed below.

The following list consists of four categories, each further divided: "Music Literature Sources," in which indexes to ten basic categories of music literature are listed; "Directories and Catalogs of Institutions," subdivided into "Libraries," "Library and Union Catalogs," "Musical Instrument Collections," "Schools of Music," and "International Music Guides"; "Music Sources," comprising five categories of reference sources pertaining to music itself; and "Selected General Bibliographies." The first category, "General Music Literature Sources," provides access to the most generally useful categories of music literature; the third, "Music Sources," gives access to music, and it is also a further avenue into prefaces in scholarly editions and recording program notes, both of which may contain valuable information.

A few of the items (e.g., OCLC, RLIN, UNCOVER/UNCOVER2) exist exclusively in the form of remote databases readable only on a computer terminal. These and another popular format, CD-ROM ("compact disk read-only memory"), are new technologies which promise to revolutionize scholarly research. Whereas remote databases can be added to on a continuing basis, CDs can hold up to 260,000 pages of text and are automatically searchable in a variety of ways that can also greatly increase the speed of the search. The holdings of such foreign libraries as the British Library and the French Bibliothèque Nationale, as well as various other bibliographic sources, are also now available on CD-ROM in addition to hard copy. For further information, consult *CD-ROMs in Print 1992: An International Guide* (Westport, Conn.: Meckler, 1992).

It must be remembered that no part of this bibliography is all-inclusive—there exist many additional sources that are specialized, regional, rare, obsolete or superseded, etc.—but a thorough consultation of the following sources, as appropriate, will take the researcher far into the existing literature in a vast range of musical topics.

MUSIC LITERATURE SOURCES

Current Writings about Music

The sources listed below each index several types of works. Each has different features and limitations, however—period of time covered, subjects included or emphasized, number and types of publications included, etc.—so wherever possible, all or more than one of them should be consulted for accuracy and completeness of coverage. Three are ongoing: the oldest is the *Bibliographie des Musikschrifttums*, a yearly listing of books, dissertations, and articles, including many in nonmusic periodicals, in all European languages. *RILM* is the most comprehensive and informative, the only one of the three that provides abstracts. It lists current scholarly writings about music in all languages: books, dissertations, articles, and prefaces to editions. The *Bibliographic Guide to Music* lists publications catalogued each year by the Research Libraries of the New York Public Library and the Library of Congress, including books, periodicals, music, and sound recordings. Of the two remaining sources, the *Bibliographia Musicologica* indexes only items published in the period 1968–76, but it is international in coverage and includes books, dissertations, musical editions, and facsimile editions. Hughes, though limited to a single era, is a selective but wide-ranging annotated index to articles, books, editions of treatises and music, etc., from and about the entire Medieval period, including the transition to the Renaissance.

Bibliographia Musicologica: A Bibliography of Musical Literature. 9 vols. Utrecht: Joachimsthal, 1970–80.

Bibliographic Guide to Music. Boston: G. K. Hall, 1975–.

Bibliographie des Musikschrifttums. Institut für Musikforschung Preussischer Kulturbesitz, Berlin. Leipzig: F. Hofmeister, 1936–38, 1950–.

Hughes, Andrew. *Medieval Music: The Sixth Liberal Art.* Rev. ed. Toronto Medieval Bibliographies, no. 4. Toronto: University of Toronto Press, 1980. First published in 1974.

RILM Abstracts of Music Literature: Répertoire international de littérature musicale/International Repertory of Music Literature/Internationales Repertorium der Musikliteratur. New York: International RILM Center, 1967–. (Also available on CD-ROM under the title *MUSE.*)

Periodicals

Robinson's bibliography is an annotated list of 1,867 current periodicals in all fields of music and dance. Basart's is an annotated list of current music research journals in English whose chief purpose is to serve as a guide to authors wishing to submit articles, but the information provided is of use to general researchers as well. Fidler and James, which comprises commissioned essays on over 150 of the most important music periodicals, historic as well as modern, constitutes a valuable source of information on topic areas, editorial policies and biases, etc.

The remaining items are lists of music periodicals that span the nearly three hundred years of the genre's history. The *MGG* and *New Grove* lists are both very comprehensive, the latter more so and also more recent. They each list periodicals by country; in *The New Grove* they are arranged chronologically (with an index), making it much easier to identify those published in a given period; in *MGG* the arrangement is alphabetical. *The New Harvard Dictionary* treats the subject in brief. Further lists of music periodicals are cited in chapter 6 of Meggett's *Music Periodical Literature* (see p. 25 below). See also the selective list of research periodicals in chapter 6 below.

Basart, Ann P. *Writing about Music: A Guide to Publishing Opportunities for Authors and Reviewers.* Fallen Leaf

Reference Books in Music, no. 11. Berkeley, Calif.: Fallen
    Leaf Press, 1989.
Fellinger, Imogen. "Periodicals." In *The New Grove Dictionary of
    Music and Musicians*. Vol. 14, pp. 407–535.
————— , comp. "Zeitschriften." In *Die Musik in Geschichte und
    Gegenwart*. Vol. 14 (1968), cols. 1041–1188.
Fidler, Linda M., and Richard S. James, eds. *International Music
    Journals*. New York: Greenwood Press, 1990.
Robinson, Doris. *Music and Dance Periodicals: An International
    Directory & Guidebook*. Voorheesville, N.Y.: Peri Press,
    1989.
Samuel, Harold E. "Periodicals." In *The New Harvard Dictionary
    of Music*. Pp. 625–28.

Periodical Articles

All of these items are indexes or bibliographies of periodical articles except Meggett's *Music Periodical Literature*, the bulk of which (chapters 3, 4, and 5) is an annotated bibliography of many such indexes, largely specialized ones. Of the other sources, *The Music Index*, begun in 1949 and international in scope, is the most standard and comprehensive index to music periodical literature; *Music Article Guide*, begun in 1966, is limited to American periodicals, only a few of which duplicate those in *The Music Index*, and includes a brief annotation for each item. *A Bibliography . . . Oct. 1938–Sept. 1940* pushes the indexing back to a brief pre-World War II period.

RIPM and Warner's *Periodical Literature on American Music* are important recent specialized indexes, the first being the beginning of a series that will "provide access to a selected corpus of 18th-, 19th- and early 20th-century periodical literature dealing with music," and the second a comprehensive bibliography of articles on American music. *A&HCI*, as its title suggests, indexes a large number of periodicals in essentially all arts and humanities fields, so while it is not the most comprehensive in music, it is of particular value in many cross-disciplinary subjects.

Of the H. W. Wilson indexes listed, one is the well-known general *Readers' Guide to Periodical Literature*, while each of the others addresses a specific area of study. Five final sources, listed under "Bibliographic Databases," are only readable on a computer terminal.

It should be recalled that the *Bibliographie des Musikschrifttums* and *RILM*, listed above under "Current Writings about Music," include periodical articles as well.

Art Index: A Cumulative Author and Subject Index to a Selected List of Fine Arts Periodicals and Museum Bulletins. New York: H. W. Wilson, 1929–.

Arts and Humanities Citation Index (A&HCI). Philadelphia: Institute for Scientific Information, 1976–. (Also available on CD-ROM.)

A Bibliography of Periodical Literature in Musicology . . . Oct. 1938–Sept. 1940. Washington, D.C.: American Council of Learned Societies, 1940–43.

Biography Index: A Cumulative Index to Biographical Material in Books and Magazines. New York: H. W. Wilson, 1946–.

Education Index. New York: H. W. Wilson, 1929–.

Humanities Index. New York: H. W. Wilson, 1974–.

Meggett, Joan M. *Music Periodical Literature: An Annotated Bibliography of Indexes and Bibliographies.* Metuchen, N.J.: Scarecrow Press, 1978.

Music Article Guide: A Comprehensive Quarterly Reference Guide to Significant Signed Feature Articles in American Music Periodicals. Philadelphia: Music Article Guide, 1966–76; Philadelphia: Information Services, 1977–.

The Music Index: A Subject-Author Guide to Music Periodical Literature. Detroit: Information Services, 1949–63; Detroit: Information Coordinators, 1963–87; Warren, Mich.: Harmonie Park Press (Information Coordinators), 1987–. (1981–89 available on CD-ROM.)

Readers' Guide to Periodical Literature. New York: H. W. Wilson, 1900–.

Répertoire international de la presse musicale: A Retrospective Index Series (RIPM). H. Robert Cohen, gen. ed. Ann Arbor, Mich.: UMI Center for Studies in Nineteenth-Century Music, University of Maryland, 1988–.

Social Sciences Index. New York: H. W. Wilson, 1974–.

Warner, Thomas E. *Periodical Literature on American Music, 1620–1920: A Classified Bibliography with Annotations.* Bibliographies in American Music, no. 12. Warren, Mich.: Harmonie Park Press, for the College Music Society, 1988.

BIBLIOGRAPHIC DATABASES

ABI/Inform. Ann Arbor, Mich.: University Microfilms International, 1989–. A database of business-related periodicals; includes articles on music that are not contained in *Music Index.* (Also available on CD-ROM.)

CAIRSS for MUSIC. Charles T. Eagle, Jr., ed. San Antonio:
    Institute for Music Research (Donald A. Hodges, director),
    University of Texas at San Antonio, 1993–. This
    "Computer-Assisted Information Retrieval Service System"
    is a bibliographic database of music research literature that
    emphasizes music education, music therapy, music
    psychology, and medicine. Currently there are fifteen
    "primary" journals in these areas that are completely
    indexed, with selected articles from more than twelve
    hundred "secondary" journals that are also in the
    database.

General Periodicals Ondisc. Ann Arbor, Mich.: University
    Microfilms, Inc., n.d. Exists only on CD-ROM; the earliest
    years indexed are 1989–90. The source may also be
    accessed under other titles, e.g., *ProQuest* and *Periodicals
    Abstracts*. Over 950 general periodicals are indexed; an
    abstract is usually included with the article citation.

SMT Online Bibliographic Database. Sponsored by the Society
    for Music Theory; Lee Rothfarb, project director.
    Cambridge: Harvard University, 1992–. A database that
    contains citations of articles and reviews in all major music
    theory journals and selected musicology journals.

UNCOVER/UNCOVER2. Denver, CARL Systems Inc., 1988–. An
    online database and document delivery service (that is,
    entire articles can be delivered via FAX to private office or
    home, or Interlibrary Loan office) that includes over ten
    thousand periodicals, general as well as musical. Includes
    a browsing function that permits the user to look at tables
    of contents of periodicals.

Music Dictionaries and Encyclopedias

Of these three lists of music dictionaries and encyclopedias,
Coover's *Music Lexicography,* in a single alphabetical list, is the most
thorough available; his article in *The New Grove Dictionary,* also comprehensive and more recent, is divided by period into several lists;
and Samuel's article in *The New Harvard Dictionary,* the most recent
of the three, is a concise treatment of the subject featuring several
lists of works. For selective lists of music dictionaries and encyclopedias, see chapter 4 below.

Coover, James B. "Dictionaries and Encyclopedias of Music." In
    The New Grove Dictionary of Music and Musicians. Vol. 5,
    pp. 430–59.

————. *Music Lexicography, Including a Study of Lacunae in Music Lexicography and a Bibliography of Music Dictionaries.* 3rd ed., rev. and enl. Carlisle, Pa.: Carlisle Books, 1971. First published in 1952.
Samuel, Harold E. "Dictionaries and Encyclopedias." In *The New Harvard Dictionary of Music.* Pp. 226–30.

Festschriften

These two sources are virtually the only available specialized indexes to musical Festschriften of any importance, Gerboth's more thorough and more recent, Krohn's shorter and earlier, both published in the 1960s.

Gerboth, Walter. *An Index to Musical Festschriften and Similar Publications.* New York: W. W. Norton, 1969.
Krohn, Ernst C. "Musical Festschriften and Related Publications." In *Notes* 21 (Winter-Spring 1963–64): 94–108.

Monographs in Series

The two important indexes to series of monographs on music are Blum's, covering 1945 to the early 1960s, and Charles's, which complements it by including both earlier series and others that go up to about 1970. One of the chief values of these sources, dated as they are, is that they list the volumes in various series that emphasize certain historical periods or subjects, thus leading the researcher to works related to a given area of investigation.

Blum, Fred. *Music Monographs in Series: A Bibliography of Numbered Monograph Series in the Field of Music Current since 1945.* New York: Scarecrow Press, 1964.
Charles, Sydney Robinson. *A Handbook of Music and Music Literature in Sets and Series.* New York: Free Press, 1972. Section C: "Music Literature Monograph and Facsimile Series," pp. 326–405.

Congress Reports

The Tyrrell and Wise volume is the only specialized index to published papers read in musicological congresses that is available at present. Briquet is a list of titles of papers on musical subjects read in congresses between 1835 and 1939.

Briquet, Marie. *La musique dans les congrès internationaux (1835–1939)*. Publications de la Société Française de Musicologie, ser. 2, vol. 10. Paris: Heugel, 1961.

Tyrrell, John, and Rosemary Wise. *A Guide to International Congress Reports in Musicology, 1900–1975*. New York: Garland Publishing, 1979.

Dissertations

Since its inception in 1951, there have been two series of *Doctoral Dissertations in Musicology* listing dissertations completed and in progress, covering only American ones up to 1971 and international ones since 1972 (the annotation in Duckles, *Music Reference and Research Materials*—see p. 32 below—covers its publication history in detail and also refers to other lists of non-American dissertations). The recent *International Directory* lists dissertations in progress not only directly related to music education but on a wide range of other musical topics as well, including biography, church music, humanities and the arts, ethnomusicology, jazz, etc.

Dissertation Abstracts International, begun in 1938 as *Microfilm Abstracts* of American dissertations and broadened to its present international status in 1969, is the well-known guide to dissertations in all fields, to which there are both author and keyword-in-title indexes. (Each monthly issue is also indexed in *The Music Index;* see p. 25 above.)

Adkins, Cecil, and Alis Dickinson, eds. *Doctoral Dissertations in Musicology*. 7th North American ed./2nd International ed. [1st ser., cumulative ed.] Philadelphia: American Musicological Society/International Musicological Society, 1984. First published in 1951.

——— . *Doctoral Dissertations in Musicology*. 2nd ser., 1st cumulative ed. Philadelphia: American Musicological Society/International Musicological Society, 1990. Suppls., 1991–.

Dissertation Abstracts International. Ann Arbor, Mich.: University Microfilms, 1938–. (Also available on CD-ROM.)

International Directory of Approved Music Education Doctoral Dissertations in Progress. Edited by Richard J. Colwell. Council for Research in Music Education, University of

Illinois, in behalf of The Graduate Program in Music Education. Urbana: University of Illinois, 1989–.

Biographies of Musicians

Of these sources, Green's *Index* differs from the others in that it is an annotated index of bibliographies on composers, and it is thus the work to consult when looking for other bibliographies than those given here. The remaining works, each addressing a different category of musician, all concern biographical materials themselves. Of these, only the Adams and Farkas books are significantly annotated. For guides to biographies in special areas, see chapter 3 below under "Bibliographies in Other Selected Areas." For further information about biographies, see the appropriate sections in Marco's *Information on Music* (see p. 32 below).

See also chapter 5 under "Biographies of Composers in English" and "Series of Composers' Biographies in English," and appropriate articles in such sources as *The New Grove Dictionary*. Selected periodicals devoted to individual composers are listed in chapter 6, "Current Research Journals—Limited to a Single Composer," p. 155 below.

Two other valuable sources of information for those composers included in them are the Garland Composer Resource Manuals series, listed alphabetically by composer in full below, and the Bio-Bibliographies in Music series (Westport, Conn.: Greenwood Press, 1984–).

Adams, John L., comp. *Musicians' Autobiographies: An Annotated Bibliography of Writings Available in English, 1800 to 1980.* Jefferson, N.C.: McFarland, 1982.

Bull, Storm. *Index to Biographies of Contemporary Composers.* 3 vols. New York: Scarecrow Press, 1964–87.

Cowden, Robert H., comp. *Concert and Opera Conductors: A Bibliography of Biographical Materials.* Music Reference Collection, no. 14. Westport, Conn.: Greenwood Press, 1987.

———, comp. *Concert and Opera Singers: A Bibliography of Biographical Materials.* Music Reference Collection, no. 5. Westport, Conn.: Greenwood Press, 1985.

———, comp. *Instrumental Virtuosi: A Bibliography of Biographical Materials.* Music Reference Collection, no. 18. Westport, Conn.: Greenwood Press, 1989.

Farkas, Andrew. *Opera and Concert Singers: An Annotated International Bibliography of Books and Pamphlets.*

Garland Reference Library of the Humanities, vol. 466.
New York: Garland Publishing, 1985.
Green, Richard D. *Index to Composer Bibliographies.* Detroit
Studies in Music Bibliography, no. 53. Detroit: Information
Coordinators, 1985.
Greene, Frank, comp. *Composers on Record: An Index to
Biographical Information on 14,000 Composers Whose
Music Has Been Recorded.* Metuchen, N.J.: Scarecrow
Press, 1985.

GARLAND COMPOSER RESOURCE MANUALS.
GUY A. MARCO, GEN. ED. NEW YORK: GARLAND
PUBLISHING, 1981–.

Adolphe Adam and Léo Delibes: A Guide to Research. By William
E. Studwell. 1987.
Béla Bartók: A Guide to Research. By Eliott Antokoletz. 1987.
Ludwig van Beethoven: A Guide to Research. By Theodore
Albrecht. 1992.
Hector Berlioz: A Guide to Research. By Jeffrey A. Langford and
Jane Denker Graves. 1989.
Ernest Bloch: A Guide to Research. By David Z. Kushner. 1988.
William Byrd: A Guide to Research. By Richard Turbet. 1987.
Claude Debussy: A Guide to Research. By James R. Briscoe. 1990.
Edward Elgar: A Guide to Research. By Christopher Kent. 1992.
Manuel de Falla: A Bibliography and Research Guide. By Gilbert
Chase. 1986.
Stephen Collins Foster: A Guide to Research. By Calvin Elliker.
1988.
Girolamo Frescobaldi: A Guide to Research. By Frederick
Hammond. 1988.
Christoph Willibald Gluck: A Guide to Research. By Patricia
Howard. 1987.
G. F. Handel: A Guide to Research. By Mary Ann Parker-Hale.
1988.
Franz Joseph Haydn: A Guide to Research. By Floyd K. Grave and
Margaret G. Grave. 1990.
Henricus Isaac: A Guide to Research. By Martin Picker. 1991.
Josquin des Prez: A Guide to Research. By Sydney Robinson
Charles. 1983.
Orlando di Lasso: A Guide to Research. By James Erb. 1990.
Franz Liszt: A Guide to Research. By Michael Saffle. 1991.
Guillaume de Machaut: A Guide to Research. By Lawrence Earp.
1993.

Gustav and Alma Mahler: A Guide to Research. By Susan M.
 Filler. 1989.
Felix Mendelssohn: A Guide to Research. By Donald Mintz. 1993.
Claudio Monteverdi: A Guide to Research. By Gary K. Adams and
 Dyke Kiel. 1989.
Wolfgang Amadeus Mozart: A Guide to Research. By Baird
 Hastings. 1989.
Carl Nielsen: A Guide to Research. By Mina Miller. 1987.
Johannes Ockeghem and Jacob Obrecht: A Guide to Research. By
 Martin Picker. 1988.
Giovanni Battista Pergolesi: A Guide to Research. By Marvin E.
 Paymer and Hermine W. Williams. 1989.
Henry Purcell: A Guide to Research. By Franklin B. Zimmerman.
 1989.
Sergei Vasil'evich Rachmaninoff: A Guide to Research. By Robert
 Palmieri. 1985.
Jean-Philippe Rameau: A Guide to Research. By Donald H.
 Foster. 1989.
Nikolai Andreevich Rimsky-Korsakov: A Guide to Research. By
 Gerald R. Seaman. 1988.
Alessandro and Domenico Scarlatti: A Guide to Research. By
 Carole F. Vidall. 1992.
Heinrich Schütz: A Guide to Research. By Allen B. Skei. 1981.
Edgard Varèse: A Guide to Research. By Anne F. Parks. 1993.
Ralph Vaughan Williams: A Guide to Research. By Neil
 Butterworth. 1990.
Antonio Vivaldi: A Guide to Research. By Michael Talbot. 1988.
Carl Maria von Weber: A Guide to Research. By Donald G.
 Henderson and Alice H. Henderson. 1990.
Hugo Wolf: A Guide to Research. By David Ossenkop. 1988.

Other Bibliographies of Music Literature Sources

The sources listed here are of several kinds. Brockman, Duckles, and Marco are all annotated bibliographies of reference materials in the field of music; Duckles and Marco aim at near-
comprehensiveness, while Brockman is more selective. The *Basic
Music Library* offers suggestions for the stocking of a music library;
Baily and *Performing Arts Books* are specialized bibliographies.

Baily, Dee. *A Checklist of Music Bibliographies and Indexes in
 Progress and Unpublished.* 4th ed. MLA Index and
 Bibliography Series, vol. 3. Philadelphia: Music Library
 Association, 1982. First published in 1974.

A Basic Music Library: Essential Scores and Books. 2nd ed., rev. and enl. Compiled by the Music Library Association, Committee on the Basic Music Collection, under the direction of Pauline S. Bayne. Edited by Robert Michael Fling. Chicago: American Library Association, 1983. First published in 1978.

Brockman, William S. *Music: A Guide to the Reference Literature.* Reference Sources in the Humanities Series. Littleton, Colo.: Libraries Unlimited, 1987.

Duckles, Vincent H., and Michael A. Keller. *Music Reference and Research Materials: An Annotated Bibliography.* 4th ed., rev. New York: Schirmer Books, 1993. First published in 1964.

Marco, Guy A., ed. *Information on Music: A Handbook of Reference Sources in European Languages.* 8 vols. projected. Littleton, Colo.: Libraries Unlimited, 1975–.

> 1. *Basic and Universal Sources.* By Guy A. Marco. 1975.
> 2. *The Americas.* By Guy A. Marco and Ann M. Garfield. 1977.
> 3. *Europe.* By Guy A. Marco with the assistance of Sharon Paugh Ferris and Ann G. Olszewski. 1984.
> 4. *Africa, Asia, Oceania.*
> 5. *Specific Topics.*
> 6, 7. *Sources for Individual Musicians.*
> 8. *Guide to Musical Editions.*

Performing Arts Books, 1876–1981, Including an International Index of Current Serial Publications. New York: R. R. Bowker, 1981.

DIRECTORIES AND CATALOGS
OF INSTITUTIONS

Libraries

The *Directory of Music Research Libraries,* begun by Rita Benton, series C of *RISM,* is the standard international guide in the area, and it is now complete except for the sixth volume. In the meantime, for libraries to be covered in that volume, consult her *New Grove* article "Libraries." Penney gives similar information for British libraries. While the chief focus in Bradley is chronicling the growth of music collections in American libraries, it does list special collections where they exist.

Benton, Rita, et al. "Libraries." In *The New Grove Dictionary of Music and Musicians.* Vol. 10, pp. 719–821.

Bradley, Carol June, comp. *Music Collections in American Libraries: A Chronology.* Detroit Studies in Music Bibliography, no. 46. Detroit: Information Coordinators, 1981.

Directory of Music Research Libraries. **Répertoire international des sources musicales (RISM)** ser. C. [2nd ed., rev. and enl.] Kassel: Bärenreiter, 1983–.

1. *Canada and the United States.* 2nd rev. ed. Kassel: Bärenreiter, 1983. First published in 1967.
2. *Thirteen European Countries.* Preliminary ed. Iowa City: University of Iowa, 1970.
3. *Spain, France, Italy, Portugal.* Preliminary ed. Iowa City: University of Iowa, 1972.
4. *Australia, Israel, Japan, New Zealand.* Kassel: Bärenreiter, 1979.
5. *Czechoslovakia, Hungary, Poland, Yugoslavia.* Edited by Lillian Pruett. Kassel: Bärenreiter, 1985.
6. *South America, Central America, Mexico and the Caribbean.*

Penney, Barbara, comp. and ed. *Music in British Libraries: A Directory of Resources.* 4th ed. London: Library Association Publishing, 1991. First published in 1971.

Library and Union Catalogs

The items in the American section pertain to the printed card catalogs of three of the largest and most important U.S. libraries. The next section includes catalogs of three major research libraries in Europe. The international items, all online union catalogs, represent an immense repository of information from cooperating libraries located primarily in America and Europe.

AMERICAN

Boston Public Library. *Dictionary Catalog of the Music Collection of the Boston Public Library.* 20 vols. Boston: G. K. Hall, 1972. First Suppl., 4 vols., 1977.

Library of Congress. *National Union Catalog: Music and Phonorecords: A Cumulative Author List Representing Library of Congress Printed Cards and Titles Reported by Other American Libraries.* Ann Arbor, Mich.: J. W. Edwards, [1956]-.

————. *National Union Catalog: Music and Phonorecords 1953–72.* Washington, D.C.: Library of Congress, 1966–73. (Also available on CD-ROM.)

————. *National Union Catalog: Music, Books on Music, and Sound Recordings 1973–.* Washington, D.C.: Library of Congress, 1978–. Continuation of previous item. (Also available on CD-ROM.)

————. *The National Union Catalog: Pre-1956 Imprints.* 754 vols. London: Mansell, 1968–81.

Music Library Association Catalog of Cards and Printed Music 1953–1972: A Supplement to the Library of Congress Catalogs. Edited by Elizabeth H. Olmstead. 2 vols. Totowa, N.J.: Rowman and Littlefield, 1974.

The New York Public Library. Reference Department. *Dictionary Catalog of the Music Collection, New York Public Library.* 2nd ed. 45 vols. Boston: G. K. Hall, 1982. First published in 1964. (See *Bibliographic Guide to Music*, p. 23 above.)

EUROPEAN

Bavarian State Library. *Bayerische Staatsbibliothek, Katalog der Musikdrucke: BSB-Musik.* 17 vols. Munich: K. G. Saur, 1988–90.

British Library. *The British Library General Catalogue of Printed Books to 1975.* 360 vols. London: Bingley; London: K. G. Saur, 1979–84. (Also available on CD-ROM.)

————. *The Catalogue of Printed Music in the British Library to 1980.* 62 vols. London: K. G. Saur, 1981–87.

Paris. Bibliothèque Nationale. *Catalogue général des livres imprimés: Auteurs.* 231 vols. Paris: Imprimerie Nationale, 1900–1981. (Also available on CD-ROM.)

————. *Catalogue général des livres imprimés: auteurs— collectivités-auteurs—anonymes, 1960–1969.* 27 vols. Paris: Imprimerie Nationale, 1972–78.

INTERNATIONAL

LC MARC. Washington, D.C.: Library of Congress, n.d. Contains bibliographic information on nearly three million publications (books, music, serials, etc.) published worldwide since 1968 from LC Machine Readable Cataloging (MARC) records. Corresponds in part to the *National Union Catalog*. Updated weekly and accessible through several online services. (Also available on CD-ROM as *CDMARC*.)

LC Foreign MARC. Washington, D.C.: Library of Congress, n.d. Contains bibliographic information on more than 250,000 publications in languages other than English compiled from records in the British Library, National Library of Canada, and National Library of New Zealand.

REMARC (REtrospective MARC). Toronto: UTLAS International, n.d. A companion file to *LC MARC* containing over five million bibliographic records on international publications, primarily in English, catalogued by the Library of Congress from 1897 to 1980 but not included in *LC MARC*. (Also available on CD-ROM.)

OCLC Online Union Catalog (OLUC). Dublin, Ohio: OCLC Online Computer Library Center, Inc., 1971–. The first online union library database in the United States, and the world's largest, with data storage (books, music, recordings, etc.) from nearly five thousand libraries in some forty countries and territories worldwide (including the Eastman School of Music, Florida State University, Indiana University, University of Illinois at Champaign/Urbana, Oberlin College Conservatory, the Newberry Library, University of Texas, and the University of California at Los Angeles); overall there are more than fifteen thousand libraries with access to the OCLC system. Through *WorldCat* it is possible to search the holdings of the entire database by author and title; subject searching of the database is available through OCLC Cataloging, Interlibrary Loan, and Reference Services (*EPIC* and *FirstSearch*). Library of Congress acquisitions are being added continuously to the database. (The database is available in part on CD-ROM.)

RLIN (Research Libraries Information Network). Stanford, Calif.: Research Libraries Group, Inc., 1974–. An online union database located at Stanford University that contains bibliographic references to the holdings of more than 250 libraries (constituting the Research Libraries Group) located primarily in the United States (e.g., Harvard University, Yale University, Princeton University, Cornell University, University of Michigan, University of California at Berkeley, Stanford University, and the New York Public Library). Library of Congress acquisitions are being added continuously to the database.

Musical Instrument Collections

The following sources are the standard ones in the area. The MLA *Survey* and the *International Directory,* both dating from the 1970s, complement each other; the former covers North American collections and catalogues, the latter the rest of the world, with an American addendum that supplements the former. Coover's book is more recent, is worldwide in coverage, includes catalogues of expositions as well as collections, and is much more thorough on private collections than either of the other sources. The Libin article in *The New Grove Dictionary* is a particularly accessible listing of instrument collections around the world. None of the directories, however, is all-inclusive, and to be thorough one should consult them all.

Coover, James B. *Musical Instrument Collections: Catalogues and Cognate Literature.* Detroit Studies in Music Bibliography, vol. 47. Detroit: Information Coordinators, 1981.
International Council of Museums. *International Directory of Musical Instrument Collections.* Edited by Jean Jenkins. Buren, The Netherlands: Frits Knuf for the International Council of Museums, 1977.
Libin, Laurence. "Instruments, Collections of." In *The New Grove Dictionary of Music and Musicians.* Vol. 9, pp. 245–54.
Music Library Association. *A Survey of Musical Instrument Collections in the United States and Canada.* Chapel Hill, N.C.: Music Library Association, 1974.

Schools of Music

Uscher's *Schirmer Guide* stands alone as an international guide to music schools. The other three sources apply to North America, the CMS *Directory* listing music faculty members, and the CMS *Index* and the NASM *Directory* listing academic degrees granted.

The College Music Society. *Directory of Music Faculties in Colleges and Universities, U.S. and Canada.* Published biennially. Boulder, Colo.: College Music Society, 1967–.

Lincoln, Harry B., comp. and ed. *Index to Graduate Degrees in Music, U.S. and Canada.* Binghamton, N.Y.: College Music Society, 1971.

National Association of Schools of Music. *Directory.* Published annually. N.p.: 19[6–]-.

Uscher, Nancy. *The Schirmer Guide to Schools of Music and Conservatories throughout the World.* New York: Schirmer Books, 1988.

International Music Guides

These useful guides are annotated lists of concert halls, festivals, famous musicians' residences, instrument collections, archives and libraries, conservatories, etc., in various European countries. For further information concerning music festivals and the like, see chapter 8 under "Performing Arts, Competitions, and Festivals," p. 196 below.

Adelmann, Marianne, ed. *Musical Europe: An Illustrated Guide to Musical Life in 18 European Countries.* New York: Paddington Press, 1974.

British Music Yearbook. London: Classical Music, 1975–; New York: Schirmer Books, 1984–.

Brody, Elaine, and Claire Brook. *The Music Guide to Austria and Germany.* New York: Dodd, Mead, 1975.

———. *The Music Guide to Belgium, Luxembourg, Holland and Switzerland.* New York: Dodd, Mead, 1977.

———. *The Music Guide to Great Britain: England, Scotland, Wales, Ireland.* New York: Dodd, Mead, 1975.

———. *The Music Guide to Italy.* New York: Dodd, Mead, 1978.

Goertz, Harald. *Musikhandbuch für Österreich: Struktur und Organisation in 2500 Stichworten, Namen, Adressen, Information.* Vienna: Doblinger, 1983.

Gottesman, Roberta, ed. *The Music Lover's Guide to Europe: A Compendium of Festivals, Concerts, and Opera.* New York: John Wiley & Sons, 1992.

Musik-Almanach. Kassel: Bärenreiter, 1986–.

Norris, Gerald. *A Musical Gazetteer of Great Britain and Ireland.* Newton Abbot, England: David and Charles, 1981.

Steinbeck, Hans. *Schweizer Musik-Handbuch: Informationen über Struktur und Organisation des Schweizer Musiklebens/ Guide musicale suisse: Informations sur la structure et l'organisation de la vie musicale suisse/Guida musicale*

*svizzera: Informazioni sulla struttura e l'organizzazione
della vita musicale svizzera.* Zurich: Atlantis Musikbuch,
1983.

MUSIC SOURCES

Primary Sources of Early Music:
Manuscripts and Prints

In the "General" list of bibliographies of primary sources,
RISM stands out from all the others in its all-inclusiveness. When
finished, its series A and B will constitute an international index of
all known sources of manuscript and printed music and writings
about music up to 1800 (for further information, see *The New Harvard Dictionary* article "RISM," as well as Duckles, *Music Reference
and Research Materials*—p. 32 above—where the individually annotated volumes in the series are listed under the full title: *Répertoire
international des sources musicales*). Wettstein's *Thematische Sammelverzeichnisse,* an annotated list of catalogues of selected music collections in libraries and archives arranged alphabetically by city, is
the only such source in print.

The *New Grove* article "Sources, MS" is also large in scope, listing in numerous separate bibliographies the manuscript sources of
Western vocal music through the Renaissance. The *Census-
Catalogue* is a more thorough treatment of polyphonic music in the
period 1400–1550. The three other *New Grove* articles list both
manuscript and printed sources of early instrumental music. The
Brown and Vogel works are fundamentally important as representative bibliographies of early printed music. Samuel's article in *The
New Harvard Dictionary* is a useful brief list of the chief manuscript
sources of polyphonic music before 1500. The two Eitner sources,
though largely superseded by *RISM*, are still of some value.

The "American" category consists of six principal bibliographies of sacred and secular music in prints and manuscripts col-
lectively covering music up into the first quarter of the nineteenth
century.

GENERAL

Boorman, Stanley, et al. "Sources, MS." In *The New Grove
    Dictionary of Music and Musicians.* Vol. 17, pp. 590–702.
Brown, Howard Mayer. *Instrumental Music Printed before 1600: A
    Bibliography.* Cambridge: Harvard University Press, 1965.

Bryden, John R., and David G. Hughes. *An Index of Gregorian Chant*. 2 vols. Cambridge: Harvard University Press, 1969.

Caldwell, John. "Sources of Keyboard Music to 1660." In *The New Grove Dictionary of Music and Musicians*. Vol. 17, pp. 717–33.

Census-Catalogue of Manuscript Sources of Polyphonic Music, 1400–1550. Compiled by the University of Illinois Musicological Archives for Renaissance Manuscript Studies. 5 vols. Stuttgart: Hänssler, for the American Institute of Musicology, 1979–88.

Edwards, Warwick. "Sources of Instrumental Ensemble Music to 1630." In *The New Grove Dictionary of Music and Musicians*. Vol. 17, pp. 702–17.

Eitner, Robert. *Bibliographie der Musik-Sammelwerke des XVI. und XVII. Jahrhunderts*. In collaboration with Franz X. Haberl, A. Lagerberg, and C. F. Pohl. Berlin: L. Liepmannssohn, 1877. Suppls. in *Monatshefte für Musikgeschichte* 14 (1882): 152–55, 161–64.

———. *Biographisch-bibliographisches Quellen-Lexikon der Musiker und Musikgelehrten christlicher Zeitrechnung bis Mitte des neunzehnten Jahrhunderts*. 2nd ed., improved and enl. 11 vols. Graz: Akademische Druck- und Verlagsanstalt, 1959. First published in 1898–1904.

Ness, Arthur J. "Sources of Lute Music." In *The New Grove Dictionary of Music and Musicians*. Vol. 17, pp. 733–53.

Répertoire international des sources musicales/Internationales Quellen-lexikon der Musik/International Inventory of Musical Sources (RISM). Ser. A, individual composers, Kassel: Bärenreiter, 1971–; ser. B, multiple-composer collections, music manuscripts, and writings about music, Munich: G. Henle, 1960–.

Samuel, Harold E. "Sources (Pre-1500)." In *The New Harvard Dictionary of Music*. Pp. 773–78.

Vogel, Emil, Alfred Einstein, François Lesure, and Claudio Sartori. *Bibliografia della musica italiana vocale profana pubblicata dal 1500 al 1700*. New ed. 2 vols. + suppl. Staderini, Switzerland: Minkoff, 1977–82. First published in 1892.

Wettstein, Hermann. *Thematische Sammelverzeichnisse der Musik: Ein bibliographischer Führer durch Musikbibliotheken und -archive*. [Laaber, Germany]: Laaber-Verlag, 1982.

AMERICAN

Britton, Allen Perdue, and Irving Lowens, completed by Richard
    Crawford. *American Sacred Music Imprints, 1698–1810: A
    Bibliography.* Worcester, Mass.: American Antiquarian
    Society, 1990.
Fuld, James J., and Mary Wallace Davidson. *18th-Century
    American Secular Music Manuscripts: An Inventory.* MLA
    Index and Bibliography Series, no. 20. Philadelphia: Music
    Library Association, 1980.
Heard, Priscilla S. *American Music, 1698–1800: An Annotated
    Bibliography.* Waco, Tex.: Baylor University Press, 1975.
Heintze, James R. "Music in Performance and Other Editions,"
    "Music in Facsimile Reprints." In *American Music before
    1865 in Print and on Records: A Biblio-Discography.* Rev.
    ed. I.S.A.M. Monographs, no. 30. Brooklyn: Institute for
    Studies in American Music, Conservatory of Music,
    Brooklyn College of the City University of New York, 1990.
    Pp. 1–67, 68–87. First published in 1976.
Sonneck, Oscar George Theodore. *A Bibliography of Early
    Secular American Music (18th Century).* Rev. and enl. ed.
    Revised by William Treat Upton. Washington, D.C.:
    Library of Congress, Music Division, 1945; reprint with
    new preface by Irving Lowens, New York: DaCapo Press,
    1964. First published in 1902.
Wolfe, Richard J. *Secular Music in America, 1801–1825: A
    Bibliography.* 3 vols. New York: New York Public Library,
    1964.

Editions of Music

Each of these indexes is different in its organization, comprehensiveness, amount of information, and recentness; none of them
covers absolutely everything, and there is some degree of overlap
among them. The recent index by Hill and Stephens, covering over
five thousand items, supersedes all other such sources, including
Heyer, which was long the standard one. The 1991 *Monuments of
Music* catalog of the European bookseller Otto Harrassowitz is also
recent though limited to series published in Europe. Samuel's *New
Harvard Dictionary* article and the two items by Charles are included
for the sake of completeness; in Charles's book, section A lists sets
and monuments, and section B, complete works as well as the-

matic catalogues. Her *New Grove* article is a bibliography only and is differently organized: complete works, other collected editions, editions of theoretical works, and anthologies.

Of the two sources that concern composers' complete works only, Coover's list is of limited value because of its age; Harrassowitz's 1992 *Composers' Collected Editions* catalogue is a practical update presenting works from European publishers.

The remaining two sources are indexes of anthologies of music. Hilton's is older, shorter, and limited to early music; it covers fewer anthologies, but some of them are as old as the late 19th century. Murray's is more recent and covers many more anthologies, emphasizing current ones.

Charles, Sydney Robinson. *A Handbook of Music and Music Literature in Sets and Series.* New York: Free Press, 1972. Section A: "Sets and Series Containing Music of Several Composers and Sets and Series Containing Both Music and Music Literature," pp. 1–144; section B: "Sets and Series Devoted to One Composer," pp. 145–325.

Charles, Sydney Robinson, with Julie Woodward. "Editions, Historical." In *The New Grove Dictionary of Music and Musicians.* Vol. 5, pp. 848–69.

Composers' Collected Editions from Europe. 7th rev. ed. Special Music Catalog no. 15. Wiesbaden: Otto Harrassowitz, 1992.

Coover, James B. *Gesamtausgaben: A Checklist.* N.p.: Distant Press, 1970.

Heyer, Anna Harriet. *Historical Sets, Collected Editions, and Monuments of Music: A Guide to Their Contents.* 3rd ed. 2 vols. Chicago: American Library Association, 1980. First published in 1957.

Hill, George R., and Norris L. Stephens. *Collected Editions, Historical Series and Sets, and Monuments of Music: A Bibliography.* Fallen Leaf Reference Books in Music, no. 14. Berkeley, Calif.: Fallen Leaf Press, 1994. (Forthcoming indexes to be published on CD-ROM.)

Hilton, Ruth B. *An Index to Early Music in Selected Anthologies.* Music Indexes and Bibliographies, no. 13. Clifton, N.J.: European American Music, 1978.

Monuments of Music from Europe. 2nd rev. ed. Special Music Catalog no. 13. Wiesbaden: Otto Harrassowitz, 1991.

Murray, Sterling E. *Anthologies of Music: An Annotated Index.* 2nd ed. Detroit Studies in Music Bibliography, no. 68. Warren, Mich.: Harmonie Park Press, 1992. First published in 1987.

Samuel, Harold E. "Editions, Historical." In *The New Harvard Dictionary of Music.* Pp. 264–76.

Thematic Catalogues

There are two standard lists of thematic catalogues of individual composers' works, Brook's *Thematic Catalogues* and Wettstein's *Bibliographie,* both originating in the 1970s and both annotated. The 1992 edition of Brook's catalogue, coauthored by Richard J. Viano, is now by far the more complete source of such information. (Recall that thematic catalogues are also included in section B of Charles's *A Handbook of Music and Music Literature in Sets and Series;* see p. 41 above).

Brook, Barry S., and Richard J. Viano. *Thematic Catalogues in Music: An Annotated Bibliography.* 2nd ed. RILM Retrospectives, no. 4. Stuyvesant, N.Y.: Pendragon Press, 1992. First published in 1972.
Wettstein, Hermann. *Bibliographie musikalischer thematischer Werkverzeichnisse.* [Laaber, Germany]: Laaber-Verlag, 1978.

Catalogues of Librettos

Following are three essential listings of opera librettos: the classic catalogue by Sonneck; its new Italian counterpart; and the recent, ongoing, comprehensive *U.S.-RISM* database. See also chapter 5 under "Dramatic Music—Libretto Studies," p. 124 below.

Sartori, Claudio. *I libretti italiani a stampa dalle origini al 1800: catalogo analitico con 16 indici.* Cuneo, Italy: Bertola & Locatelli, 1990–. (Also exists as a database at the University of Michigan.)
Sonneck, Oscar. *Catalogue of Opera Librettos Printed before 1800.* Washington, D.C.: Government Printing Office, 1914; reprint, New York: Johnson Reprints, 1970.
U.S.-RISM Libretto Project. 1982–. An online database "established at the University of Virginia in 1982 in order to coordinate the cataloguing and indexing of all historical librettos in libraries and private collections in the United States. The objective of the project is not only to catalogue these librettos as bibliographic entities, but also to index much of the information about the productions for which

these librettos were produced." (From "Searching for U.S.-RISM Libretto Project Records in RLIN: A Guide," prepared by John Andrus and Diane Parr Walker, October 1990.) All data are being entered into the *RLIN* database. (See *RLIN [Research Libraries Information Network]*, p. 35 above).

Discographies

These items were selected from many such sources and represent those primarily concerned with "serious" or "classical" and ethnic music. The first category is "Bibliographies of Discographies," works that are—or contain, in the case of *Brian Rust's Guide*—lists of discographies. *The Bibliography of Discographies* promises to be the most extensive such work; when complete, it will comprise five volumes, the final two containing ethnic and folk music discographies and miscellaneous ones, such as of the spoken word.

The second category, "Guides to Currently Available Recordings," consists of the most important periodically updated lists of available recordings—four American, one English, and one German.

The third category, "Specialized Discographies," lists some important sources with special emphases—classical and opera, early music, women composers, etc.—some of them annotated, some not. Holmes's two discographies of performances organized by conductors' names, virtually the only such specialized works on the subject, are particularly detailed; the same may be said for the more recent lists of ethnic and Gregorian chant recordings, by Spottswood and Weber respectively.

BIBLIOGRAPHIES OF DISCOGRAPHIES

Bibliography of Discographies. 5 vols. projected. New York: R. R. Bowker, 1977–.

1. *Classical Music, 1925–1975.* By Michael H. Gray and Gerald D. Gibson. 1977. Suppl.: *Classical Music Discographies, 1976–1988: A Bibliography.* Compiled by Michael H. Gray. Discographies no. 34. New York: Greenwood Press, 1989.
2. *Jazz.* By Daniel Allen. 1981.
3. *Popular Music.* By Michael H. Gray. 1983.

Cooper, David Edwin. *International Bibliography of Discographies: Classical Music and Jazz and Blues, 1962–1972: A Reference Book for Record Collectors, Dealers, and Libraries.* Littleton, Colo.: Libraries Unlimited, 1975.

Gray, Michael, comp. *Classical Music Discographies, 1976–1988: A Bibliography.* Discographies, no. 34. Westport, Conn.: Greenwood Press, 1989.

Rust, Brian A. L. *Brian Rust's Guide to Discography.* Discographies, no. 4. Westport, Conn.: Greenwood Press, 1980.

Guides to Currently Available Recordings

Bielefelder Katalog Klassik. Published semiannually. Stuttgart: Vereinigte Motor-Verlage, 1953–.

Gramophone Classical Catalogue. Published quarterly. Harrow, Middlesex, England: General Gramophone Publications, 1953–.

Opus: America's Guide to Classical Music. Published quarterly. Santa Fe: Stereophile, 1990–. Originally began publication as *Schwann Record and Tape Guide* in 1949.

Phonolog. Looseleaf service, updated monthly. Los Angeles: Trade Services Publications, 1948–. (CD-ROM version: *Billboard/Phonolog Music Reference Library.* New York: BPI Communications, 1992–.)

Schwann Artist Issue. Published triennially. Santa Fe: Stereophile, 1949–.

Spectrum: Your Guide to Today's Music. Published quarterly. Santa Fe: Stereophile, 1990–. Originally began publication as *Schwann Record and Tape Guide* in 1949; limited to jazz and vernacular music.

Specialized Discographies

Classical and Opera

Cohn, Arthur. *Recorded Classical Music: A Critical Guide to Compositions and Performances.* New York: Schirmer Books, 1981.

Mordden, Ethan. *A Guide to Opera Recordings.* New York: Oxford University Press, 1987.

Rosenberg, Kenyon C. *A Basic Classical and Operatic Recordings Collection for Libraries.* Metuchen, N.J.: Scarecrow Press, 1987.

———— . *A Basic Classical and Operatic Recordings Collection on Compact Discs for Libraries: A Buying Guide.* Metuchen, N.J.: Scarecrow Press, 1990.

Gregorian Chant and Early Music

Croucher, Trevor, comp. *Early Music Discography: From Plainsong to the Sons of Bach.* 2 vols. Phoenix: Oryx Press, 1981.

Weber, Jerome F., comp. *A Gregorian Chant Discography.* 2 vols. Discography Series, no. 20. New York: J. F. Weber, 1990.

American Music

Davis, Elizabeth A. *Index to the New World Recorded Anthology of American Music: A User's Guide to the Initial One Hundred Records.* New York: W. W. Norton, 1981.

Heintze, James R. "Discography." In *American Music before 1865 in Print and on Records: A Biblio-Discography.* Rev. ed. I.S.A.M. Monographs, no. 30. Brooklyn: Institute for Studies in American Music, Conservatory of Music, Brooklyn College of the City University of New York, 1990. Pp. 88–144. First published in 1976.

Oja, Carol J., ed. *American Music Recordings: A Discography of 20th-Century U.S. Composers.* A Project of the Institute for Studies in American Music for the Koussevitzky Music Foundation. Brooklyn: Institute for Studies in American Music, Conservatory of Music, Brooklyn College of the City University of New York, 1982.

Conductors

Holmes, John L. *Conductors: A Record Collector's Guide, Including Compact Discs.* London: Victor Gollancz, 1988.

———— . *Conductors on Record.* Westport, Conn.: Greenwood Press, 1982.

Women Composers

Cohen, Aaron I., comp. *International Discography of Women Composers.* Discographies, no. 10. Westport, Conn.: Greenwood Press, 1984.

Frasier, Jane. *Women Composers: A Discography.* Detroit Studies in Music Bibliography, no. 50. Detroit: Information Coordinators, 1983.

Mitchell, Charles, ed. *Discography of Works by Women Composers*. Paterson, N.J.: Paterson Free Public Library, 1975.

Ethnomusicology

Spottswood, Richard K. *Ethnic Music on Record: A Discography of Ethnic Recordings Produced in the United States, 1893–1942*. 7 vols. Urbana: University of Illinois Press, 1990.

    1. *Western Europe.*
    2. *Slavic.*
    3. *Eastern Europe.*
    4. *Spanish, Portuguese, Philippine, Basque.*
    5. *Mid-East, Far East, Scandinavian, English Language, American Indian, International.*
    6. Indexes.
    7. Indexes.

Jazz

Bielefelder Katalog Jazz. Published annually. Stuttgart: Vereinigte Motor-Verlage, 1963–.
Harrison, Max, et al. *The Essential Jazz Records.* Discographies, no. 12. Westport, Conn.: Greenwood Press, 1984–.

    1. *Ragtime to Swing.* 1984.

SELECTED GENERAL BIBLIOGRAPHIES

Music research is often cross-disciplinary, necessitating work in other fields. The sources listed here are among the most widely known and comprehensive listings of general sources. Sheehy and Walford are both standard guides to reference works in all fields. Mixter introduces the music researcher to general reference works outside the field of music, and the *Bibliographical Index* is a serial publication that lists current bibliographies that are either published separately or appear in books or periodicals.

The four remaining sources represent what are probably the most important current book-trade publications in the English-speaking world. *Books in Print* and *Subject Guide to Books in Print* cover American publishers, and *British National Bibliography*, British publishers; the *Cumulative Book Index* lists all English-language publications.

*Bibliographical Index: A Cumulative Bibliography of
    Bibliographies, 1937–.* New York: H. W. Wilson, 1938–.
*Books in Print: An Author-Title-Series Index to the Publishers'
    Trade List Annual.* New York: R. R. Bowker, 1948–. (Also
    available on CD-ROM as *Books in Print Plus.*)
British National Bibliography. London: Council of the British
    National Bibliography, British Museum, 1950–. (Also
    available on CD-ROM.)
Cumulative Book Index. New York: H. W. Wilson, 1898–.
Mixter, Keith E. *General Bibliography for Music Research.* 2nd ed.
    Detroit Studies in Music Bibliography, no. 33. Detroit:
    Information Coordinators, 1975. First published in 1962;
    3rd ed. forthcoming from Harmonie Park Press.
Sheehy, Eugene P., et al., eds. *Guide to Reference Books.* 10th ed.
    Chicago: American Library Association, 1986. First
    published in 1902.
*Subject Guide to Books in Print: An Index to the Publishers'
    Trade List Annual, 1957–.* New York: R. R. Bowker, 1957–.
    (Also available on CD-ROM as *Books in Print Plus.*)
Walford's Guide to Reference Material. 5th ed. London: Library
    Association, 1989–. First published in 1959.

CHAPTER THREE

Area Bibliographies and Other Reference Sources

This chapter includes lists of basic sources in five fundamental areas of music research—general musicology, ethnomusicology, performance practice, music theory, and music education. Then follow short lists of bibliographies, guides, and indexes of reference value for researching certain other selected topic areas.

MUSICOLOGY

Musicology, since its early recognition and definition in the late 1800s, has produced an extensive literature concerned with itself as a discipline. The following bibliography is a list of basic discussions of the theory and practice of musicology, intended to serve as an introduction to its content, organization, and history. The emphasis is largely on more recent sources, but selected older classics have also been included.

Listed in the first category, "The History of Musicology," are two standard accounts of the history of the discipline. Under "Comprehensive Overviews" are sources that are primarily systematic presentations of the field and its philosophy and methodology. Some of the most significant and influential early treatments are included, most notably the one by Adler, whose division into systematic and historical musicology has largely been observed ever since.

"Selected Discussions of the Discipline in Chronological Order" begins with Chrysander's preface in 1863 in which the word "Musikwissenschaft" was first presented, proceeds to Adler's pioneering article on the subject and Pratt's introduction of it to American readers, and continues with various writings that treat matters of definition, philosophical interpretation, trends, problems, challenges, etc., in musicology up to 1992. "Discussions of Musicology in the United States" brings together varied sources that deal with the history and practice of musicology in this country, including Crawford's history of the American Musicological Society and Steinzor's bibliography of the writings of the leading earlier American musicologists. The sources listed under "Music Historiography" are concerned with the techniques, theories, and principles of historical research and presentation.

Under "Miscellaneous Sources" are the conference papers published as *Musicology and the Computer,* and the introductions to musicological materials and applications by Davies, Spiess, and Stevens (the first two now mostly of historical value); presentations by Spencer and Wallin of newly conceived aspects of the discipline; and two collections of essays: Seeger's, many of which are discussions of musicological theory and practice; and Wiora's, which amount to a virtual overview of the field.

The final item, under "Bibliographic Database," is the *SMT Online Database,* which includes some musicological journals although its emphasis is music theory.

Monographs on musicological subjects are often published in series, such as the substantial Musicological Studies and Documents series of the American Institute of Musicology, and the many German series, such as Beiträge zur rheinischen Musikgeschichte. Apart from Steinzor's *American Musicologists,* no bibliographies are listed here, but virtually all the bibliographies appearing in chapter 2 and the present chapter are applicable to the field of musicology in its broadest sense. There are also series of bibliographies that pertain to musicology, such as the Detroit Studies in Music Bibliography. For a list of standard musicological journals, see chapter 6, "Current Research Journals in Music," p. 152 below.

The History of Musicology

Harrison, Frank Ll., Mantle Hood, and Claude V. Palisca.
   Musicology (Harrison: "American Musicology and the
   European Tradition," pp. 1–85; Palisca: "American
   Scholarship in Western Music," pp. 87–213). Englewood
   Cliffs, N.J.: Prentice Hall, 1963.
Krohn, Ernst C. "The Development of Modern Musicology." In
   Historical Musicology: A Reference Manual for Research in

Music. Musicological Studies, no. 4. Brooklyn, N.Y.:
Institute of Mediaeval Music, [1963]. Pp. 153–72.

Comprehensive Overviews

Adler, Guido. *Methode der Musikgeschichte.* Leipzig: Breitkopf &
Härtel, 1919.
Chailley, Jacques, ed. *Précis de musicologie.* New ed., rev. Paris:
Presses Universitaires de France, 1984. First published in
1958.
Dahlhaus, Carl, and Helga de la Motte-Haber, eds. *Systematische
Musikwissenschaft.* Neues Handbuch der Musik-
wissenschaft, vol. 10. Laaber, Germany: Laaber-
Verlag, 1982.
Duckles, Vincent, et al. "Musicology." In *The New Grove
Dictionary of Music and Musicians.* Vol. 12, pp. 836–63.
Fellerer, Karl G. *Einführung in die Musikwissenschaft.* 2nd rev.
and enl. ed. Münchberg, Germany: B. Hahnefeld, 1953.
First published in 1942.
Haydon, Glen. *Introduction to Musicology: A Survey of the
Fields, Systematic and Historical, of Musical Knowledge
and Research.* Rev. ed. Chapel Hill: University of North
Carolina Press, 1959. First published in 1941.
Husmann, Heinrich. *Einführung in die Musikwissenschaft.* 2nd
ed. Taschenbücher zur Musikwissenschaft, no. 40.
Wilhelmshaven: Heinrichshofen's Verlag, 1975. First
published in 1958.
Kimmey, John A., Jr. *A Critique of Musicology: Clarifying the
Scope, Limits, and Purposes of Musicology.* Studies in the
History and Interpretation of Music, vol. 12. Lewiston,
N.Y.: Edwin Mellen Press, 1988.
"Musicology." In *The New Harvard Dictionary of Music.* Pp.
520–22.
Riemann, Hugo. *Grundriss der Musikwissenschaft.* 4th ed.
Revised by Johannes Wolff. Musikwissenschaft und
Bildung, Einzeldarstellungen aus allen Gebieten des
Wissens, no. 34. Leipzig: Quelle & Meyer, 1928. First
published in 1908.
Weber, Edith. *Recherche musicologique: objet, méthodologie,
normes de présentation.* Guides musicologiques, no. 1.
Paris: Beauchesne, 1980.
Wiora, Walter, et al. "Musikwissenschaft." In *Die Musik in
Geschichte und Gegenwart.* Vol. 9 (1961), cols. 1192–1220.

Selected Discussions of the Discipline in
Chronological Order

Chrysander, Friedrich. "Vorwort und Einleitung." *Jahrbücher für musikalische Wissenschaft* 1 (1863): 9–16.

Adler, Guido. "Umfang, Methode und Ziel der Musikwissenschaft." *Vierteljahrsschrift für Musikwissenschaft* 1, no. 1 (1885): 5–20.

Pratt, Waldo S. "On Behalf of Musicology." *The Musical Quarterly* 1 (January 1915): 1–16.

Harap, Louis. "On the Nature of Musicology." *The Musical Quarterly* 23 (January 1937): 18–25.

Seeger, Charles L. "Systematic and Historical Orientations in Musicology." *Acta Musicologica* 11 (September-December 1939): 121–28.

——— . "Systematic Musicology: Viewpoints, Orientations, and Methods." *Journal of the American Musicological Society* 4 (Fall 1951): 240–48.

Mendel, Arthur, Curt Sachs, and Carroll C. Pratt. *Some Aspects of Musicology: Three Essays* (Mendel: "The Services of Musicology to the Practical Musician"; Sachs: "The Lore of Non-Western Music"; Pratt: "Musicology and Related Disciplines"). New York: Liberal Arts Press, 1957.

Hibberd, Lloyd. "Musicology Reconsidered." *Acta Musicologica* 31 (January-March 1959): 25–31.

Lippman, Edward A. "What Should Musicology Be?" *Current Musicology*, no. 1 (1965): 55–60.

Ernst, Viet. "Über die Einheit von historischer und systematischer Musikwissenschaft." *Beiträge zur Musikwissenschaft* 9, no. 2 (1967): 91–97.

Tischler, Hans. "And What Is Musicology?" *Music Review* 30 (November 1969): 253–60.

Brook, Barry S., Edward O. D. Downes, and Sherman Van Solkema, eds. *Perspectives in Musicology*. New York: W. W. Norton, 1972.

Chase, Gilbert. "Musicology, History, and Anthropology: Current Thoughts." In *Current Thought in Musicology*, edited by John W. Grubbs et al. Symposia in the Arts and Humanities, no. 4. Austin: University of Texas Press, 1976. Pp. 231–46.

Holoman, D. Kern, and Claude V. Palisca, eds. *Musicology in the 1980s: Methods, Goals, Opportunities*. Da Capo Press Music Series. New York: Da Capo Press, 1982.

Kerman, Joseph. *Contemplating Music: Challenges to Musicology.* Cambridge: Harvard University Press, 1985.

Citron, Marcia J. "Gender, Professionalism and the Musical Canon." *Journal of Musicology* 8 (Winter 1990): 102–17.

Newman, William S. "Musicology among the Humanities." In *Essays in Musicology: A Tribute to Alvin Johnson,* edited by Lewis Lockwood and Edward Roesner. N.p.: American Musicological Society, 1990. Pp. 292–302.

Bergeron, Katherine, and Philip V. Bohlman, eds. *Disciplining Music: Musicology and Its Canons.* Chicago: University of Chicago Press, 1992.

Discussions of Musicology in the United States in Chronological Order

Bukofzer, Manfred. *The Place of Musicology in American Institutions of Higher Learning.* New York: Liberal Arts Press, 1957.

Goldthwaite, Scott. "The Growth and Influence of Musicology in the United States." *Acta Musicologica* 33 (April-December 1961): 72–79.

Kerman, Joseph. "A Profile for American Musicology." *Journal of the American Musicological Society* 18 (Spring 1965): 60–69.

Lowinsky, Edward E. "Character and Purposes of American Musicology: A Reply to Joseph Kerman." *Journal of the American Musicological Society* 18 (Summer 1965): 222–34.

McPeek, Gwynn. "Musicology in the United States: A Survey of Recent Trends." In *Studies in Musicology: Essays in the History, Style, and Bibliography of Music, in Memory of Glen Haydon,* edited by James W. Pruett. Chapel Hill: University of North Carolina Press, 1969. Pp. 260–75.

Crawford, Richard. *The American Musicological Society, 1934–1984: An Anniversary Essay.* Philadelphia: American Musicological Society, 1984.

Pruett, James W., and Thomas P. Slavens. *Research Guide to Musicology.* Sources of Information in the Humanities, no. 4. Chicago: American Library Association, 1985.

Steinzor, Curt Efram, comp. *American Musicologists, c. 1890–1945: A Bio-Bibliographical Sourcebook to the Formative Period.* Music Reference Collection, no. 17. Westport, Conn.: Greenwood Press, 1989.

Kerman, Joseph. "American Musicology in the 1990s." *Journal of Musicology* 9 (Spring 1991): 131–44.

Music Historiography

Adler, Guido. *Methode der Musikgeschichte.* Leipzig: Breitkopf & Härtel, 1919.

Allen, Warren Dwight. *Philosophies of Music: A Study of General Histories of Music, 1600–1960.* New York: Dover Publications, 1962. First published in 1939. Ph.D. diss., Columbia University, 193?.

Chase, Gilbert. "The Musicologist as Historian: A Matter of Distinction." *Notes* 29 (September 1972): 10–16.

Dahlhaus, Carl. *Foundations of Music History.* Translated by J. B. Robinson. Cambridge: Cambridge University Press, 1983. First published in 1967.

Eggebrecht, Hans Heinrich. "Historiography." In *The New Grove Dictionary of Music and Musicians.* Vol. 8, pp. 592–600.

Grout, Donald J. "Current Historiography and Music History." In *Studies in Music History: Essays for Oliver Strunk,* edited by Harold Powers. Princeton: Princeton University Press, 1968. Pp. 23–40.

Lenneberg, Hans. *Witnesses and Scholars: Studies in Musical Biography.* Musicology Book Series, vol. 5. New York: Gordon and Breach, 1988.

Treitler, Leo. "On Historical Criticism." *The Musical Quarterly* 53 (April 1967): 188–205.

Westrup, J. A. *An Introduction to Musical History.* 2nd ed. London: Hutchinson University Library, 1973. First published in 1955.

Wiora, Walter, ed. *Die Ausbreitung des Historismus über die Musik.* Studien zur Musikgeschichte des 19. Jahrhunderts, vol. 14. Regensburg: Gustav Bosse, 1969.

Miscellaneous Sources

Brook, Barry S., ed. *Musicology and the Computer: Musicology 1966–2000: A Practical Program—Three Symposia.* American Musicological Society, Greater New York Chapter, Publications, no. 2. New York: City University of New York Press, 1970.

Davies, J. H. *Musicalia: Sources of Information in Music.* Oxford: Pergamon Press, 1966.

Seeger, Charles. *Studies in Musicology 1935–1975.* Berkeley: University of California Press, 1977.

Spencer, Jon Michael. *Theological Music: Introduction to Theomusicology.* Contributions to the Study of Music and Dance, no. 23. Westport, Conn.: Greenwood Press, 1991.

Spiess, Lincoln Bunce. *Historical Musicology: A Reference Manual for Research in Music.* Brooklyn, N.Y.: Institute of Mediaeval Music, 1963.

Stevens, Denis. *Musicology: A Practical Guide.* Yehudi Menuhin Music Guides. New York: Schirmer Books, 1980.

Wallin, Nils L. *Biomusicology: Neurophysiological, Neuropsychological, and Evolutionary Perspectives on the Origins and Purposes of Music.* Stuyvesant, N.Y.: Pendragon Press, 1992.

Wiora, Walter. *Historische und systematische Musikwissenschaft: Ausgewählte Aufsätze.* Edited by Hellmut Kühn and Christoph-Hellmut Mahling. Tutzing: Hans Schneider, 1972.

Bibliographic Database

SMT Online Bibliographic Database. Sponsored by the Society for Music Theory; Lee Rothfarb, project director. Cambridge: Harvard University, 1992–. A database that contains citations of articles and reviews in all major music theory journals and selected musicology journals.

ETHNOMUSICOLOGY

The relative newness of what has come to be known as ethnomusicology is indicated by the fact that the term was coined, by Jaap Kunst, only in 1950, although the study of non-Western and folk music predates it by centuries and the origins of the field as it is now understood go back to the 1880s. The English-language sources listed below, dating with few exceptions from more recent decades, have been selected from this vast and multifaceted field not only to present some of its basic texts, overviews, and surveys, but to give some notion of its scope and extent by listing examples of more specific studies.

Thus, under "General Sources" are four "Classic Presentations of the Field," beginning with Kunst's in 1950; several "Works about Ethnomusicology as a Field of Research," comprising résumés of the discipline or discussions of areas within it; some "Surveys of

World Music," basic coverages of the music of the world or large regions of it, of which the twelve–volume *Universe of Music* will be by far the most comprehensive when completed; and four important representative sources on world instruments. Then, under "Selected Monographs and Studies," are two highly selective lists, each of a very few representative studies from an extensive literature of such sources: "Examplars of Ethnomusicological Method," works demonstrating some of the varied analytical approaches or methodologies employed in the field; and a selection from the numerous "General Works about Individual Cultures or Cultural Areas" that exist.

"Bibliographies and Other Reference Guides" constitutes the final category. The regularly featured "Current Bibliography, Discography, and Filmography" sections in *Ethnomusicology* cumulatively form the most complete list of sources in the field. Nettl's and Briegleb Schuursma's bibliographies are also generalized in their coverage, as is the latter author's *Directory* of sound recording archives in North America. All the remaining sources relate to particular regions of the world.

For other bibliographies related to ethnomusicology, see under "Bibliographies in Other Selected Areas—African-American Music," p. 85 below. For further coverage of the field, see *The Garland Encyclopedia of World Music*, listed on p. 92 below; further coverage of instruments may be found in the dictionaries listed in chapter 4 under "Specialized Dictionaries and Encyclopedias—Musical Instruments and Makers," p. 100 below. Standard ethnomusicological research journals are listed in chapter 6, "Current Research Journals in Music," p. 152 below. See also articles on individual countries, instruments, etc., in *The New Grove Dictionary*.

General Sources

Classic Presentations of the Field

Hood, Mantle. *The Ethnomusicologist.* New ed. Kent, Ohio: Kent State University Press, 1982. First published in 1971.
Kunst, Jaap. *Ethnomusicology: A Study of Its Nature, Its Problems, Methods, and Representative Personalities, to Which Is Added a Bibliography.* 3rd ed., enl. The Hague: Martinus Nijhoff, 1959. Suppl., 1960. First published in 1950.
Merriam, Alan P. *The Anthropology of Music.* Evanston, Ill.: Northwestern University Press, 1964.

Nettl, Bruno. *Theory and Method in Ethnomusicology.* New York: Free Press of Glencoe, 1964.

Works about Ethnomusicology as a Field of Research

Blum, Stephen, et al. *Ethnomusicology and Modern Music History.* Urbana: University of Illinois Press, 1991.

The Garland Library of Readings in Ethnomusicology: A Core Collection of Ethnomusicology Articles. 7 vols. Complied by Kay Kaufman Shelemay. New York: Garland Publishing, 1990.

Hood, Mantle. "Music, the Unknown." In *Musicology,* by Frank Ll. Harrison, Mantle Hood, and Claude V. Palisca. Englewood Cliffs, N.J.: Prentice Hall, 1963. Pp. 215–326.

Krader, Barbara. "Ethnomusicology." In *The New Grove Dictionary of Music and Musicians.* Vol. 6, pp. 275–82.

McAllester, David P., comp. *Readings in Ethnomusicology.* Landmarks in Anthropology. New York: Johnson Reprint, 1971.

Merriam, Alan P. "Definitions of 'Comparative Musicology' and 'Ethnomusicology': An Historical-Theoretical Perspective." *Ethnomusicology: Journal of the Society for Ethnomusicology* 21 (1977): 189–204.

Myers, Helen, ed. *Ethnomusicology: An Introduction.* The Norton/Grove Handbooks in Music. New York: W. W. Norton, 1992.

Nettl, Bruno. "Ethnomusicology." In *The New Harvard Dictionary of Music.* Pp. 291–93.

———. *The Study of Ethnomusicology: Twenty-Nine Issues and Concepts.* Urbana: University of Illinois Press, 1983.

Nettl, Bruno, and Philip V. Bohlman, eds. *Comparative Musicology and Anthropology of Music: Essays on the History of Ethnomusicology.* Chicago: University of Chicago Press, 1991.

Surveys of World Music

Malm, William P. *Music Cultures of the Pacific, the Near East, and Asia.* 2nd ed. The Prentice Hall History of Music Series. Englewood Cliffs, N.J.: Prentice Hall, 1977. First published in 1967.

May, Elizabeth, ed. *Musics of Many Cultures: An Introduction.* Berkeley: University of California Press, 1980.

Nettl, Bruno, with Gerard Béhague. *Folk and Traditional Music of the Western Continents*. 3rd ed. Revised and edited by Valerie Woodring Goertzen. The Prentice Hall History of Music Series. Englewood Cliffs, N.J.: Prentice Hall, 1990. First published in 1965.

Nettl, Bruno, et al. *Excursions in World Music*. Englewood Cliffs, N.J.: Prentice Hall, 1992.

Reck, David. *Music of the Whole Earth*. New York: Charles Scribner's Sons, 1977.

Schneider, Marius. *Non-European Folklore and Art Music*. Anthology of Music, vol. 44. Cologne: Arno Volk Verlag, 1972.

Titon, Jeff Todd, gen. ed. *Worlds of Music: An Introduction to the Music of the World's Peoples*. 2nd ed. New York: Schirmer Books, 1992. First published in 1984.

The Universe of Music: A History. A UNESCO/International Music Council Project. 12 vols. projected. Washington, D.C.: Smithsonian Institution Press, 1993–.

INSTRUMENTS

Buchner, Alexander. *Folk Music Instruments*. Translated by Alzbeta Nováková. New York: Crown Publishers, 1972. First published in 1968.

Hornbostel, Erich M. von, and Curt Sachs. "Classification of Musical Instruments." Translated by Anthony Baines and Klaus P. Wachsmann. *Galpin Society Journal*, no. 14 (March 1961): 3–29. First published in 1914.

Kartomi, Margaret J. *On Concepts and Classifications of Musical Instruments*. Chicago Studies in Ethnomusicology. Chicago: University of Chicago Press, 1990.

Wachsmann, Klaus, Erich M. Hornbostel, and Curt Sachs. "Instruments, Classification of." In *The New Grove Dictionary of Music and Musicians*. Vol. 9, pp. 237–45.

Selected Monographs and Studies

EXAMPLARS OF ETHNOMUSICOLOGICAL METHOD

Ames, David W., and Anthony V. King. *Glossary of Hausa Music and Its Social Contexts*. Evanston, Ill.: Northwestern University Press, 1971.

Blacking, John. *Venda Children's Songs: A Study in Ethnomusicological Analysis.* Johannesburg: Witwatersrand University Press, 1967.

Feld, Steven. *Sound and Sentiment: Birds, Weeping, Poetics and Song in Kaluli Expression.* 2nd ed. Publications of the American Folklore Society, new ser., vol. 5. Philadelphia: University of Pennsylvania Press, 1990. First published in 1982.

Kaufmann, Walter. *Musical Notations of the Orient: Notational Systems of Continental, East, South, and Central Asia.* Indiana University Humanities Series, no. 60. Bloomington: Indiana University Press, 1967.

Koskoff, Ellen, ed. *Women and Music in Cross-Cultural Perspective.* Contributions in Women's Studies, no. 79. New York: Greenwood Press, 1987.

Lomax, Alan. *Folk Song Style and Culture.* Publication no. 88. Washington, D.C.: American Association for the Advancement of Science, 1968.

Lord, Albert B. *The Singer of Tales.* Cambridge: Harvard University Press, 1960.

Manuel, Peter. *Popular Musics of the Non-Western World: An Introductory Survey.* New York: Oxford University Press, 1988.

Powers, Harold. "An Historical and Comparative Approach to the Classification of Ragas (with an Appendix on Ancient Indian Tunings)." In *Selected Reports: Publication of the Institute of Ethnomusicology of the University of California at Los Angeles* 1, no. 3 (1970): 1–78.

General Works about Individual Cultures or Cultural Areas

Arom, Simha. *African Polyphony and Polyrhythm: Musical Structure and Methodology.* Translated by Martin Thom et al. Cambridge: Cambridge University Press, 1991. First published in 1985.

Baily, John. *Music of Afghanistan: Professional Musicians in the City of Herat.* Cambridge Studies in Ethnomusicology. New York: Cambridge University Press, 1988.

Becker, Judith. *Traditional Music in Modern Java: Gamelan in a Changing Society.* Honolulu: University Press of Hawaii, 1980.

Herndon, Marcia. *Native American Music.* Norwood, Pa.: Norwood Editions, 1980.

Jairazbhoy, Nazir A. *The Rāgs of North Indian Music, Their Structure and Evolution.* Middletown, Conn.: Wesleyan University Press, 1971.

Kunst, Jaap. *Music in Java, Its History, Its Theory and Its Technique.* 3rd, enl. ed. 2 vols. Edited by E. L. Heins. The Hague: Martinus Nijhoff, 1973.

McPhee, Colin. *Music in Bali: A Study in Form and Instrumental Organization in Balinese Orchestral Music.* New Haven: Yale University Press, 1966.

Malm, William. *Japanese Music and Musical Instruments.* Rutland, Vt.: Charles E. Tuttle, 1959.

Merriam, Alan P. *Ethnomusicology of the Flathead Indians.* Viking Fund Publications in Anthropology, no. 44. Chicago: Aldine Publishing Company, 1967.

Morton, David. *The Traditional Music of Thailand.* Berkeley: University of California Press, 1976.

Myers, Helen, ed. *Ethnomusicology: Historical and Regional Studies.* New York: W. W. Norton, 1992.

Nettl, Bruno. *Folk Music in the United States: An Introduction.* 3rd ed., rev. and exp. by Helen Myers. Detroit: Wayne State University Press, 1976. First published in 1960.

Nketia, Joseph H. Kwabena. *The Music of Africa.* New York: W. W. Norton, 1974.

Slobin, Mark. *Music in the Culture of Northern Afghanistan.* Viking Fund Publications in Anthropology, no. 54. Tucson: University of Arizona Press, 1976.

Sutton, R. Anderson. *Traditions of Gamelan Music in Java: Musical Pluralism and Regional Identity.* Cambridge Studies in Ethnomusicology. New York: Cambridge University Press, 1991.

Tenzer, Michael. *Balinese Music.* Berkeley, Calif.: Periplus Editions, 1991.

Wade, Bonnie C. *Music in India: The Classical Traditions.* The Prentice Hall History of Music Series. Englewood Cliffs, N.J.: Prentice Hall, 1978.

Waterman, Christopher A. *Jùjú: A Social History and Ethnography of an African Popular Music.* Chicago: University of Chicago Press, 1990.

Yung, Bell. *Cantonese Opera: Performance as Creative Process.* Cambridge Studies in Ethnomusicology. Cambridge: Cambridge University Press, 1989.

Zonis, Ella. *Classical Persian Music: An Introduction.* Cambridge: Harvard University Press, 1973.

Bibliographies and Other Reference Guides

Briegleb, Ann, ed. *Directory of Ethnomusicological Sound Recording Collections in the U.S. and Canada.* Special Series, no. 2. Ann Arbor, Mich.: Society for Ethnomusicology, 1971.

"Current Bibliography, Discography, and Filmography." Edited by Joseph C. Hickerson et al. In *Ethnomusicology: Journal of the Society for Ethnomusicology* 1– (1953–).

Gray, John. *African Music: A Bibliographical Guide to the Traditional, Popular, Art and Liturgical Musics of Sub-Saharan Africa.* African Special Bibliographic Series, no. 14. New York: Greenwood Press, 1991.

Lieberman, Fredric. *Chinese Music: An Annotated Bibliography.* 2nd ed., rev. and enl. Garland Bibliographies in Ethnomusicology, vol. 1. New York: Garland Publishing, 1979. First published in 1970.

McLean, Mervyn. *An Annotated Bibliography of Oceanic Music and Dance.* Memoir no. 41. Wellington, New Zealand: The Polynesian Society, 1977. Suppl., 1981.

Musikethnologische Jahresbibliographie Europas/Annual Bibliography of European Ethnomusicology. Edited by Oskár Elschek et al. 10 vols. Bratislava: Slovenské Národné Múzeum, 1967–76.

Nettl, Bruno. *Reference Materials in Ethnomusicology: A Bibliographic Essay on Primitive, Oriental and Folk Music.* 2nd ed., rev. Detroit Studies in Music Bibliography, no. 1. Detroit: Information Coordinators, 1967. First published in 1961.

Schuursma, Ann Briegleb. *Ethnomusicology Research: A Select Annotated Bibliography.* Garland Library of Music Ethnology, vol. 1. New York: Garland Publishing, 1992.

Song, Bang-Song. *An Annotated Bibliography of Korean Music.* Asian Music Publications, ser. A, no. 2. Providence: Brown University Press, 1971.

Tsuge, Gen'ichi. *Japanese Music: An Annotated Bibliography.* Garland Bibliographies in Ethnomusicology, vol. 2. New York: Garland Publishing, 1986.

PERFORMANCE PRACTICE

Until about the mid-20th century "performance practice" was little more than the translation of an obscure German term, *Auf-*

führungspraxis, that represented the few ground-breaking studies in the area written prior to that time. Since then this field has grown, especially in just the last few years, into one of the most visible, influential, and controversial branches of music scholarship, affecting live and recorded performances of music of every historical period.

The following bibliography includes basic general texts and a representative selection of other important sources in the area. The first list, "General Treatments," offers three recent comprehensive coverages of the subject: Donington's classic treatise (whose chief, but not exclusive, concern is actually the Baroque era), the *New Grove* article by Brown, and the completely new and much more comprehensive two-volume Norton/Grove study edited by Brown and Sadie. The *Performance Practice Encyclopedia,* when published, will be the only such source in the field. The second list, "Studies Specific to an Era," brings together four sources that each apply to a single historical period. Next comes a much longer but far more selective list, "Examples of More Specialized Discussions," combining a sampling of monographs and *New Grove* articles, each on a specific subject, together illustrating something of the wide scope and variety of interests in the field.

There then follow two lists that are more concerned with matters of performance itself. Under "Discussions of the Performance Practice Movement" are two treatments (Cohen/Snitzer and Haskell) of the history and evolution of the "authentic performance" revival, Kottick's practical guide to the setting up and running of a Collegium Musicum, the texts of papers read at a conference on performance practice (Kenyon), and six other discussions of the movement. Under "Guides for Performers" are more recent creditable examples of the many performance practice sources addressed directly to performers.

The next two lists are of older sources: "Studies of Historical Interest," presenting a few of the pioneering earlier-20th-century works, and "Editions of Selected Primary Sources," comprising some of the best-known treatises that are valuable for the information they contain about the performance of music of their time. The list of "Anthologies" contains two collections (Ferand, Mather/Lasocki, and Schmitz) of musical works with contemporaneous written-out ornamentation or improvisation, and MacClintock's unique anthology of excerpts from primary-source writings that pertain to performance practice. The concluding list is of the two standard bibliographies in the field, Vinquist/Zaslaw and the more recent one by Jackson, which is updated annually.

For a list of journals in the area, see chapter 6, "Current Research Journals in Music," p. 152 below.

General Treatments

Brown, Howard Mayer. "Performing Practice." In *The New Grove Dictionary of Music and Musicians*. Vol. 14, pp. 370–93.

Brown, Howard Mayer, and Stanley Sadie, eds. *Performance Practice*. 1st American ed. 2 vols. The Norton/Grove Handbooks in Music. New York: W. W. Norton, 1990. First published in 1989.

Donington, Robert. *The Interpretation of Early Music*. New rev. ed. New York: W. W. Norton, 1989. First published in 1963.

Performance Practice Encyclopedia. Edited by Roland John Jackson. New York: Garland Publishing, forthcoming.

Studies Specific to an Era

Boorman, Stanley, ed. *Studies in the Performance of Late Medieval Music*. Cambridge: Cambridge University Press, 1983.

Donington, Robert. *Baroque Music: Style and Performance*. New York: W. W. Norton, 1982.

Page, Christopher. *Voices and Instruments of the Middle Ages: Instrumental Practice and Songs in France, 1100–1300*. Berkeley: University of California Press, 1986.

Saint-Arroman, Jean. *L'interprétation de la musique française, 1661–1789*. Vol. 1: *Dictionnaire d'interprétation (initiation)*. 6 vols. projected. Paris: Honoré Champion, 1983–.

Examples of More Specialized Discussions

Arnold, Frank Thomas. *The Art of Accompaniment from a Thorough-Bass as Practised in the XVIIth and XVIIIth Centuries*. Reprint, with a new introduction by Denis Stevens. 2 vols. New York: Dover, 1965. First published in 1931.

Badura-Skoda, Eva. "Cadenza." In *The New Grove Dictionary of Music and Musicians*. Vol. 3, pp. 586–93.

Badura-Skoda, Eva, and Paul Badura-Skoda. *Interpreting Mozart on the Keyboard*. Translated by Leo Black. London: Barrie and Rockliff, 1962.

Barbour, J. Murray. *Tuning and Temperament: A Historical Survey.* East Lansing, Mich.: Michigan State College Press, 1951; reprint, New York: Da Capo Press, 1972. Ph.D. diss., Cornell University, 1932.

Bent, Margaret, et al. "Musica Ficta." In *The New Grove Dictionary of Music and Musicians.* Vol. 12, pp. 802–11.

Borgir, Tharald. *The Performance of the Basso Continuo in Italian Baroque Music.* Studies in Musicology, no. 90. Ann Arbor, Mich.: UMI Research Press, 1977. Revision of Ph.D. diss., University of California, 1971.

Boyden, David D. *The History of Violin Playing from Its Origins to 1761 and Its Relationship to the Violin and Violin Music.* London: Oxford University Press, 1965.

Brown, Howard Mayer. *Sixteenth-Century Instrumentation: The Music for the Florentine Intermedii.* Musicological Studies and Documents, no. 30. N.p.: American Institute of Musicology, 1973.

Buelow, George J. *Thorough-Bass Accompaniment According to Johann David Heinichen.* Los Angeles: University of California Press, 1966. Revision of Ph.D. diss., New York University, 1961.

Donington, Robert. "Ornaments." In *The New Grove Dictionary of Music and Musicians.* Vol. 13, pp. 827–67.

Eppelsheim, Jürgen. *Das Orchester in den Werken Jean-Baptiste Lullys.* Münchner Veröffentlichungen zur Musikgeschichte, vol. 7. Tutzing: Hans Schneider, 1961. Revision of Ph.D. diss., University of Munich, 1958.

Fallows, David. "Tempo and Expression Marks." In *The New Grove Dictionary of Music and Musicians.* Vol. 18, pp. 677–84.

Fuller, David. "Notes inégales." In *The New Grove Dictionary of Music and Musicians.* Vol. 13, pp. 420–27.

———. "Ornamentation." In *The New Harvard Dictionary of Music.* Pp. 594–99.

Hefling, Stephen E. *Rhythmic Alteration in Seventeenth- and Eighteenth-Century Music: Notes inégales and Overdotting.* New York: Schirmer Books, 1992.

Horsley, Imogene, et al. "Improvisation." In *The New Grove Dictionary of Music and Musicians.* Vol. 9, pp. 31–56.

Houle, George. *Meter in Music, 1600–1800: Performance, Perception, and Notation.* Bloomington: Indiana University Press, 1987.

Kelly, Thomas Forrest, ed. *Plainsong in the Age of Polyphony.*
    Cambridge Studies in Performance Practice, no. 2.
    Cambridge: Cambridge University Press, 1992.
Koury, Daniel J. *Orchestral Performance Practices in the
    Nineteenth Century: Size, Proportions, and Seating.* Studies
    in Musicology, no. 85. Ann Arbor, Mich.: UMI Research
    Press, 1986. Revision of Ph.D. diss., Boston University,
    1981.
Le Huray, Peter. *Authenticity in Performance: Eighteenth-Century
    Case Studies.* Cambridge: Cambridge University Press, 1990.
Lindley, Mark. *Lutes, Viols and Temperaments.* Cambridge:
    Cambridge University Press, 1984.
———— . "Temperaments." In *The New Grove Dictionary of Music
    and Musicians.* Vol. 18, pp. 660–74.
Lindley, Mark, et al. "Pitch." In *The New Grove Dictionary of
    Music and Musicians.* Vol. 14, pp. 779–86.
Neumann, Frederick. *Essays in Performance Practice.* Studies in
    Musicology, no. 58. Ann Arbor, Mich.: UMI Research
    Press, 1982.
———— . *New Essays in Performance Practice.* Studies in Music,
    no. 108. Ann Arbor, Mich.: UMI Research Press, 1989.
———— . *Ornamentation and Improvisation in Mozart.* Princeton:
    Princeton University Press, 1986.
———— . *Ornamentation in Baroque and Post-Baroque Music with
    Special Emphasis on J. S. Bach.* Princeton: Princeton
    University Press, 1978.
Newman, William S. *Beethoven on Beethoven: Playing His Piano
    Music His Way.* New York: W. W. Norton, 1988.
Westrup, Jack, with Neal Zaslaw. "Orchestra." In *The New Grove
    Dictionary of Music and Musicians.* Vol. 13, pp. 679–91.
Whitmore, Philip J. *Unpremeditated Art: The Cadenza in the
    Classical Keyboard Concerto.* Oxford Monographs on
    Music. New York: Oxford University Press, 1991.
Williams, Peter. "Continuo [Basso continuo]." In *The New Grove
    Dictionary of Music and Musicians.* Vol. 4, pp. 685–99.
Williams, Peter, ed. *Bach, Handel, Scarlatti: Tercentenary Essays.*
    Cambridge: Cambridge University Press, 1985.

Discussions of the Performance Practice Movement

Cohen, Joel, and Herb Snitzer. *Reprise: The Extraordinary
    Revival of Early Music.* Boston: Little, Brown, 1985.

Dreyfus, Laurence. "Early Music Defended against Its Devotees: A Theory of Historical Performance in the Twentieth Century." *The Musical Quarterly* 59 (Summer 1983): 297–322.

Haskell, Harry. *The Early Music Revival: A History.* London: Thames and Hudson, 1988.

Kenyon, Nicholas, ed. *Authenticity and Early Music: A Symposium.* London: Oxford University Press, 1988.

Kerman, Joseph. "The Historical Performance Movement." In *Contemplating Music: Challenges to Musicology.* Cambridge: Harvard University Press, 1985. Pp. 182–217.

Kottick, Edward. *The Collegium: A Handbook.* Stonington, Conn.: October House, 1977.

Taruskin, Richard. "On Letting the Music Speak for Itself: Some Reflections on Musicology and Performance." *Journal of Musicology* 1 (July 1982): 338–49.

——— . "The Musicologist and the Performer." In *Musicology in the 1980s: Methods, Goals, Opportunities.* New York: Da Capo Press, 1982. Pp. 101–17.

——— . "Tradition and Authority." *Early Music* 20 (May 1992): 311–25.

Taruskin, Richard, et al. "The Limits of Authenticity: A Discussion." *Early Music* 12 (February 1984): 3–25.

Guides for Performers

Brown, Howard Mayer. *Embellishing 16th-Century Music.* Early Music Series, no. 1. London: Oxford University Press, 1976.

Collins, Fletcher, Jr. *The Production of Medieval Church Music-Drama.* Charlottesville: University Press of Virginia, 1972.

Cyr, Mary. *Performing Baroque Music.* Portland, Ore.: Amadeus Press, 1992.

Donington, Robert. *A Performer's Guide to Baroque Music.* New York: Charles Scribner's Sons, 1973.

——— . *String Playing in Baroque Music.* London: Faber and Faber, 1977.

Jorgensen, Owen H. *Tuning, Containing the Perfection of Eighteenth-Century Temperament, the Lost Art of Nineteenth-Century Temperament, and the Science of Equal Temperament, Complete with Instructions for Aural and*

Electronic Tuning. East Lansing: Michigan State University Press, 1991.

————. *Tuning the Historical Temperaments by Ear: A Manual of Eighty-nine Methods of Tuning Fifty-one Scales on the Harpsichord, Piano, and Other Keyboard Instruments.* Marquette: Northern Michigan University Press, 1977.

Knighton, Tess, and David Fallows, eds. *Companion to Medieval and Renaissance Music.* 1st American ed. New York: Schirmer Books, 1992.

Krausz, Michael. *The Interpretation of Music: Philosophical Essays.* New York: Oxford University Press, 1993.

Lasocki, David, and Betty Bang Mather. *The Classical Woodwind Cadenza: A Workbook.* New York: McGinnis & Marx, 1978.

Loft, Abram. *Ensemble! A Rehearsal Guide to Thirty Great Works of Chamber Music.* Portland, Ore.: Amadeus Press, 1992.

McGee, Timothy J. *Medieval and Renaissance Music: A Performer's Guide.* Toronto: University of Toronto Press, 1985.

Mather, Betty Bang. *Interpretation of French Music from 1675 to 1775 for Woodwind and Other Performers.* New York: McGinnis & Marx, 1973.

Mather, Betty Bang, and David Lasocki. *The Art of Preluding, 1700–1830, for Flutists, Oboists, Clarinettists and Other Performers.* New York: McGinnis & Marx, 1984.

Mather, Betty Bang, with the assistance of Dean M. Karns. *Dance Rhythms of the French Baroque: A Handbook for Performance.* Bloomington: Indiana University Press, 1988.

Moens-Haenen, Greta. *Das Vibrato in der Musik des Barock: Ein Handbuch zur Aufführungspraxis für Vokalisten und Instrumentalisten.* Graz: Akademische Druck- und Verlagsanstalt, 1988.

Neumann, Frederick. *Performance Practices of the Seventeenth and Eighteenth Centuries.* New York: Schirmer Books, 1993.

Newman, Anthony. *Bach and the Baroque: A Performing Guide to Baroque Music with Special Emphasis on the Music of J. S. Bach.* Stuyvesant, N.Y.: Pendragon Press, 1985.

North, Nigel. *Continuo Playing on the Lute, Archlute and Theorbo: A Comprehensive Guide for Performers.* Bloomington: Indiana University Press, 1987.

Performers' Guides to Early Music. Jeffery Kite-Powell, gen. ed. New York: Early Music America and Schirmer Books, 1994–.

The Middle Ages. Edited by Ross Duffin.
The Renaissance. Edited by Jeffery Kite-Powell. (Earlier edition published as *Practical Guide to Historical*

Performance: The Renaissance, New York: Early
Music America, 1989.)
The Seventeenth Century. Edited by Stewart Carter.
The Eighteenth-Century Baroque. Edited by Stephen
Hefling.
The Classic Period. Edited by Neal Zaslaw and Malcolm
Bilson.

Phillips, Elizabeth V., and John-Paul Christopher Jackson.
*Performing Medieval and Renaissance Music: An
Introductory Guide.* New York: Schirmer Books, 1986.
Rosenblum, Sandra P. *Performance Practices in Classic Piano
Music: Their Principles and Applications.* Bloomington:
Indiana University Press, 1988.
Rowland-Jones, Anthony. *Playing Recorder Sonatas:
Interpretation and Technique.* New York: Oxford University
Press, 1992.
Stevens, Denis. "Applied Musicology." Part 3 of *Musicology: A
Practical Guide.* New York: Schirmer Books, 1980.
Stowell, Robin. *Violin Technique and Performance Practice in the
Late-Eighteenth and Early-Nineteenth Centuries.*
Cambridge: Cambridge University Press, 1990.
Williams, Peter. *Figured Bass Accompaniment.* 2 vols. Edinburgh:
Edinburgh University Press, 1970.

Studies of Historical Interest

Aldrich, Putnam C. "The Principal Agréments of the
Seventeenth and Eighteenth Centuries: A Study
in Musical Ornamentation." Ph.D. thesis, Harvard
University, 1942.
Arger, Jane. *Les agréments et le rythme: leur représentation
graphique dans la musique vocale française du XVIIIe
siècle.* Paris: Rouart, Lerolle, [1921].
Borrel, Eugène. *L'interprétation de la musique française (de Lully
à la Révolution).* Les maîtres de la musique, new ser.
Paris: Félix Alcan, 1934.
Dart, Thurston. *The Interpretation of Music.* 4th ed., rev.
reimpression. London: Hutchinson's University Library,
1960. First published in 1954.
Dolmetsch, Arnold. *The Interpretation of the Music of the XVIIth
and XVIIIth Centuries Revealed by Contemporary Evidence.*
New ed. London: Novello, 1969. First published in 1915.

Haas, Robert. *Aufführungspraxis der Musik.* Handbuch der
    Musikwissenschaft, vol. 6. Potsdam: Akademische
    Verlagsgesellschaft Athenaion, 1931.
Schering, Arnold. *Aufführungspraxis alter Musik.* Leipzig: Quelle
    und Meyer, 1931.

Editions of Selected Primary Sources

Arbeau, Thoinot. *Orchesography* [1589]. Translated by Mary
    Stewart Evans. With a new introduction and notes by Julia
    Sutton. New York: Dover Publications, 1967. First
    published in 1948.
Bach, Carl Philipp Emanuel. *Essay on the True Art of Playing
    Keyboard Instruments* [original and rev. eds., 1753–97].
    2nd ed. Translated and edited by William J. Mitchell.
    London: Cassell and Company, 1951. First published in
    1949.
Caccini, Giulio. *Le nuove musiche* [1602]. Translated and edited by
    H. Wiley Hitchcock. Recent Researches in the Music of the
    Baroque Era, vol. 9. Madison, Wis.: A-R Editions, 1970.
Couperin, François. *L'art de toucher le clavecin/Die Kunst das
    Klavier zu spielen/The Art of Playing the Harpsichord*
    [1716]. English translation by Mevanwy Roberts; German
    translation by Anna Linde. Leipzig: Breitkopf & Härtel,
    1933.
Hotteterre, Jacques. *Principles of the Flute, Recorder & Oboe*
    [1707]. Translated and edited by David Lasocki. New York:
    Frederick A. Praeger, 1968.
Mace, Thomas. *Musick's Monument; or, a Remembrancer of the
    Best Practical Musick Both Divine and Civil, That Has
    Ever Been Known, to Have Been in the World* [1676]. Facs.
    ed. 2 vols. Paris: Editions du Centre National de la
    Recherche Scientifique, 1958–66.
Mersenne, Marin. *Harmonie universelle: The Books on
    Instruments* [1636]. Translated by Roger E. Chapman. The
    Hague: Martinus Nijhoff, 1957.
Morley, Thomas. *A Plain and Easy Introduction to Practical
    Music* [1597]. 2nd ed. Edited by R. Alec Harman, with a
    foreword by Thurston Dart. London: J. M. Dent & Sons,
    1963. First published in 1952.
Praetorius, Michael. *Syntagma Musicum II* [1618]: *De
    Organographia, Parts I and II.* Translated and edited by
    David Z. Crookes. Early Music Series, no. 7. Oxford:
    Clarendon Press, 1986.

————— . "A Translation of *Syntagma Musicum* III [1619] by
Michael Praetorius." Translated and edited by Hans Lampl.
D.M.A. diss., University of Southern California, 1957.
Quantz, Johann Joachim. *On Playing the Flute* [1752]. Translated,
with an introduction and notes, by Edward R. Reilly. 2nd
ed. New York: Schirmer Books, 1985. First published in
1966.

Anthologies

Ferand, Ernst Thomas. *Improvisation in Nine Centuries of
Western Music: An Anthology with a Historical
Introduction.* Anthology of Music, vol. 12. Cologne: Arno
Volk Verlag, 1961.
MacClintock, Carol. *Readings in the History of Music in
Performance.* Bloomington: Indiana University Press, 1979.
Mather, Betty Bang, and David Lasocki. *Free Ornamentation in
Woodwind Music, 1700–1775: An Anthology with
Introduction.* New York: McGinnis & Marx, 1976.
Schmitz, Hans-Peter. *Die Kunst der Verzierung im 18. Jahrhundert:
Instrumentale und vokale Musizierpraxis in Beispielen.* 2nd
ed. Kassel: Bärenreiter, 1965. First published in 1955.

Bibliographies of the Literature

Jackson, Roland John. *Performance Practice, Medieval to
Contemporary: A Bibliographic Guide.* Music Research and
Information Guides, vol. 9. New York: Garland Publishing,
1988. Annual suppl. in Fall issue of *Performance Practice
Review* (see chapter 6).
Vinquist, Mary, and Neal Zaslaw, eds. *Performance Practice: A
Bibliography.* New York: W. W. Norton, 1971. Suppls.:
Current Musicology no. 12 (1971): 129–49, no. 15 (1973):
126–33.

MUSIC THEORY

Only in the past generation, and especially in America, has
music theory become a discipline with its own separate identity,
rather than being considered an aspect of musicology. Furthermore, this period has seen the development of more specialized

fields within the discipline, such as set theory, methodologies for explaining tonal music (Schenker's being generally regarded as the most important), and specific studies in the history of theory. The following bibliography of basic sources reflects within its nine main divisions some of the principal emphases in the field. Books designed specifically as course texts have been excluded, and more recent sources have been emphasized.

Of the sources listed under "History of Theory," Bent's book (a revision and expansion of his *New Grove* article) is the most comprehensive, and Palisca's *New Grove* article is also substantial; Riemann and Shirlaw are included because both are classic early studies.

With regard to "General Issues of Style and Analysis," the studies by Bent, Cook, and Dunsby/Whittall may be singled out as surveys of the field of analysis, Bent's being the most complete. De la Motte's *Study of Harmony* is unique in its historical approach to the topic.

In "Twentieth-Century Theories of Tonal Music," the sources listed under "Theories of Tonality and Tonal Music" run from the early studies by Schoenberg, Hindemith, and Kurth (as discussed by Rothfarb) to the more current cognitive studies, the most notable new approach being that of Lerdahl and Jackendoff; the sources under "Schenkerian Analysis" similarly range from Schenker's chief treatises through the earliest explanation of *Der freie Satz* by Jonas, and Forte's later treatment of it, to the most recent Schenkerian studies.

Under "Twentieth-Century Theories of Nontonal Music," "Atonality, Serialism, and Set Theory" brings together a variety of treatments and viewpoints, including Hanson, now superseded by other points of view; Perle, one of the earliest studies in the field; the pioneering works of Forte and Rahn; and what are perhaps the most important current studies, those by Lewin and Morris. Under "Modality and Octatonicism," van den Toorn's *The Music of Igor Stravinsky* is probably the most significant item. Only older sources treat "Microtonality," a field that has failed to attract more recent scholarly attention.

"Musical Time: Theories of Rhythm and Meter" includes the classic study by Sachs, the pioneering modern treatment by Cooper/Meyer, and the particularly significant recent study by Kramer. The "Theories of Musical Timbre" list is necessarily brief because the entire field is new. "Aesthetics and Semiotics of Music" ranges from the early works by Hanslick and Busoni through various standard 20th-century studies to more recent ones, such as those by Meyer and Nattiez, the latter perhaps the most prominent scholar in the emerging field of musical semiotics. "Texts of Theoretical Treatises" and "Bibliographies and Guides to the Literature" complete this section.

For a list of journals specializing in theory, see chapter 6, "Current Research Journals in Music," p. 152 below.

The History of Theory

Bent, Ian D. "Analysis." In *The New Grove Dictionary of Music and Musicians.* Vol. 1, pp. 340–88.

———. *Analysis.* With a Glossary by William Drabkin. 1st American ed. The Norton/Grove Handbooks in Music. New York: W. W. Norton, 1987.

Brown, Matthew. "Theory." In *The New Harvard Dictionary of Music.* Pp. 844–54.

Dahlhaus, Carl. *Die Musiktheorie im 18. und 19. Jahrhundert: Grundzüge einer Systematik.* Geschichte der Musiktheorie, vol. 10. Darmstadt: Wissenschaftliche Buchgesellschaft, 1984.

———. *Untersuchungen über die Entstehung der harmonischen Tonalität.* Saarbrücker Studien zur Musikwissenschaft, vol. 2. Kassel: Bärenreiter, 1968.

Forte, Allen. "Theory." In *Dictionary of Contemporary Music,* by John Vinton. New York: E. P. Dutton, 1974. Pp. 753–61.

Gushee, Lawrence. "Anonymous Theoretical Writings." In *The New Grove Dictionary of Music and Musicians.* Vol. 1, pp. 441–46.

Lester, Joel. *Compositional Theory in the Eighteenth Century.* Cambridge: Harvard University Press, 1992.

———. *Modes and Keys: German Theory, 1592–1802.* Stuyvesant, N.Y.: Pendragon Press, 1992.

Palisca, Claude V. "Theory, Theorists." In *The New Grove Dictionary of Music and Musicians.* Vol. 18, pp. 741–62.

Riemann, Hugo. *Geschichte der Musiktheorie im IX.-XIX. Jahrhundert.* 2nd ed. Berlin: Max Hesse, 1921. First published in 1898. English transl.: (1) *History of Music Theory, Books I and II: Polyphonic Theory to the Sixteenth Century.* Translated, with preface, commentary, and notes, by Raymond H. Haggh. Lincoln: University of Nebraska Press, 1962. (2) *Hugo Riemann's Theory of Harmony: A Study . . . , and History of Music Theory, Book III.* Translated and edited by William C. Mickelsen. Lincoln: University of Nebraska Press, 1977.

Rummenhöller, Peter. *Musiktheoretisches Denken im 19. Jahrhundert: Versuch einer Interpretation erkenntnistheoretischer Zeugnisse in der Musiktheorie.* Regensburg: Gustav Bosse, 1967.

Shirlaw, Matthew. *The Theory of Harmony: An Inquiry into the Natural Principles of Harmony, with an Examination of the Chief Systems of Harmony from Rameau to the Present Day.* 2nd ed. De Kalb, Ill.: Dr. Birchard Coar, 1955. First published in 1917.

Thompson, David M. *A History of Harmonic Theory in the United States.* Kent, Ohio: Kent State University Press, 1980.

Wason, Robert. *Viennese Harmonic Theory from Albrechtsberger to Schenker and Schoenberg.* Ann Arbor, Mich.: UMI Research Press, 1984.

General Issues of Style and Analysis

Bent, Ian D. *Analysis.* With a Glossary by William Drabkin. 1st American ed. The Norton/Grove Handbooks in Music. New York: W. W. Norton, 1987.

Bonds, Mark Evan. *Wordless Rhetoric: Musical Form and the Metaphor of the Oration.* Cambridge: Harvard University Press, 1991.

Cone, Edward T. *Musical Form and Musical Performance.* New York: W. W. Norton, 1968.

Cook, Nicholas. *A Guide to Musical Analysis.* New York: W. W. Norton, 1992. First published in 1987.

Dunsby, Jonathan, and Arnold Whittall. *Music Analysis in Theory and Practice.* New Haven: Yale University Press, 1988.

Ferrara, Lawrence. *Philosophy and the Analysis of Music: Bridges to Musical Sound, Form, and Reference.* Contributions to the Study of Music and Dance, no. 24. New York: Greenwood Press, 1991.

LaRue, Jan. *Guidelines for Style Analysis.* 2nd ed. Detroit Monographs in Musicology/Studies in Music, no. 12. Warren, Mich.: Harmonie Park Press, 1992. First published in 1970.

Motte, Diether de la. *The Study of Harmony: An Historical Perspective.* Translated by Jeffrey L. Prater. Dubuque, Iowa: Wm. C. Brown, 1991.

Sessions, Roger. *Questions about Music.* Cambridge: Harvard University Press, 1970.

Stein, Erwin. *Form and Performance.* New York: Alfred A. Knopf, 1962.

Twentieth-Century Theories of Tonal Music

THEORIES OF TONALITY AND TONAL MUSIC

Browne, Richmond. *Music Theory: Special Topics.* New York: Academic Press, 1981.

Carpenter, Patricia, and Severine Neff, eds. and trans. *The Musical Idea and the Logic, Technique, and Art of Its Presentation by Arnold Schoenberg.* New York: Columbia University Press, 1993.

Dahlhaus, Carl. *Studies on the Origin of Harmonic Tonality.* Translated by Robert D. Gjerdingen. Princeton: Princeton University Press, 1990.

————. "Tonality." In *The New Grove Dictionary of Music and Musicians.* Vol. 19, pp. 51–55.

Epstein, David. *Beyond Orpheus: Studies in Musical Structure.* Cambridge: MIT Press, 1979.

Hindemith, Paul. *The Craft of Musical Composition.* [Rev. ed.] Translated by Arthur Mendel and Otto Ortmann. 2 vols. London: B. Schott, 1945. First published in 1937.

Komar, Arthur. *Theory of Suspensions.* Princeton: Princeton University Press, 1971. Ph.D. diss., Princeton University, 1968.

Lerdahl, Fred, and Ray Jackendoff. *A Generative Theory of Tonal Music.* Cambridge: MIT Press, 1983.

Narmour, Eugene. *The Analysis and Cognition of Basic Melodic Structures: The Implication-Realization Model.* Chicago: University of Chicago Press, 1990.

————. *Beyond Schenkerism: The Need for Alternatives in Music Analysis.* Chicago: University of Chicago Press, 1977.

Neff, Severine, ed. *Coherence, Counterpoint, Instrumentation, Instruction in Form by Arnold Schoenberg.* Translated by Charlotte M. Cross and Severine Neff. Lincoln: University of Nebraska Press, 1993.

Neumeyer, David. *The Music of Paul Hindemith.* New Haven: Yale University Press, 1986.

Norton, Richard. *Tonality in Western Culture: A Critical and Historical Perspective.* University Park: Pennsylvania State University Press, 1984.

Réti, Rudolph. *The Thematic Process in Music.* London: Faber and Faber, 1961.

Rothfarb, Lee. *Ernst Kurth as Theorist and Analyst.* Philadelphia: University of Pennsylvania Press, 1988.

Serafine, Mary Louise. *Music as Cognition.* New York: Columbia
    University Press, 1988.
Straus, Joseph N. *Remaking the Past: Musical Modernism and
    the Influence of the Tonal Tradition.* Cambridge: Harvard
    University Press, 1990.

Schenkerian Analysis

Beach, David, ed. *Aspects of Schenkerian Theory.* New Haven:
    Yale University Press, 1983.
Cadwallader, Allen, ed. *Trends in Schenkerian Research.* New
    York: Schirmer Books, 1990.
Forte, Allen, and Steven E. Gilbert. *Introduction to Schenkerian
    Analysis.* New York: W. W. Norton, 1982.
Jonas, Oswald. *Introduction to the Theory of Heinrich Schenker:
    The Nature of the Musical Work of Art.* Translated and
    edited by John Rothgeb. New York: Longman, 1987. First
    published in 1934.
Neumeyer, David, and Susan Tepping. *A Guide to Schenkerian
    Analysis.* Englewood Cliffs, N.J.: Prentice Hall, 1992.
Salzer, Felix. *Structural Hearing: Tonal Coherence in Music.* 2
    vols. New York: Dover Publications, 1962. First published
    in 1952.
Salzer, Felix, and Carl Schachter. *Counterpoint in Composition:
    The Study of Voice Leading.* Morningside Edition, with
    new preface. New York: Columbia University Press, 1989.
    First published in 1969.
Salzer, Felix, and Carl Schachter, eds. *The Music Forum.* 6 vols.
    New York: Columbia University Press, 1967–82.
Schenker, Heinrich. *Counterpoint: A Translation of Kontrapunkt
    by Heinrich Schenker.* Edited by John Rothgeb. Translated
    by John Rothgeb and Jürgen Thym. 2 vols. New York:
    Schirmer Books, 1987. First published in 1922.
————. *Free Composition [Der freie Satz].* Translated and edited
    by Ernst Oster. New York: Longman, 1979. First published
    in 1935.
————. *Harmony [Harmonielehre].* Edited and annotated by
    Oswald Jonas. Translated by Elisabeth Mann Borgese.
    Chicago: University of Chicago Press, 1954. First published
    in 1906.
Siegel, Heidi, ed. *Schenker Studies.* Cambridge: Cambridge
    University Press, 1990.
Yeston, Maury, ed. *Readings in Schenker Analysis and Other
    Approaches.* New Haven: Yale University Press, 1977.

Twentieth-Century Theories of Nontonal Music

Atonality, Serialism, and Set Theory

Boretz, Benjamin, and Edward T. Cone, eds. *Perspectives on Contemporary Music Theory.* New York: W. W. Norton, 1972.

Forte, Allen. *The Structure of Atonal Music.* New Haven: Yale University Press, 1973.

Griffiths, Paul. "Serialism." In *The New Grove Dictionary of Music and Musicians.* Vol. 17, pp. 162–69.

Hanson, Howard. *Harmonic Materials of Modern Music.* New York: Appleton-Century Crofts, 1960.

Lansky, Paul, and George Perle. "Atonality." In *The New Grove Dictionary of Music and Musicians.* Vol. 1, pp. 669–73.

Lewin, David. *Generalized Musical Intervals and Transformations.* New Haven: Yale University Press, 1987.

Morris, Robert. *Composition with Pitch-Classes: A Theory of Compositional Design.* New Haven: Yale University Press, 1987.

Perle, George. *Serial Composition and Atonality: An Introduction to the Music of Schoenberg, Berg, and Webern.* 5th ed., rev. Berkeley: University of California Press, 1981. First published in 1962.

Rahn, John. *Basic Atonal Theory.* New York: Longman, 1980.

Rufer, Joseph. *Composition with Twelve Notes Related Only to One Another.* Rev. ed. Translated by Humphrey Searle. London: Barrie and Rockliff, Cresset Press, 1969. First published in 1952.

Schoenberg, Arnold. *Style and Idea.* Edited by Leonard Stein. New York: St. Martin's Press, 1975.

Straus, Joseph N. *Introduction to Post-Tonal Theory.* Englewood Cliffs, N.J.: Prentice Hall, 1990.

Webern, Anton. *The Path to New Music.* Translated by Leo Black. Bryn Mawr, Pa.: Theodore Presser, 1963. First published in 1960.

Wittlich, Gary, ed. *Aspects of Twentieth-Century Music.* Englewood Cliffs, N.J.: Prentice Hall, 1975.

Wuorinen, Charles. *Simple Composition.* New York: Longman, 1979.

Modality and Octatonicism

Bacon, Ernst. *Our Musical Idiom.* Chicago: Open Court Press, 1917.

Lendvai, Ernö. *Béla Bartók: An Analysis of His Music.* London: Kahn and Averill, 1971.

Messiaen, Olivier. *Technique of My Musical Language.* Translated by John Satterfield. Paris: A. Leduc, 1956. First published in 1950.

van den Toorn, Pieter C. *The Music of Igor Stravinsky.* New Haven: Yale University Press, 1983.

Microtonality

Hába, Alois. *Neue Harmonielehre des diatonischen, chromatischen Viertel-, Drittel-, Sechstel- und Zwölftel-Tonsystems.* Revised by Erich Steinhard. Leipzig: Fr. Kistner & C. F. W. Siegel, 1927.

Partch, Harry. *Genesis of a Music.* 2nd ed., enl. New York: Da Capo Press, 1974. First published in 1949.

Yasser, Joseph. *A Theory of Evolving Tonality.* New York: American Library of Musicology, 1932.

Musical Time: Theories of Rhythm and Meter

Barry, Barbara. *The Sense of Order: Perceptual and Analytical Studies in Musical Time.* Harmonologia Series, no. 5. Stuyvesant, N.Y.: Pendragon Press, 1990.

Cooper, Grosvenor, and Leonard B. Meyer. *The Rhythmic Structure of Music.* Chicago: University of Chicago Press, 1960.

Kramer, Jonathan D. *The Time of Music: New Meanings, New Temporalities, New Listening Strategies.* New York: Schirmer Books, 1988.

Lester, Joel. *The Rhythms of Tonal Music.* Carbondale: Southern Illinois University Press, 1986.

Rothstein, William Nathan. *Phrase Rhythm in Tonal Music.* New York: Schirmer Books, 1989.

Sachs, Curt. *Rhythm and Tempo: A Study in Music History.* New York: Columbia University Press, 1953.

Yeston, Maury. *The Stratification of Rhythm.* New Haven: Yale University Press, 1976.

Theories of Musical Timbre

Cogan, Robert. *New Images of Music Sound.* Cambridge: Harvard University Press, 1984.

Slawson, Wayne. *Sound Color.* Berkeley: University of California Press, 1985.

Aesthetics and Semiotics of Music

Agawu, V. Kofi. *Playing with Signs: A Semiotic Interpretation of Classic Music.* Princeton: Princeton University Press, 1991.

Burrows, David. *Sound, Speech, and Music.* Amherst: University of Massachusetts Press, 1990.

Busoni, Ferruccio. *Sketch of a New Esthetic of Music.* Translated by Thomas Baker. New York: Dover, 1962. First published in 1907.

Clifton, Thomas. *Music as Heard: A Study in Applied Phenomenology.* New Haven: Yale University Press, 1983.

Coker, Wilson. *Music and Meaning: A Theoretical Introduction to Musical Aesthetics.* New York: Free Press, 1972.

Cone, Edward. *The Composer's Voice.* Berkeley: University of California Press, 1974.

Hanslick, Eduard. *On the Musically Beautiful: A Contribution towards the Revision of the Aesthetics of Music.* Translated and edited by Geoffrey Poyzant. Indianapolis: Hackett Publishing, 1986. First published in 1854.

Kivy, Peter. *The Corded Shell: Reflections on Musical Expression.* Princeton: Princeton University Press, 1980.

———. *Osmin's Rage: Philosophical Reflections on Opera, Drama, and Text.* Princeton: Princeton University Press, 1988.

———. *Sound and Semblance: Reflections on Music Representation.* Princeton: Princeton University Press, 1984.

Langer, Susanne. *Feeling and Form: A Theory of Art.* New York: Charles Scribner's Sons, 1953.

———. *Philosophy in a New Key: A Study in the Symbolism of Reason, Rite, and Art.* 3rd ed. Cambridge: Harvard University Press, 1976. First published in 1942.

Lippman, Edward A. *A History of Western Musical Aesthetics.* Lincoln: University of Nebraska Press, 1992.

Meyer, Leonard B. *Emotion and Meaning in Music.* Chicago: University of Chicago Press, 1956.

———. *Music, the Arts, and Ideas: Patterns and Predictions in Twentieth-Century Culture.* Chicago: University of Chicago Press, 1967.

———. *Style and Music: Theory, History, and Ideology.*
Philadelphia: University of Pennsylvania Press, 1989.
Monelle, Raymond. *Linguistics and Semiotics in Music.*
Contemporary Music Studies, vol. 5. New York: Gordon
and Breach Publishers, 1992.
Nattiez, Jean-Jacques. *Music and Discourse: Toward a Semiology
of Music.* Translated and revised by Carolyn Abbate.
Princeton: Princeton University Press, 1990. First
published in 1987.
Rowell, Lewis. *Thinking about Music: An Introduction to the
Philosophy of Music.* Amherst: University of
Massachusetts Press, 1983.
Sparshott, F. E. "Aesthetics of Music." In *The New Grove
Dictionary of Music and Musicians.* Vol. 1, pp. 120–34.
Zuckerkandl, Victor. *The Sense of Music.* Princeton: Princeton
University Press, 1959.
———. *Sound and Symbol.* 2 vols. Translated by Willard R. Trask
and Norbert Guterman. New York: Pantheon Books,
1956–73.

Texts of Theoretical Treatises

*Thesaurus Musicarum Latinarum: A Comprehensive Database of
Latin Music Theory of the Middle Ages and the
Renaissance (TML).* Thomas J. Mathiesen, project director.
Bloomington: Indiana University, 1990–. "An evolving
database that will eventually contain the entire corpus of
Latin music theory written during the Middle Ages and
the early Renaissance"; the joint effort of a consortium of
universities.

Bibliographies and Guides to the Literature

Basart, Ann Phillips. *Serial Music: A Classified Bibliography of
Writings on Twelve-Tone and Electronic Music.* Berkeley:
University of California Press, 1961.
Beach, David, ed. "A Schenker Bibliography." *Journal of Music
Theory* 13 (Spring 1969): 2–37.
———. "A Schenker Bibliography: 1969–1979." *Journal of Music
Theory* 23 (Spring 1979): 275–86.

Coover, James. "Music Theory in Translation: A Bibliography."
   Journal of Music Theory 3 (April 1959): 70–96; 13 (Spring
   1969): 230–48.
Damschroeder, David A., and David Russell Williams. *Music
   Theory from Zarlino to Schenker: A Bibliography and
   Guide.* Harmonologia Series, no. 4. Stuyvesant, N.Y.:
   Pendragon Press, 1990. First published in 1970.
Diamond, Harold J. *Music Analyses: An Annotated Guide to the
   Literature.* New York: Schirmer Books, 1991.
"Index of Music Theory in the United States, 1955–1970."
   Richmond Browne, supervising ed. *In Theory Only* 3, nos.
   7–11 (October 1977–February 1978): entire issue.
Kramer, Jonathan D. "Studies of Time and Music: A
   Bibliography." *Music Theory Spectrum* 7 (1985): 72–106.
Laskowski, Larry, comp. and annot. *Heinrich Schenker: An
   Annotated Index to His Analyses of Musical Works.* New
   York: Pendragon Press, 1978.
Mathiesen, Thomas J. *Ancient Greek Music Theory: A Catalogue
   Raisonné of Manuscripts.* Munich: G. Henle, 1988.
Reese, Gustave. *Fourscore Classics of Music Literature: A Guide
   to Selected Original Sources on Theory and Other Writings
   on Music Not Available in English, with Descriptive
   Sketches and Bibliographical References.* New York: Liberal
   Arts Press, 1957.
*Répertoire international des sources musicales/Internationales
   Quellen-lexikon der Musik/International Inventory of
   Musical Sources (RISM).* Historical treatises contained in
   ser. B. Munich: G. Henle, 1961–.
SMT Online Bibliographic Database. Sponsored by the Society
   for Music Theory; Lee Rothfarb, project director.
   Cambridge: Harvard University, 1992–. A database that
   contains citations of articles and reviews in all major music
   theory journals and selected musicology journals.
"The Society for Music Theory: The First Decade." Special Issue,
   Music Theory Spectrum 11, no. 1 (Spring 1989).
Vander Weg, John D. "An Annotated Bibliography of Articles on
   Serialism: 1955–1980." *In Theory Only* 5, no. 1 (April 1979):
   entire issue.
Wenk, Arthur B., comp. *Analyses of Nineteenth- and
   Twentieth-Century Music: 1940–1985.* MLA Index and
   Bibliography Series, no. 25. Boston: Music Library
   Association, 1987. First published as separate vols. in
   1975–76.

Winick, Steven D. *Rhythm: An Annotated Bibliography.*
Metuchen, N.J.: Scarecrow Press, 1974.

MUSIC EDUCATION

The following sources are largely, but not exclusively, concerned with the field of music education in the United States. In the first category, "The History of Music Education," for example, the article by Anderson et al. in *The New Grove* covers the entire history of the field from ancient Greece on; the other sources contain general overviews of music education in the United States and Canada. Under "Research Methodology," Borg and Gall is a comprehensive overview of what research in the social sciences entails, drawing examples from the many disciplines involved in the broad field of education. The remaining sources are focused primarily on how research has and can be conducted specifically in music education—Barnes contains actual examples of different types of such research.

"General Reference Sources" brings together works that constitute a general orientation to the field of music education, paying some attention to the past as well as assessing current issues and directions. Nelson is a classic reference work in its pioneering attempt to examine the field. Leonhard and House remains a primary study in its comprehensive attention to the philosophy and curriculum of public school music. Mark is an excellent summary and bibliographic resource on the main people, ideas, and literature of the field.

The sources listed under "Research Overviews" are evaluative reflections on the results of research efforts in both general and music education; each is based on the review of a substantial number of research projects and offers direction for future efforts. The three handbooks sponsored by AERA (Gage, Travers, Wittrock) are monumental attempts to examine the current status of the field of educational research and illustrate how it has changed drastically over a period of twenty-five years. Colwell's *Handbook* is the first similar project devoted specifically to music, containing fifty-five essays on topics pertaining to all age levels and related to all areas of music teaching and learning.

The final list, "Bibliographies, Directories, and Indexes," is of important bibliographic tools in music education, including the major sources from the Educational Resources Information Center (ERIC), located in Washington, D.C.

For a list of research journals in the field, see chapter 6, "Current Research Journals in Music," p. 152 below.

The History of Music Education

Anderson, Warren, et al. "Education in Music." In *The New Grove Dictionary of Music and Musicians*. Vol. 6, pp. 1–58.

Birge, Edward Bailey. *History of Public School Music in the United States*. New and augm. ed. Bryn Mawr, Pa.: Oliver Ditson, 1937; reprint, Reston, Va.: Music Educators National Conference, 1988. First published in 1928.

Colwell, Richard, et al. "Education in Music." In *The New Grove Dictionary of American Music*. Edited by H. Wiley Hitchcock and Stanley Sadie. 4 vols. New York: Grove's Dictionaries of Music, 1986. Vol. 2, pp. 11–21.

"Education in the United States." In *The New Harvard Dictionary of Music*. Pp. 276–78.

Goodman, A. Harold. *Music Education: Perspectives and Perceptions*. Dubuque, Iowa: Kendall-Hunt, 1982.

Green, J. Paul, and Nancy F. Vogan. *Music Education in Canada: A Historical Account*. Toronto: University of Toronto Press, 1991.

Keene, James A. *A History of Music Education in the United States*. Hanover, N.H.: University Press of New England, 1982.

Mark, Michael L. *Source Readings in Music Education History*. New York: Schirmer Books, 1982.

Mark, Michael L., and Charles L. Gary. *A History of American Music Education*. New York: Schirmer Books, 1992.

Tellstrom, A. Theodore. *Music in American Education: Past and Present*. New York: Holt, Rinehart and Winston, 1971.

Research Methodology

Barnes, Stephen H., ed. *A Cross Section of Research in Music Education*. Washington, D.C.: University Press of America, 1982.

Borg, Walter R., and Meredith Damien Gall. *Educational Research: An Introduction*. 5th ed. New York: Longman, 1989. First published in 1963.

Phelps, Roger P. *A Guide to Research in Music Education.* 3rd ed. Metuchen, N.J.: Scarecrow Press, 1986. First published in 1969.

Rainbow, Edward L., and Hildegard C. Froehlich. *Research in Music Education: An Introduction to Systematic Inquiry.* New York: Schirmer Books, 1987.

Weimer, George William. "Trends in Topics, Methods, and Statistical Techniques Employed in Dissertations Completed for Doctor's Degrees in Music Education 1963–1978." Ed.D. diss., University of Illinois at Urbana-Champaign, 1980.

General Reference Sources

Campbell, Patricia Shehan. *Lessons from the World: A Cross-Cultural Guide to Music Teaching and Learning.* New York: Schirmer Books, 1991.

Colwell, Richard J. *Basic Concepts of Music Education, II.* Niwot: University Press of Colorado, 1991.

Fletcher, Peter. *Education and Music.* New York: Oxford University Press, 1987.

Gates, J. Terry, ed. *Music Education in the United States: Contemporary Issues.* Tuscaloosa: University of Alabama Press, 1988.

Handbook of Music Psychology. Edited by Donald A. Hodges. Lawrence, Kans.: National Association for Music Therapy, 1980.

Leonhard, Charles, and Robert W. House. *Foundations and Principles of Music Education.* 2nd ed. New York: McGraw-Hill, 1972. First published in 1959.

Mark, Michael L. *Contemporary Music Education.* 2nd ed. New York: Schirmer Books, 1986. First published in 1978.

Nelson, Henry, ed. *Basic Concepts in Music Education.* Fifty-seventh Yearbook of the National Society for the Study of Education, part 1. Chicago: The National Society for the Study of Education, 1958.

Research Overviews

Colwell, Richard, ed. "Symposium on K-12 Music Education." *Design for Arts in Education* 91, no. 5 (1990): 14–52.

Encyclopedia of Educational Research. 6th ed. Edited by Marvin
    Alkin. 4 vols. A Project of the American Educational
    Research Association. New York: Macmillan, 1992. First
    published in 1941.
Fowler, Charles, ed. *The Crane Symposium: Toward an
    Understanding of the Teaching and Learning of Musical
    Performance.* Potsdam: Potsdam College of the State
    University of New York, 1988.
Handbook of Research on Curriculum. Edited by Philip Jackson.
    New York: Macmillan, 1992.
Handbook of Research on Music Teaching and Learning. Edited by
    Richard Colwell. A Project of the Music Educators
    National Conference. New York: Schirmer Books, 1992.
Handbook of Research on Teaching. Edited by Nathaniel Lees
    Gage. A Project of the American Educational Research
    Association. Chicago: Rand McNally, 1963.
Second Handbook of Research on Teaching. Edited by Robert
    M. W. Travers. A Project of the American Educational
    Research Association. Chicago: Rand McNally, 1973.
Handbook of Research on Teaching. 3rd ed. Edited by Merlin C.
    Wittrock. A Project of the American Educational Research
    Association. New York: Macmillan, 1986.
Leonhard, Charles, and Richard Colwell. "Research in Music
    Education." In *Arts and Aesthetics: An Agenda for the
    Future Based on a Conference Held at Aspen, Colorado,
    June 22–25, 1976.* Edited by Stanley Madeja. St. Louis:
    CEMREL, 1977.
Madson, Clifford K., and Carol A. Prickett, eds. *Applications of
    Research in Music Behavior.* Tuscaloosa: University of
    Alabama Press, 1987.
Schneider, Erwin H., and Henry L. Cady. *Evaluation and
    Synthesis of Research Studies Related to Music Education.*
    Columbus: Ohio State University, 1965.
Sloboda, John A. *The Musical Mind: The Cognitive Psychology of
    Music.* New York: Oxford University Press, 1985.

Bibliographies, Directories, and Indexes

Bibliography of Research Studies in Music Education, 1932–1948.
    Rev. ed. Prepared by William S. Larson and presented by
    The Music Education Research Council. Washington, D.C.:
    Music Educators National Conference, 1949. First
    published in 1944.

Bibliography of Research Studies in Music Education, 1949–1956.
    Washington, D.C.: Music Educators National Conference,
    1957.
Brookhart, Edward. *Music in American Higher Education: An
    Annotated Bibliography.* Bibliographies in American Music,
    no. 10. Warren, Mich.: Harmonie Park Press, 1988.
CAIRSS for MUSIC. Charles T. Eagle, Jr., ed. San Antonio:
    Institute for Music Research (Donald A. Hodges, director),
    University of Texas at San Antonio, 1993–. This "Computer-
    Assisted Information Retrieval Service System" is a
    bibliographic database of music research literature that
    emphasizes music education, music therapy, music
    psychology, and medicine. Currently there are fifteen
    "primary" journals in these areas that are completely
    indexed, with selected articles from more than twelve
    hundred "secondary" journals that are also in the
    database.
Complete Guide and Index to ERIC *Reports through December
    1969.* Compiled by the Prentice-Hall Editorial Staff.
    Englewood Cliffs, N.J.: Prentice Hall, 1970.
Current Index to Journals in Education (CIJE). Phoenix: Oryx
    Press for Educational Resources Information Center (ERIC)
    of the National Institute of Education, U.S. Department of
    Education, 1969–. (Also available on CD-ROM as *ERIC.*)
*Education Index: A Cumulative Author-Subject Index to a Selected
    List of Educational Periodicals and Yearbooks.* New York:
    H. W. Wilson, 1929–.
Gordon, Roderick D. "Doctoral Dissertations in Music and Music
    Education, 1957–1963." *Journal of Research in Music
    Education* 13 (Spring 1965): 45–55.
Harris, Ernest E., ed. *Music Education: A Guide to Information
    Sources.* Education Information Guide Series, vol. 1.
    Detroit: Gale Research, 1978.
Heller, George N. *Historical Research in Music Education: A
    Bibliography.* 2nd ed. Lawrence: Department of Art and
    Music Education and Music Therapy, University of Kansas,
    1992. First published in 1988.
*International Directory of Approved Music Education Doctoral
    Dissertations in Progress.* Edited by Richard J. Colwell.
    Council for Research in Music Education, University of
    Illinois, in behalf of The Graduate Program in Music
    Education. Urbana: University of Illinois, 1989–.
Resources in Education (RIE). Washington, D.C.: Educational
    Resources Information Center (ERIC), U.S. Department of

Health, Education, and Welfare, National Institute of
Education, 1974–. (Formerly *Research in Education,*
1966–73.) (Also available on CD-ROM as *ERIC.*)
Thesaurus of **ERIC** *Descriptors.* 11th ed. Edited by James
Houston. Phoenix: Oryx Press, 1987. First published in
1968. (See current issues of *Resources in Education* for
"Thesaurus Additions and Changes.")

BIBLIOGRAPHIES IN OTHER SELECTED AREAS

This section consists of important bibliographical sources of
music literature through which to initiate research in other selected
subject areas. Only five areas are given here; the number could be
expanded to include separate countries, individual genres, popular
and rock music, folk song, etc., bibliographies of which may be
found in Duckles's *Music Reference and Research Materials* and in
Marco's *Information on Music* (see p. 32 above). It should be noted
that sources appearing in one category may also apply to another,
most notably those pertaining to various aspects of American music, e.g., sources in the "African-American Music" section that concern "Jazz."

African-American Music

de Lerma, Dominique-René. *Bibliography of Black Music.* 4 vols.
The Greenwood Encyclopedia of Black Music. Westport,
Conn.: Greenwood Press, 1981–84.

1. *Reference Materials.* 1981.
2. *Afro-American Idioms.* 1981.
3. *Geographical Studies.* 1981.
4. *Theory, Education, and Related Studies.* 1984.

de Lerma, Dominique-René, and Marsha J. Reisser. *Black Music
and Musicians in The New Grove Dictionary of American
Music and The New Harvard Dictionary of Music.* CBMR
Monographs, no. 1. Chicago: Center for Black Music
Research, Columbia College Chicago, 1989.

Floyd, Samuel A., Jr. "Books on Black Music by Black Authors: A
Bibliography." *The Black Perspective in Music* 14 (Fall
1986): 215–32.

Floyd, Samuel A., Jr., and Marsha J. Reisser. *Black Music
Biography: An Annotated Bibliography.* White Plains, N.Y.:
Kraus International Publications, 1987.

————. *Black Music in the United States: An Annotated Bibliography of Selected Reference and Research Materials.* Millwood, N.Y.: Kraus International Publications, 1983.

Gray, John, comp. *Blacks in Classical Music: A Bibliographical Guide to Composers, Performers, and Ensembles.* Music Reference Collection, no. 15. Westport, Conn.: Greenwood Press, 1988.

Johnson, James Peter, comp. *Bibliographic Guide to the Study of Afro-American Music.* Washington, D.C.: Howard University Libraries, 1973.

Skowronski, JoAnn. *Black Music in America: A Bibliography.* Metuchen, N.J.: Scarecrow Press, 1981.

Southern, Eileen, and Josephine Wright, comps. *African-American Traditions in Song, Sermon, Tale, and Dance, 1600s–1920: An Annotated Bibliography of Literature, Collections, and Artworks.* The Greenwood Encyclopedia of Black Music. Westport, Conn.: Greenwood Press, 1990.

Szwed, John F., Roger D. Abrahams, et al. *Afro-American Folk Culture: An Annotated Bibliography of Materials from North, Central, and South America, and the West Indies.* Publications of the American Folklore Society, Bibliographical and Special Series, no. 31. Philadelphia: Institute for the Study of Human Issues, 1978.

Vann, Kimberly R., et al. *Black Music in* Ebony: *An Annotated Guide to the Articles on Music in* Ebony *Magazine, 1945–1985.* CBMR Monographs, no. 2. Chicago: Center for Black Music Research, Columbia College Chicago, 1990.

Wright, Josephine. "Research in Afro-American Music, 1968–88: A Survey with Selected Bibliography of the Literature." In *New Perspectives on Music: Essays in Honor of Eileen Southern,* edited by Josephine Wright, with Samuel A. Floyd, Jr. Detroit Monographs in Musicology/Studies in Music, no. 11. Warren, Mich.: Harmonie Park Press, 1992. Pp. 481–515.

American Music

Bibliographies in American Music. Published for the College Music Society. Warren, Mich.: Harmonie Park Press, 1974–.

Brookhart, Edward. *Music in American Higher Education: An Annotated Bibliography.* Bibliographies in American Music, no. 10. Warren, Mich.: Harmonie Park Press, 1988.

District of Columbia Historical Records Survey. *Bio-Biblio-graphical Index of Musicians in the United States of America since Colonial Times/Indice bio-bibliográfico de músicos de los Estados Unidos de America desde la época de la colonia.* 2nd ed. Washington, D.C.: Music Section, Pan American Union, 1956. First published in 1940.

Heintze, James R. *Early American Music: A Research and Information Guide.* Music Research and Information Guides, no. 13. New York: Garland Publishing, 1990.

Horn, David. *The Literature of American Music in Books and Folk Music Collections: A Fully Annotated Bibliography.* Metuchen, N.J.: Scarecrow Press, 1977. Suppl. 1, by David Horn, with Richard Jackson, 1988.

I.S.A.M. Monographs. Brooklyn: Institute for Studies in American Music, Department of Music, Brooklyn College of the City University of New York, 1973–.

Jackson, Richard. *United States Music: Sources of Bibliography and Collective Biography.* I.S.A.M. Monographs, no. 1. Brooklyn: Institute for Studies in American Music, Department of Music, Brooklyn College of the City University of New York, 1973.

Krummel, D. W. *Bibliographical Handbook of American Music.* Music in American Life. Urbana: University of Illinois Press, 1987.

Krummel, D. W., et al. *Resources of American Music History: A Directory of Source Materials from Colonial Times to World War II.* Urbana: University of Illinois Press, 1981.

Mead, Rita H. *Doctoral Dissertations in American Music: A Classified Bibliography.* I.S.A.M. Monographs, no. 3. Brooklyn: Institute for Studies in American Music, Department of Music, School of Performing Arts, Brooklyn College of the City University of New York, 1974.

Warner, Thomas E. *Periodical Literature on American Music, 1620–1920: A Classified Bibliography with Annotations.* Bibliographies in American Music, no. 12. Warren, Mich.: Harmonie Park Press, 1988.

Dance

Adamczyk, Alice J. *Black Dance: A Bibliography.* New York: Garland Publishing, 1989.

Bopp, Mary S. *Research in Dance: A Guide to Research.* New York: G. K. Hall Reference, 1993.

Forbes, Fred R., Jr. *Dance: An Annotated Bibliography, 1965–1982.* Music Research and Information Guides, vol. 3. New York: Garland Publishing, 1986.

Johnson, Thomas J. *Review and Index to Research in Dance Relevant to Aesthetic Education, 1900–1968.* St. Ann, Mo.: CEMREL, 1970.

New York Public Library. Research Libraries. *Dictionary Catalog of the Dance Collection: A List of Authors, Titles, and Subjects of Multi-Media Materials in the Dance Collection of the Performing Arts Research Center of the New York Public Library.* 10 vols. + yearly suppls. Boston: New York Public Library et al., 1974.

Schwartz, Judith L., and Christena L. Schlundt. *French Court Dance and Dance Music: A Guide to Primary Source Writings 1643–1789.* Dance and Music Series, no. 1. Stuyvesant, N.Y.: Pendragon Press, 1987.

Jazz

Carner, Gary, comp. *Jazz Performers: An Annotated Bibliography of Biographical Materials.* Music Reference Collection, no. 26. Westport, Conn.: Greenwood Press, 1990.

Gray, John, comp. *Fire Music: A Bibliography of the New Jazz, 1959–1990.* Music Reference Collection, no. 31. Westport, Conn.: Greenwood Press, 1991.

Gregor, Carl, Duke of Mecklenburg. *International Bibliography of Jazz Books.* Compiled with the assistance of Norbert Ruecker. 4 vols. projected. Collection d'études musicologiques/Sammlung musikwissenschaftlicher Abhandlungen. Baden-Baden: Valentin Koerner, 1983–.

1. *1921–1949.* No. 67 in series. 1983.
2. *1950–1959.* No. 76 in series. 1988.

――――― . *International Jazz Bibliography: Jazz Books from 1919 to 1968.* Suppls., 1970 to 1975. Strasbourg: P. H. Heitz, 1969.

Hefele, Bernhard. *Jazz-Bibliography: International Literature on Jazz, Blues, Spirituals, Gospel and Ragtime Music. . . .* New York: K. G. Saur, 1981.

Jazz Index: Bibliographie unselbständiger Jazzliteratur/ Bibliography of Jazz Literature in Periodicals and Collections. Compiled by Norbert Ruecker and C. Reggentin-Scheidt. Frankfurt: N. Ruecker, 1977–.

Kennington, Donald, and Danny Read. *The Literature of Jazz: A Critical Guide.* 2nd ed., rev. Chicago: American Library Association, 1980. First published in 1970.

Meadows, Eddie S. *Jazz Reference and Research Materials: A Bibliography.* Critical Studies on Black Life and Culture, no. 22; Garland Reference Library of the Humanities, vol. 251. New York: Garland Publishing, 1981.

Merriam, Alan P., with the assistance of Robert J. Banford. *A Bibliography of Jazz.* Publications of the American Folklore Society, Bibliographical Series, vol. 4. Philadelphia: The American Folklore Society, 1954.

Reisner, Robert G. *The Literature of Jazz: A Selective Bibliography.* New York: New York Public Library, 1959.

Women in Music

Block, Adrienne Fried, and Carol Neuls-Bates, comps. and eds. *Women in American Music: A Bibliography of Music and Literature.* Westport, Conn.: Greenwood Press, 1979.

Hixon, Don L., and Don Hennesee. *Women in Music: A Biobibliography.* Metuchen, N.J.: Scarecrow Press, 1975.

LePage, Jane Weiner. *Women Composers, Conductors, and Musicians of the Twentieth Century: Selected Bibliographies.* 3 vols. Metuchen, N.J.: Scarecrow Press, 1980–88.

The Musical Woman: An International Perspective. Judith Lang Zaimont, editor-in-chief. New York: Greenwood Press, 1984–.

Resource Guide on Women in Music. Edited by Judith Cody. Materials compiled by Laura M. Gilliard. San Francisco: Bay Area Congress on Women in Music, 1981.

Skowronski, JoAnn. *Women in American Music: A Bibliography.* Metuchen, N.J.: Scarecrow Press, 1978.

Stern, Susan. *Women Composers: A Handbook.* Metuchen, N.J.: Scarecrow Press, 1978.

Women's Studies/Women's Status. By the Committee on the Status of Women in Music (1984–1986). CMS Report no. 5. Boulder, Colo.: College Music Society, 1988.

CHAPTER FOUR

Dictionaries and Encyclopedias of Music

The dictionaries and encyclopedias of music listed in this chapter have been divided by type into (1) the recent large sources and selected concise ones that contain articles on people as well as on terms, (2) selected sources, international and North American, that contain only biographical articles, (3) the chief sources that contain only articles on terms, and (4) selected specialized dictionaries—those treating specific areas or subjects, regardless of approach. In all but one category, the names of certain older sources of historical interest are also included. For comprehensive lists of such sources, see under "Dictionaries and Encyclopedias of Music" in chapter 2 above. As an addendum to this chapter, a representative list of articles in what is probably the most common single-volume dictionary of terms, *The New Harvard Dictionary of Music*, has been added as an indication of the variety of information that it contains. Similar articles can be found in *The New Grove Dictionary* and other such sources.

GENERAL DICTIONARIES AND ENCYCLOPEDIAS

These sources are "general" dictionaries and encyclopedias of music in that all of them (with the exception of the *Encyclopedia of World Music*) include articles on both biographical and nonbiographical subjects, on people as well as terms, forms, genres, countries, etc. Beyond that, however, there are considerable differences among them in size, comprehensiveness, and recentness. There are sometimes specified limitations (e.g., *Dictionary of Contemporary Music, Encyclopedia of Music in Canada, Garland Encyclopedia of World Music,* and *New Grove Dictionary of American Music*). Less obvious in the international sources is that there are often differences of emphasis, e.g., more detailed coverage of subjects pertaining to the country in which the work originated.

By far the most comprehensive sources in any language in this category are the well-known *Die Musik in Geschichte und Gegenwart* [*MGG*] and *New Grove Dictionary.* The latter is more recent, but a new edition of *MGG* is now in preparation. *Das grosse Lexikon der Musik,* the greatly enlarged translation into German of Honegger's four-volume French original, and the *Dizionario enciclopedico* should also be mentioned as quite lengthy and thorough works, both slightly more recent than *The New Grove.*

The Lavignac/La Laurencie *Encyclopédie,* though dating back to earlier in the century, still holds a place of importance; not in alphabetical order, it consists of a series of book-length articles on a wide variety of musical subjects. The *Brockhaus Riemann Musik-Lexikon* (formerly *Riemann Musik-Lexikon,* which went through twelve editions), *New Oxford Companion to Music* (the continuation of Percy Scholes's *Oxford Companion to Music,* which went through eleven editions), and *International Cyclopedia* are especially worthy of mention as standard sources of medium length. The Westrup/Harrison *New College Encyclopedia, Norton/Grove Concise Encyclopedia,* and *Oxford Dictionary of Music* are all short one-volume works.

Under "Of Historical Interest" are two of the many earlier dictionaries of music, each an important first: Walther's venerable *Musicalisches Lexicon* (1732), the earliest example of the genre, and Moore's *Encyclopedia* (1854), the earliest major American one.

Brockhaus Riemann Musik-Lexikon. Edited by Carl Dahlhaus. 5
   vols. Serie Musik Piper-Schott. Mainz: Schott, 1989.
Dictionary of Contemporary Music. Edited by John Vinton. New
   York: E. P. Dutton, 1974.
Dictionnaire de la musique en France aux XVIIe et XVIIIe siècles.
   Marcelle Benoit, gen. ed. Paris: Fayard, 1992.
Dizionario enciclopedico universale della musica e dei musicisti.
   Edited by Alberto Basso. 13 vols. Turin: Unione
   Tipografico-Editrice Torinese, 1983–90.

   [Part 1, vols. 1–4.] *Il lessico.* 1983–84.
   [Part 2, vols. 1–8.] *Le biografie.* 1985–88.
   Appendice. 1990.

Enciclopedia della musica. New ed. Edited by Claudio Sartori. 4
vols. Milan: Ricordi, 1972–74. First published in 1963–64.

Encyclopedia of Music in Canada. 2nd ed. Edited by Helmut
Kallman et al. Toronto: University of Toronto Press, 1992.
First published in 1981.

Encyclopédie de la musique. Edited by François Michel et al. 3
vols. Paris: Fasquelle, 1958–61.

Encyclopédie de la musique et dictionnaire du Conservatoire.
Founded by Albert Lavignac. Edited by Lionel de La
Laurencie. 11 vols. Paris: Delagrave, 1913–31.

Garland Encyclopedia of World Music. Timothy Rice and James
Porter, gen. eds.; Bruno Nettl, advisory ed. 10 vols.
projected. New York: Garland Publishing, 1993–.

1. *Europe.* By James Porter and Timothy Rice.
2. *Africa.* By Ruth Stone.
3. *Inner and East Asia.* By Yoshihiko Tokumaru and Bell
   Yung.
4. *Southeast Asia.* By Terry Miller.
5. *South Asia.* By Charles Capwell.
6. *Middle East.* By Lorraine Sakata and Philip Schuyler.
7. *The Pacific.* By Adrienne Kaeppler and Jacob Love.
8. *North America.* By Jeff Todd Titon.
9. *Latin Ameria.* By Dale Olsen and Daniel Sheehy.
10. *Global Perspectives.* By James Porter and Timothy Rice.

Griffiths, Paul. *The Thames and Hudson Encyclopaedia of
20th-Century Music.* London: Thames and Hudson, 1986.

Das grosse Lexikon der Musik. Edited by Marc Honegger and
Günther Massenkeil. Translated into German from the
original French, and enl. 8 vols. Freiburg: Herder, 1978–82.
First published in 1970–76.

The International Cyclopedia of Music and Musicians. Oscar
Thompson, gen. ed. 11th ed. Edited by Bruce Bohle. New
York: Dodd, Mead, 1985. First published in 1939.

Jablonski, Edward. *The Encyclopedia of American Music.* Garden
City, N.Y.: Doubleday, 1981.

Kennedy, Michael. *The Oxford Dictionary of Music.* Rev. and enl.
ed. of *The Concise Oxford Dictionary of Music,* 3rd ed.,
1980. London: Oxford University Press, 1985.

Morehead, Philip D., with Anne MacNeal. *The New American
Dictionary of Music.* New York: Dalton, 1991.

Die Musik in Geschichte und Gegenwart [*MGG*]. Edited by
Friedrich Blume. 14 vols. Kassel: Bärenreiter, 1949–68.
Suppls., 1973 and 1979. Index, 1986.

The New Grove Dictionary of American Music. Edited by H.
    Wiley Hitchcock and Stanley Sadie. 4 vols. New York:
    Grove's Dictionaries of Music, 1986.
The New Grove Dictionary of Music and Musicians. Edited by
    Stanley Sadie. 20 vols. London: Macmillan, 1980.
The New Oxford Companion to Music. Edited by Denis Arnold. 2
    vols. London: Oxford University Press, 1983.
The Norton/Grove Concise Encyclopedia of Music. Edited by
    Stanley Sadie. 1st American ed. New York: W. W. Norton,
    1988.
Performance Practice Encyclopedia. Edited by Roland John
    Jackson. New York: Garland Publishing, forthcoming.
Roche, Jerome, and Elizabeth Roche. *A Dictionary of Early
    Music: From the Troubadours to Monteverdi.* London:
    Oxford University Press, 1981.
Westrup, Jack A., and Frank Ll. Harrison. *The New College
    Encyclopedia of Music.* Rev. ed. Revised by Conrad Wilson.
    New York: W. W. Norton, 1976. First published in 1959.

Of Historical Interest

Moore, John W. *Complete Encyclopedia of Music, Elementary,
    Technical, Historical, Biographical, Vocal and Instrumental.*
    New York: Sheldon, Lamport and Blakeman, 1854.
Walther, Johann Gottfried. *Musicalisches Lexicon oder
    musicalische Bibliothec.* Leipzig: Wolffgang Deer, 1732;
    facsimile, edited by Richard Schaal, Documenta
    Musicologica, 1. Reihe: Druckschriften-Faksimiles, no. 3.
    Kassel: Bärenreiter, 1953.

BIOGRAPHICAL DICTIONARIES
AND ENCYCLOPEDIAS

The first of the following lists, "International," includes the
two most comprehensive international dictionaries devoted exclusively to biographies of musicians, *Baker's Biographical Dictionary*
and the *International Who's Who in Music*. The remaining sources are
specialized biographical works, representative of many such
sources that have some specific delimitation such as period, style of
music, gender or race, or type of musical figure (composer, performer, music educator, etc.).

The works in the next list, "North American," are fairly recent and each is slightly different in scope; under "English" Pulver's work is given because it is still of value in researching pre-18th-century English music.

The several sources listed as being "Of Historical Interest" include two monuments of 19th-century single-author scholarship, Fétis and Eitner, neither completely out-of-date although their biographical portions are now largely superseded by more recent sources. The remaining works by Mattheson and Gerber represent the beginnings of purely biographical dictionaries in music, dating back to the mid- and late 18th century respectively.

For further information, see chapter 2 under "Biographies of Musicians," p. 29 above. See also the sections "Biographies of Composers in English," p. 133, and "Series of Composers' Biographies in English," p. 143, in chapter 5 below. (Other national biographical dictionaries, including American, are listed in Duckles, *Music Reference and Research Materials;* see p. 32 above.)

International

Baker's Biographical Dictionary of Musicians. 8th ed., rev. Edited by Nicholas Slonimsky. New York: Schirmer Books, 1991. First published in 1900.

Berry, Lemuel, Jr. *Biographical Dictionary of Black Musicians and Music Educators.* Vol. 1. N.p.: Educational Book Publishers, 1978–.

Carlson, Effie B. *A Bio-Bibliographical Dictionary of Twelve-Tone and Serial Composers.* Metuchen, N.J.: Scarecrow Press, 1970.

Chilton, John. *Who's Who of Jazz: Storyville to Swing Street.* 4th ed. New York: Da Capo Press, 1985. First published in 1970.

Claghorn, Charles Eugene. *Biographical Dictionary of Jazz.* Englewood Cliffs, N.J.: Prentice Hall, 1982.

———. *Women Composers and Hymnists: A Concise Biographical Dictionary.* Metuchen, N.J.: Scarecrow Press, 1984.

Cohen, Aaron I. *International Encyclopedia of Women Composers.* 2nd ed., rev. and enl. 2 vols. New York: Books & Music, 1987. First published in 1981.

Companion to Baroque Music. Compiled and edited by Julie Anne Sadie. New York: Schirmer Books, 1990.

Contemporary Composers. Edited by Brian Morton and Pamela
    Collins. Detroit: St. James Press, 1992.
International Who's Who in Music and Musicians' Directory. 13th
    ed. Cambridge, England: Melrose Press, 1992/93. First
    published in 1935.
LePage, Jane Weiner. *Women Composers, Conductors, and
    Musicians of the Twentieth Century: Selected Biographies.*
    3 vols. Metuchen, N.J.: Scarecrow Press, 1980–88.
The New Grove Dictionary of Women Composers. Edited by Julie
    Anne Sadie and Rhian Samuel. London: Macmillan, 1994.
Southern, Eileen. *Biographical Dictionary of Afro-American and
    African Musicians.* The Greenwood Encyclopedia of Black
    Music. Westport, Conn.: Greenwood Press, 1982.
Stern, Susan. *Women Composers: A Handbook.* Metuchen, N.J.:
    Scarecrow Press, 1978.
Thompson, Kenneth. *A Dictionary of Twentieth-Century
    Composers, 1911–1971.* London: Faber and Faber, 1973.
Who's Who in Black Music. Edited by Robert E. Rosenthal and
    Portia K. Maultsby. New Orleans: Edwards Printing, 1985.
*Who's Who in Opera: An International Biographical Dictionary
    of Singers, Conductors, Directors, Designers, and
    Administrators, also Including Profiles of 101 Opera
    Companies.* Edited by Maria F. Rich. New York: Arno
    Press, 1976.

North American

American Society of Composers, Authors, and Publishers.
    ASCAP Biographical Dictionary. 4th ed. Compiled for the
    American Society of Composers, Authors, and Publishers
    by Jaques Cattell Press. New York: R. R. Bowker, 1980.
    First published in 1948.
Butterworth, Neil. *A Dictionary of American Composers.* Garland
    Reference Library of the Humanities, vol. 296. New York:
    Garland Publishing, 1984.
Claghorn, Charles Eugene. *Biographical Dictionary of American
    Music.* West Nyack, N.Y.: Parker Publishing, 1973.
Contemporary American Composers: A Biographical Dictionary.
    2nd ed. Compiled by E. Ruth Anderson. Boston: G. K.
    Hall, 1982. First published in 1976.
Contemporary Canadian Composers. Edited by Keith MacMillan
    and John Beckwith. London: Oxford University Press, 1975.

Ewen, David. *American Composers: A Biographical Dictionary.*
New York: G. P. Putnam's Sons, 1982.
Who's Who in American Music: Classical. 2nd ed. Edited by
Jaques Cattell Press. New York: R. R. Bowker, 1985. First
published in 1983.

English

Pulver, Jeffrey. *A Biographical Dictionary of Old English Music.*
Reprint, with an introduction by Gilbert Blount. New York:
Da Capo Press, 1973. First published in 1927.

Of Historical Interest

Eitner, Robert. *Biographisch-bibliographisches Quellen-Lexikon
der Musiker und Musikgelehrten christlicher Zeitrechnung
bis zur Mitte des neunzehnten Jahrhunderts.* 2nd ed.,
improved and enl. 11 vols. Graz: Akademische Druck- und
Verlagsanstalt, 1959. First published in 1898–1904.
Fétis, François-Joseph. *Biographie universelle des musiciens et
bibliographie générale de la musique.* 2nd ed. 8 vols. Paris:
Firmin-Didot, 1866–70. First published in 1835–44.
Gerber, Ernst Ludwig. *Historisch-biographisches Lexikon der
Tonkünstler, welches Nachrichten von dem Leben und
Werken musikalischer Schriftsteller, berühmter
Componisten, Sänger, usw. . . . enthält.* 2 vols. Leipzig:
J. G. I. Breitkopf, 1790–92.
————. *Neues historisch-biographisches Lexikon der
Tonkünstler. . . .* 4 vols. Leipzig: A. Kühnel, 1812–14.
Mattheson, Johann. *Grundlage einer Ehren-Pforte, woran der
tüchtigsten Capellmeister, Componisten, Musikgelehrten,
Tonkünstler, usw., erscheinen sollen.* Rev. and enl. ed.
Edited by Max Schneider. Kassel: Bärenreiter, 1969. First
published in 1740.

DICTIONARIES OF TERMS

In this list of dictionaries of musical terms—tempo markings,
forms, genres, even names of compositions, instruments, countries, etc., the diversity and quantity of terms varying from one

source to the next—the key word is variety. The most detailed and elaborate is Eggebrecht's *Handwörterbuch*, still unfinished and growing in its unique looseleaf format, to which additional pages continue to be added. *The New Harvard Dictionary of Music* is perhaps the most widely used one-volume general dictionary of terms; Slonimsky's even more recent *Lectionary*, though similar in scope, bears the unmistakable stamp of its author. Ammer's recent *A to Z*, equally recent, gives definitions in English of terms from French, German, Italian, Latin, Portuguese, and Spanish musical scores, as well as pronunciation guides to Italian, German, and French. Schaal's *Abkürzungen* consists entirely of abbreviations commonly used in music, emphasizing German terms. The remaining items are all concerned with the equivalence of terms in various languages and thus include no definitions, except for an occasional one in the *Terminorum Musicae*.

The works listed under "Individual Subject Areas" are each limited to a particular area; in Levarie and Levy there is a lengthy essay addressing matters of musical form and structure that precedes the dictionary of terms that concern formal principles.

Under "Of Historical Interest" appear three very important older dictionaries of musical terms, those by Tinctoris (the first self-contained dictionary, which predates all others by centuries), Brossard (the model for all subsequent works of the type), and the celebrated Jean-Jacques Rousseau (whose initial efforts in this form appeared in Diderot's and d'Alembert's *Encyclopédie*, 1751–72).

Ammer, Christine. *The A to Z of Foreign Musical Terms from Adagio to Zierlich: A Dictionary for Performers and Students*. Boston: E. C. Schirmer, 1989. Rev. and exp. ed. of *Musician's Handbook of Foreign Terms*, 1971.

Eggebrecht, Hans Heinrich. *Handwörterbuch der musikalischen Terminologie*. 3 vols. Wiesbaden: Franz Steiner, 1972–.

Music Translation Dictionary: An English-Czech-Danish-Dutch-French-German-Hungarian-Italian-Polish-Portuguese-Russian-Spanish-Swedish Vocabulary of Music Terms. Compiled by Carolyn Doub Grigg. Westport, Conn.: Greenwood Press, 1978.

The New Harvard Dictionary of Music. Edited by Don Michael Randel. Cambridge: Belknap Press of Harvard University Press, 1986.

Schaal, Richard. *Abkürzungen in der Musik-Terminologie: Eine Übersicht*. Taschenbücher zur Musikwissenschaft, vol. 1. Wilhelmshaven: Heinrichshofen's Verlag, 1969.

Slonimsky, Nicolas. *Lectionary of Music.* New York: McGraw-Hill, 1989.

Smith, W. J. *A Dictionary of Musical Terms in Four Languages.* London: Hutchinson, 1961.

Terminorum Musicae Index Septem Linguis Redactus: Polyglottes Wörterbuch der musikalischen Terminologie. Edited by Horst Leuchtmann et al. Kassel: Bärenreiter, 1978.

Wörterbuch Musik: Englisch-Deutsch, Deutsch-Englisch/ Dictionary of Terms in Music: English-German, German-English. Edited by Horst Leuchtmann. 3rd ed., enl. Munich: Linnet Books, 1981. First published in 1964.

Individual Subject Areas

Carter, Henry Holland. *A Dictionary of Middle English Musical Terms.* Edited by George B. Gerhard. Indiana University Humanities Series, no. 45. Bloomington: Indiana University Press, 1961.

Cary, Tristram. *Dictionary of Musical Terminology.* New York: Greenwood Press, 1992.

Enders, Bernd. *Lexikon Musik-Elektronik.* Mainz: B. Schott's Söhne, 1985.

Fink, Robert, and Robert Ricci. *The Language of Twentieth Century Music: A Dictionary of Terms.* New York: Schirmer Books, 1975.

Kaufmann, Walter. *Selected Musical Terms of Non-Western Cultures: A Notebook-Glossary.* Warren, Mich.: Harmonie Park Press, 1990.

Levarie, Siegmund, and Ernst Levy. *Musical Morphology: A Discourse and a Dictionary.* Kent, Ohio: Kent State University Press, 1983.

Tomlyn, Bo, and Steve Leonard. *Electronic Music Dictionary: A Glossary of the Specialized Terms Relating to the Music and Sound Technology of Today.* Milwaukee: Hall Leonard Books, 1988.

Of Historical Interest

Brossard, Sébastien de. *Dictionaire de musique, contenant une explication des termes grecs, latins, italiens & françois les plus usitez dans la musique. . . .* 2nd ed. Paris: Christophe Ballard, 1705. First published in 1703. English trans.:

Dictionary of Music. . . . Translated and edited by Albion
   Gruber. Musical Theorists in Translation, vol. 12. Ottawa:
   Institut de Musique Médiévale, 1982.
Rousseau, Jean-Jacques. *Dictionnaire de musique.* Paris:
   Duchesne, 1768. English trans.: *A Complete Dictionary of
   Music.* . . . 2nd ed. Translated by William Waring. London:
   J. Murray, 1779; reprint, New York: AMS Press, 1975. First
   published in 1771.
Tinctoris, Johannes. *Terminorum Musicae Diffinitorium* [ca. 1494];
   reprint, New York: Broude Brothers, 1966. English trans.:
   *Dictionary of Musical Terms . . . Together with the Latin
   Text.* Translated and annotated by Carl Parrish. Da Capo
   Press Music Reprint Series. New York: Da Capo Press, 1978.

SPECIALIZED DICTIONARIES
AND ENCYCLOPEDIAS

Many music dictionaries and encyclopedias are organized
around a single subject or interest. Some of the most significant
and well known of these are listed here, divided into six groups
according to whether they concern instruments, opera, jazz, etc.
Some include terms only (e.g., Marcuse's *Musical Instruments*),
some are exclusively biographical (e.g., Vannes's *Dictionnaire universel des luthiers* [violin makers]), some combine the two (e.g.,
Julian's *Dictionary of Hymnology* and *The New Grove Dictionary of
Opera*), and some depart completely from the usual alphabetical arrangement in favor of some other organization, but are encyclope-
dic in their treatment of the subject (e.g., Michel's *Historical Pianos*,
which is a kind of dictionary of pictures, and Loewenberg's *Annals
of Opera*, a chronological list by date of first performance, with
indexes).

Under "Musical Themes and Compositional Devices" are dictionaries of musical themes by Barlow/Morgenstern, Burrows/
Redmond, and Parsons; Read's *Thesaurus*, a "lexicon of instrumentation"; Slonimsky's *Thesaurus of Scales* (almost one thousand of
them); and the first volume of LaRue's unfinished *Catalogue*, unique
in listing the incipits in letter notation of 16,558 symphonies
from ca. 1720 to ca. 1810 (subsequent volumes of composers' work-
lists will follow). The "Miscellaneous Sources" section contains a
sampling of other works in lexicon form, including dictionaries of
quotations and of ballet, and Slonimsky's *Lexicon of Musical Invective*, an anthology of negative reviews of music from Beethoven to
Webern.

Musical Instruments and Makers

GENERAL

Baines, Anthony N. *The Oxford Companion to Musical
    Instruments.* New York: Oxford University Press, 1993.
Bragard, Roger, and Ferdinand J. de Hen. *Musical Instruments in
    Art and History.* Translated by Bill Hopkins. New York:
    Viking Press, n.d. First published in 1967.
Marcuse, Sibyl. *Musical Instruments: A Comprehensive
    Dictionary.* Rev. ed. Garden City, N.Y.: Doubleday, 1975.
    First published in 1964.
The New Grove Dictionary of Musical Instruments. Edited by
    Stanley Sadie. 3 vols. London: Macmillan, 1984.
Sachs, Curt. *Handbuch der Musikinstrumentenkunde.* 2nd ed.
    Kleine Handbücher der Musikgeschichte nach Gattungen,
    no. 12. Leipzig: Breitkopf & Härtel, 1930. First published in
    1920.
————. *Real-Lexikon der Musikinstrumente, zugleich ein
    Polyglossar für das gesamte Instrumentengebiet.* [Rev. and
    enl. ed.] New York: Dover, 1964. First published in 1913.

OF HISTORICAL INTEREST

Mersenne, Marin. *Harmonie universelle: The Books on
    Instruments* [1636]. Translated by Roger E. Chapman. The
    Hague: Martinus Nijhoff, 1957.
Praetorius, Michael. *Syntagma Musicum II* [1618]: *De
    Organographia, Parts I and II.* Translated and edited by
    David Z. Crookes. Early Music Series, no. 7. Oxford:
    Clarendon Press, 1986.

STRINGS

Bachman, Alberto A. *An Encyclopedia of the Violin.* Edited by
    Albert E. Wier. Translated by Frederick G. Martens. New
    York: D. Appleton, 1925.
Jalovec, Karel. *Encyclopedia of Violin-Makers.* Translated by J. B.
    Kozak. Edited by Patrick Hanks. 2 vols. London: Paul
    Hamlyn, 1968. First published in 1965.
Straeten, Edmund van der. *The History of the Violin, Its
    Ancestors, and Collateral Instruments from the Earliest
    Times to the Present Day.* London: Cassell, 1933.

Vannes, René. *Dictionnaire universel des luthiers.* 2nd ed., rev. and enl. 2 vols. Brussels: Les Amis de la Musique, 1951. First published in 1932.

WINDS

Langwill, Lyndesay Graham. *An Index of Musical Wind-Instrument Makers.* New ed. Edited by William Waterhouse. London: Tony Bingham, 1993. First published in 1960.

PERCUSSION

Encylopedia of Percussion Instruments. Edited by John H. Beck. New York: Garland Publishing, 1994.

KEYBOARD

Encyclopedia of Keyboard Instruments. Edited by Robert Palmieri and Margaret W. Palmieri. 3 vols. New York: Garland Publishing, 1993–.

1. *The Piano.* Edited by Robert Palmieri and Margaret W. Palmieri. 1993.
2. *The Organ.* Edited by Douglas E. Bush. 1994.
3. *The Clavichord and Harpsichord.* Edited by Igor Kipnis.

Irwin, Stevens. *Dictionary of Pipe Organ Stops.* 2nd ed. New York: Schirmer Books, 1983. First published in 1962.
Michel, Norman Elwood. *Historical Pianos, Harpsichords and Clavichords.* Pico Rivera, Calif.: By the author, 1963.
Russell, Raymond. *The Harpsichord and Clavichord: An Introductory Study.* 2nd ed. Revised by Howard Schott. London: Faber and Faber, 1973. First published in 1959.

Opera

Dictionary-Catalogue of Operas and Operettas Which Have Been Performed on the Public Stage. Edited by John Towers. 2 vols. Morgantown, W.Va.: Acme Publishing, 1910.
The Encyclopedia of Opera. Edited by Leslie Orrey. New York: Charles Scribner's Sons, 1976.

Ewen, David. *The New Encyclopedia of Opera.* New York: Hill
and Wang, 1971.
International Dictionary of Opera. Edited by Emily McMurray. 2
vols. Detroit: St. James Press, 1992.
Loewenberg, Alfred. *Annals of Opera, 1597–1940, Compiled from
the Original Sources.* 3rd ed., rev. and corrected. Totowa,
N.J.: Rowman and Littlefield, 1978. First published in 1943.
Moore, Frank L. *Crowell's Handbook of World Opera.* New York:
Thomas Y. Crowell, 1961.
The New Grove Dictionary of Opera. Edited by Stanley Sadie. 4
vols. London: Macmillan, 1992.
Osborne, Charles. *Dictionary of Opera.* New York: Simon and
Schuster, 1983.
Parsons, Charles H. *The Mellen Opera Reference Index.* 23 vols.
projected. Lewiston, N.Y.: Edwin Mellen Press, 1986–.

> 1–4. *Opera Composers and Their Works.* 1986.
> 5–6. *Opera Librettists and Their Works.* 1987.
> 7–8. *Opera Premieres: A Geographical Index.* 1989.
> 9. *Opera Subjects.* 1989.
> 10–12. *An Opera Discography.* 1990.
> 13–14. *Opera Premieres: An Index of Casts.* 1992.
> 15–16. *Opera Premieres: Reviews.*
> 17–18. *An Opera Bibliography.*
> 19–20. *Index of Printed Scores.*
> 21. *Opera That Is Not Opera.*
> 22. *Miscellanea Operatica.*
> 23. *Opera and the Librarian.*

*Pipers Enzyklopädie des Musiktheaters: Oper, Operette, Musical,
Ballet.* Edited by Carl Dahlhaus. 8 vols. projected. Munich:
Piper, 1986–.
Rosenthal, Harold, and John Warrack. *The Concise Oxford
Dictionary of Opera.* 2nd ed. New York: Oxford University
Press, 1979. First published in 1964.
Stieger, Franz. *Opernlexikon/Opera Catalogue/Lexique des
opéras/Dizionario operistico.* 4 parts in 11 vols. Tutzing:
Hans Schneider, 1975–83.
Warrack, John, and Ewan West. *The Oxford Dictionary of Opera.*
New York: Oxford University Press, 1992.

Sacred Music

Davidson, James Robert. *A Dictionary of Protestant Church
Music.* Metuchen, N.J.: Scarecrow Press, 1975.

Encylopédie des musiques sacrées. Edited by Jacques Porte. 3 vols.
and 16 phonodiscs. Paris: Editions Labergerie, 1968–70.

Julian, John. *A Dictionary of Hymnology, Setting Forth the
Origin and History of Christian Hymns of All Ages and
Nations.* Rev. ed., with new suppl. 2 vols. London: J.
Murray, 1907. First published in 1892.

Nulman, Macy. *Concise Encyclopedia of Jewish Music.* New York:
McGraw-Hill, 1975.

Poultney, David. *Dictionary of Western Church Music.* Chicago:
American Library Association, 1991.

Zahn, Johannes. *Die Melodien der deutschen evangelischen
Kirchenlieder aus den Quellen geschöpft und mitgeteilt.* . . .
6 vols. Güttersloh, Germany: C. Bertelsmann, 1889–93.

Jazz

Feather, Leonard G. *The Encyclopedia of Jazz.* Rev. and enl. ed.
New York: Horizon Press, 1960. First published in 1955.

——— . *The Encyclopedia of Jazz in the Sixties.* New York:
Horizon Press, 1966.

Feather, Leonard G., and Ira Gitler. *The Encyclopedia of Jazz in
the Seventies.* New York: Horizon Press, 1976.

Gold, Robert S. *Jazz Talk.* Indianapolis: Bobbs-Merrill, 1975.

The New Grove Dictionary of Jazz. Edited by Barry Kernfeld. 2
vols. New York: Grove's Dictionaries of Music, 1988.

Musical Themes and Compositional Devices

Barlow, Harold, and Sam Morgenstern. *A Dictionary of Musical
Themes.* Rev. ed. New York: Crown Publishers, 1975. First
published in 1948.

——— . *A Dictionary of Opera and Song Themes, Including
Cantatas, Oratorios, Lieder and Art Songs.* Rev. ed. New
York: Crown Publishers, 1976. First published in 1950.

Burrows, Raymond M., and Bessie C. Redmond. *Concerto
Themes.* New York: Simon and Schuster, 1951.

——— . *Symphony Themes.* New York: Simon and Schuster, 1942.

LaRue, Jan. *A Catalogue of 18th-Century Symphonies.* 3 vols.
projected. Vol. 1: *Thematic Identifier.* Bloomington: Indiana
University Press, 1988–.

Parsons, Denys. *The Directory of Tunes and Musical Themes.*
Cambridge, England: Spencer Brown, 1975.

Read, Gardner. *Thesaurus of Orchestral Devices.* New York:
    Pitman, 1953.
Slonimsky, Nicolas. *Thesaurus of Scales and Melodic Patterns.*
    New York: Coleman-Ross, 1947.

Miscellaneous Sources

Berkowitz, Freda Pastor. *Popular Titles and Subtitles of Musical
    Compositions.* 2nd ed. Metuchen, N.J.: Scarecrow Press,
    1975. First published in 1962.
The Concise Oxford Dictionary of Ballet. 2nd ed. Compiled by
    Horst Koegler. London: Oxford University Press, 1982.
    First published in 1977.
A Dictionary of Musical Quotations. Compiled by Ian Crofton
    and Donald Fraser. 1st American ed. New York: Schirmer
    Books, 1985.
An Encyclopedia of Quotations about Music. Compiled and
    edited by Nat Shapiro. Garden City, N.Y.: Doubleday,
    1978.
International Dictionary of Ballet. Edited by Martha Bremser. 2
    vols. Detroit: St. James Press, 1992.
Reid, Jane Davidson. *A Guide to Classical Subjects in the Arts.* 3
    vols. New York: Oxford University Press, 1993.
Slonimsky, Nicolas. *Lexicon of Musical Invective: Critical
    Assaults on Composers since Beethoven's Time.* Seattle:
    University of Washington Press, 1953.

THE NEW HARVARD DICTIONARY OF MUSIC:
ARTICLES OF GENERAL INTEREST

Many of the music dictionaries and encyclopedias listed in the
present chapter can be useful in researching almost any topic.
Among these *The New Harvard Dictionary of Music* may well be the
one most often found in personal libraries. As a practical guide it,
or similar sources, can introduce, organize, summarize, and
provide an initial bibliography for various areas of study, such as
courses, term papers, and examinations. Many entries in such
sources, however, might be overlooked. Examples from *The
New Harvard Dictionary* are listed below, with related terms grouped
together:

Research in Music

Aesthetics
Authenticity
Autograph; Sketch
Bibliography
Computers, Musical Applications of
Dictionaries and Encyclopedias
Editions, Historical
Festschrift
Iconography of Music
Libraries
Liturgical Books
Musicology; Ethnomusicology
Notation; Paleography; Textual Criticism; Transcription;
     Transmission; Watermark
Organology
Periodicals
Printing of Music
Publishing of Music
Societies, Musical; Academy; Collegium Musicum
Sociology of Music
Sources (Pre-1500)

Music History, Style Periods, and Trends

History of Music
Ars Antiqua, Ars Vetus; Ars Nova; Mannerism
Middle Ages, Music of the; Renaissance, Music of the; Baroque;
     Rococo; Classical; Romantic
Galant Style; Empfindsam Style
Nationalism; Verismo; Impressionism; Expressionism
Aleatory Music; Neoclassical; Twelve-Tone Music
Twentieth Century, Western Art Music of the

Countries, Cities, and Musical Centers

Berlin School; Bologna School; Mannheim School; Neapolitan
     School; Venetian School; New German School; Viennese
     Classical School; Viennese School, Second
Canada; England; France; Germany; Italy; Netherlands; Spain;
     Union of Soviet Socialist Republics; United States; etc.
East Asia; South Asia; Southeast Asia; Latin America; Near and
     Middle East; Africa; Oceania and Australia

General Music Theory

Acoustics
Analysis; Harmonic Analysis
Composition
Counterpoint; Invertible Counterpoint
Harmonics
Interval
Isorhythm
Key; Mode
Melody; Harmony; Rhythm; Form; Texture
Modes, Rhythmic
Modulation
Orchestration; Instrumentation
Pitch; Pitch Class; Pitch Names
Polyphony; Homophony
Scale
Schenker Analysis
Serial Music
Solfège; Solmization
Twelve-Tone Music

Musical Forms and Genres

Bar Form; Formes fixes; Rondeau; Ballata; Caccia; etc.
Dance; Ballet; Basse danse; Gagliarda; Minuet; Polonaise; etc.
Estampie; Canzona; Ricercar; Concerto; Concerto grosso; Program
        Music; Rondo; Symphony; Suite; Sonata; Toccata; etc.
Folk Music; Jazz; Blues; etc.
Fugue; Double Fugue; Fuging Tune; Canon
Mass; Motet; Madrigal; Chanson; Opera; Cantata; Oratorio;
        Passion; Seven (Last) Words, The; Lied; Song; Song Cycle;
        etc.

Performance and Performance Practice

Affections (Affects), Doctrine of; Rhetoric
Chamber Music; Chamber Orchestra; String Quartet
Choirbook; Partbook; Chansonnier
Chorus; Choral Music; Schola (Cantorum)
Church Music; Chapel; Kapelle; Capella
Concert; Concert Hall
Conducting; Ensemble; Consort; Kantor; Kantorei
Copyright and Performance Right

Expression; Performance Marks
Fingering
Gregorian Chant; Liturgy
Interpretation; Phrasing; Style
Musica Ficta
Notation; Mensural Notation
Orchestra; Instrument [also see under individual instruments];
    Bowing; etc.
Ornamentation [also see under individual ornaments];
    Improvisation, Extemporization
Performance Practice
Piano; Organ; Harpsichord; etc.
Proportion
Psalmody, British and North American
Score; Tablature
Sight-Reading
Singing; Voice; Cantor
Temperament
Tempo; Tempus
Text and Music; Libretto
Thoroughbass, Figured Bass

The Music Profession

Conservatory
Criticism
Education in the United States; Music Appreciation
Music Therapy
Psychology of Music
Radio and Television Broadcasting
Recording

CHAPTER FIVE

Sources Treating the History of Music

The present chapter classifies many of the myriad sources in the field of music history into eleven lists with varying degrees of selectivity and a distinct emphasis on sources in English. "Historical Surveys of Western Music" is one of the most selective, with only twelve coverages of Western music in English—most quite recent and intended as course texts—followed by some miscellaneous sources and three of the most prominent older ones. "Histories in Series" lists the contents of the nine most recent series of books on periods of music history, followed by the titles of three of the most important earlier 20th-century series.

Next are found selective lists of "Single-Volume Studies in English of Historical Periods," "Histories of American Music," "English-Language Sources on Musical Genres and Forms," and "Chronologies and Outlines" of music history.

"Biographies of Composers in English" is highly selective—only a representative selection of works on prominent composers has been included; next are listed the contents of three of the most important "Series of Composers' Biographies in English."

The final lists are of the major "Collections of Excerpts from Primary Sources on Music," "Histories of Musical Instruments," and significant "Pictorial Sources on Music History."

HISTORICAL SURVEYS OF WESTERN MUSIC

The oldest of these modern single-volume histories of music in English is Lang's staple, *Music in Western Civilization*, published in

1941; the most recent are Seaton's and Stolba's generalized histories and Pendle's history of women in music.

Under "Miscellaneous Sources" are five special works: *The Garland Library* and Hays's *Twentieth-Century Views*, both anthologies of reprinted significant English-language articles and excerpts arranged in chronological order (the former also includes volumes devoted to opera and to music criticism and analysis); Bowers and Tick's collection of essays on women in music, in chronological order; Poultney's *Studying Music History*, which is more of a study guide to the subject; and Raynor's specialized approach. Finally, Burney, Forkel, and Hawkins, listed under "Of Historical Interest," are three of the most important early histories.

For historical perspective on published histories, see Eggebrecht's *New Grove* article "Historiography," and Allen's *Philosophies of Music History* (see p. 53 above); an exhaustive chronological list of music histories from Calvisius (1600) to Schering (1931) may be seen on pp. 343–65 in the latter source.

Abraham, Gerald. *The Concise Oxford History of Music.* London: Oxford University Press, 1979.

Borroff, Edith. *Music in Europe and the United States: A History.* 2nd ed. New York: Ardsley House, 1990. First published in 1971.

Crocker, Richard L. *A History of Musical Style.* New York: McGraw-Hill, 1966.

Fuller, Sarah. *The European Musical Heritage 800–1750.* New York: McGraw Hill, 1986.

Grout, Donald Jay, and Claude V. Palisca. *A History of Western Music.* 4th ed. New York: W. W. Norton, 1988. First published in 1960.

Harman, Alec, and Wilfrid Mellers. *Man and His Music: The Story of Musical Experience in the West.* London: Barrie & Rockliff, 1962.

Lang, Paul Henry. *Music in Western Civilization.* New York: W. W. Norton, 1941.

Pendle, Karin, ed. *Women and Music: A History.* Bloomington: Indiana University Press, 1991.

Schirmer History of Music. Léonie Rosenstiel, gen. ed. New York: Schirmer Books, 1982.

Seaton, Douglass. *Ideas and Styles in the Western Musical Tradition.* Mountain View, Calif.: Mayfield Publishing, 1991.

Stolba, K Marie. *The Development of Western Music: A History.* Dubuque, Iowa: Wm. C. Brown Publishers, 1990.

Ulrich, Homer, and Paul Pisk. *A History of Music and Musical Style.* New York: Harcourt, Brace & World, 1963.

Miscellaneous Sources

Bowers, Jane, and Judith Tick, eds. *Women Making Music: The Western Art Tradition, 1150–1950.* Urbana: University of Illinois Press, 1987.

The Garland Library of the History of Western Music. Ellen Rosand, gen. ed. 14 vols. New York: Garland Publishing, 1985.

Hays, William, ed. *Twentieth-Century Views of Music History.* New York: Charles Scribner's Sons, 1972.

Poultney, David. *Studying Music History: Learning, Reasoning, and Writing about Music History and Literature.* Englewood Cliffs, N.J.: Prentice Hall, 1983.

Raynor, Henry. *A Social History of Music from the Middle Ages to Beethoven/Music and Society since 1815.* 2 vols in one. New York: Taplinger Publishing, 1978. First published as single volumes in 1972 and 1976 respectively.

Of Historical Interest

Burney, Charles. *A General History of Music, from the Earliest Ages to the Present Period* [1776–89]. Edited by Frank Mercer. 4 vols. in 2. London: G. T. Foulis, 1935; reprint, New York: Dover Publications, 1957.

Forkel, Johann Nikolaus. *Allgemeine Geschichte der Musik.* . . . 2 vols. Leipzig: Schwikertschen Verlag, 1788–1801.

Hawkins, Sir John. *A General History of the Science and Practice of Music* [1776]. With a new introduction by Charles Cudworth. 2 vols. American Musicological Society, Music Library Association Reprint Series. New York: Dover Publications, 1963.

HISTORIES IN SERIES

This bibliography lists the most important recent multivolume histories of music (two of which, the Neues Handbuch der Musik-wissenschaft and The Prentice Hall History of Music Series, also include volumes organized in some other way—by country, for example; The Universe of Music is unique in being organized exclusively by major geographical region). Of special value in such histories is the bringing together of the contributions of various specialists in different fields, although sometimes the result is criticized for lacking a totally unified approach.

The three oldest series are The Norton History of Music Series, The New Oxford History of Music, and The Prentice Hall History of Music Series, but none of them appears to be complete—the long-announced Norton book on the Classical period has yet to appear, and Prentice Hall continues to bring out revised versions or replacements of its original volumes.

The remaining series were begun more recently, and of these, the Heritage of Music Series, the Neues Handbuch der Musikwissenschaft, and the Storia della musica are complete, although some volumes of the Storia della musica have not yet been published in English translations. The Music and Society Series and The Norton Introduction to Music History Series are still incomplete at this time.

Under "Of Historical Interest" are the titles of three major earlier series. Ambros's monumental work was not conceived as a multivolume set to be written in collaboration with other authors, like the other sources listed here, but it is virtually that because of its period-by-period breakdown into volumes and its having been completed and/or revised by others. Bücken's Handbuch der Musikwissenschaft series is historically important, but it is gradually being superseded by the Neues Handbuch series. The Kleine Handbücher series is different from the others in that it is organized by subject rather than by period, e.g., histories of the oratorio, of the cantata, of conducting; some volumes are still quite useful while others are outdated.

Heritage of Music Series. Michael Raeburn and Alan Kendall, gen. eds. 4 vols. Oxford: Oxford University Press, 1989.

1. *Classical Music and Its Origins.* Edited by Roger Blanchard, Denis Arnold, and H. C. Robbins Landon.
2. *The Romantic Era.* Edited by Denis Matthews, Ludwig Finscher, and Robert Donington.
3. *The Nineteenth-Century Legacy.* Edited by Martin Cooper and Heinz Becker.
4. *Music in the Twentieth Century.* Edited by Felix Aprahamian and Wilfrid Mellers.

Music and Society Series/Man and Music Series. Stanley Sadie, gen. ed. 8 vols. projected. Englewood Cliffs, N.J.: Prentice Hall, 1989–.

Antiquity and the Middle Ages: From Ancient Greece to the 15th Century. Edited by James W. McKinnon. 1st North American ed. 1991.

The Renaissance: From the 1470s to the End of the 16th Century. Edited by Iain Fenlon. 1st North American ed. 1989.

The Early Baroque Era: From the Late 16th Century to the 1660s. Edited by Curtis A. Price. 1st North American ed. 1992.

The Late Baroque Era. Edited by George J. Buelow.

The Classical Era: From the 1740s to the End of the 18th Century. Edited by Neal Zaslaw. 1st North American ed. 1989.

The Early Romantic Era: Between Revolutions: 1789 and 1848. Edited by Alexander Ringer. 1st North American ed. 1991.

The Late Romantic Era: From the Mid-19th Century to World War I. Edited by Jim Samson. 1st North American ed. 1991.

Modern Times. Edited by Robert P. Morgan.

Neues Handbuch der Musikwissenschaft. Carl Dahlhaus, gen. ed. 11 vols. projected. Laaber, Germany: Laaber-Verlag, 1980–.

1. *Die Musik des Altertums.* Edited by Albrecht Riethmüller and Frieder Zaminer, in collaboration with Ellen Hickmann. 1989.

2. *Die Musik des Mittelalters.* Edited by Hartmut Möller and Rudolf Stephan. 1991.

3. *Die Musik des 15. und 16. Jahrhunderts.* Edited by Ludwig Finscher et al. 2 vols. 1989–90.

4. *Die Musik des 17. Jahrhunderts.* By Werner Braun. 1981.

5. *Die Musik des 18. Jahrhunderts.* Edited by Carl Dahlhaus. 1985.

6. *Die Musik des 19. Jahrhunderts.* By Carl Dahlhaus. 1980. Translation by J. Bradford Robinson: *Nineteenth-Century Music.* California Studies in Nineteenth-Century Music, vol. 5. Berkeley: University of California Press, 1989.

7. *Die Musik des 20. Jahrhunderts.* By Hermann Danuser. 1984.
8. *Aussereuropäische Musik. (Teil 1.)* By Hans Oesch et al. 1984.
9. *Aussereuropäische Musik. (Teil 2.)* By Hans Oesch et al. 1987.
10. *Systematische Musikwissenschaft.* Edited by Carl Dahlhaus and Helga de la Motte-Haber. 1982.
11. *Musikalische Interpretation.* Edited by Hermann Danuser. 1992.

The New Oxford History of Music. 10 vols. London: Oxford University Press, 1954–.

1. *Ancient and Oriental Music.* Edited by Egon Wellesz. 1957.
2. *The Early Middle Ages to 1300.* 2nd ed. Edited by Richard Crocker and David Hiley. 1990. First published in 1954.
3. *Ars Nova and the Renaissance, 1300–1450.* Edited by Anselm Hughes and Gerald Abraham. Reprint with corrections, 1986. First published in 1960.
4. *The Age of Humanism, 1540–1630.* Edited by Gerald Abraham. 1968.
5. *Opera and Church Music, 1630–1750.* Edited by Anthony Lewis and Nigel Fortune. 1975.
6. *Concert Music, 1630–1750.* Edited by Gerald Abraham. 1986.
7. *The Age of Enlightenment, 1745–1790.* Edited by Egon Wellesz and Frederick Sternfeld. 1973.
8. *The Age of Beethoven, 1790–1830.* Edited by Gerald Abraham. 1982.
9. *Romanticism, 1830–1890.* Edited by Gerald Abraham. 1990.
10. *The Modern Age, 1890–1960.* Edited by Martin Cooper. 1974.

The Norton History of Music Series. 7 vols. projected. New York: W. W. Norton, 1940–.

The Rise of Music in the Ancient World. By Curt Sachs. 1943.
Music in the Middle Ages. By Gustave Reese. 1940.
Music in the Renaissance. By Gustave Reese. Rev. ed. 1959. First published in 1954.

Music in the Baroque Era, from Monteverdi to Bach. By
  Manfred Bukofzer. 1947.
Music in the Classic Era. 2 vols. By Daniel Heartz.
Music in the Romantic Era. By Alfred Einstein. 1947.
*Music in the 20th Century from Debussy through
  Stravinsky.* By William W. Austin. 1966.

The Norton Introduction to Music History. Paul Henry Lang,
  gen. ed. 6 vols. projected. New York: W. W. Norton,
  1978–.

Medieval Music. By Richard H. Hoppin. 1978.
Renaissance Music. By Leeman L. Perkins.
Baroque Music. By George Buelow.
Classical Music: The Era of Haydn, Mozart, and Beethoven.
  By Philip G. Downs. 1992.
Romantic Music. By Leon Plantinga. 1984.
*Twentieth-Century Music: A History of Musical Style in
  Modern Europe and America.* By Robert P. Morgan.
  1991.

The Prentice Hall History of Music Series. Edited by H. Wiley
  Hitchcock. 11 vols. Englewood Cliffs, N.J.: Prentice Hall,
  1965–.

Music in Medieval Europe. By Jeremy Yudkin. 1989.
Music in the Renaissance. By Howard M. Brown. 1976.
Baroque Music. By Claude V. Palisca. 3rd ed. 1991. First
  published in 1968.
Music in the Classic Period. By Reinhard G. Pauly. 3rd ed.
  1988. First published in 1973.
Nineteenth-Century Romanticism in Music. By Rey M.
  Longyear. 3rd ed. 1988. First published in 1969.
Twentieth-Century Music: An Introduction. By Eric
  Salzman. 3rd ed. 1988. First published in 1967.
Folk and Traditional Music of the Western Continents. By
  Bruno Nettl, with Gerard Béhague. 3rd ed. Revised
  and edited by Valerie Woodring Goertzen. 1990.
  First published in 1965.
Music Cultures of the Pacific, the Near East, and Asia. By
  William P. Malm. 2nd ed. 1977. First published in
  1967.
Music in the United States: A Historical Introduction. By
  H. Wiley Hitchcock. 3rd ed. 1988. First published in
  1969.

Music in India: The Classical Traditions. By Bonnie C. Wade. 1979.

Music in Latin America: An Introduction. By Gerard Béhague. 1979.

Storia della musica. 10 vols. in 12. Turin: Edizioni di Torino, 1976–82.

    1/i. *La musica nella cultura greca e romana.* By Giovanni Comotti. 1979. Translation by Rosaria V. Munson: *Music in Greek and Roman Culture.* Baltimore: Johns Hopkins University Press, 1989.

    1/ii. *Il medioevo I.* By Giulio Cattin. 1979. Translation by Steven Botterill: *Music of the Middle Ages I.* Cambridge: Cambridge University Press, 1984.

    2. *Il medioevo II.* By F. Alberto Gallo. 1977. Translation by Karen Eales: *Music of the Middle Ages II.* Cambridge: Cambridge University Press, 1985.

    3. *L'età dell'umanesimo e del rinascimento.* By Claudio Gallico. 1978.

    4. *Il seicento.* By Lorenzo Bianconi. 1982. Translation by David Bryant: *Music in the Seventeenth Century.* Cambridge: Cambridge University Press, 1987.

    5. *L'età di Bach e di Haendel.* By Alberto Basso. 1976.

    6. *L'età di Mozart e di Beethoven.* By Giorgio Pestelli. 1979. Translation by Eric Cross: *The Age of Mozart and Beethoven.* Cambridge: Cambridge University Press, 1984.

    7. *L'ottocento I.* By Renato Di Benedetto. 1982.

    8. *L'ottocento II.* By Claudio Casini. 1978.

    9. *Il novecento I.* By Guido Salvetti. 1977.

    10/i. *Il novecento II.* By Gianfranco Vinay. 1978.

    10/ii. *Il novecento III.* By Andrea Lanza. 1980.

The Universe of Music: A History. A UNESCO/International Music Council Project. 12 vols. projected. Washington, D.C.: Smithsonian Institution Press, 1993–.

Of Historical Interest

Ambros, August Wilhelm. *Geschichte der Musik. . . .* 5 vols. Leipzig: Leuckart, 1887–1911. Continued by Wilhelm

Langhans as *Die Geschichte der Musik des 17. 18. und 19.*
Jahrhunderts in chronologischen Anschlusse an die
Musikgeschichte von A. W. Ambros. 2 vols. Leipzig:
Leuckart, 1884.
Handbuch der Musikwissenschaft. Edited by Ernst Bücken. 13
vols. in 10. Potsdam: Akademische Verlagsgesellschaft
Athenaion, [1927–31].
Kleine Handbücher der Musikgeschichte nach Gattungen.
Edited by Hermann Kretzschmar. 14 vols. in 15. Leipzig:
Breitkopf & Härtel, 1905–22.

SINGLE-VOLUME STUDIES IN ENGLISH OF
HISTORICAL PERIODS

This list completes the previous one with mostly recent histories of periods in English or English translation that do not belong
to multivolume sets (except for the two volumes edited by Sternfeld, which were originally intended to form part of a series that
was later abandoned). Sadie's valuable new *Companion to Baroque
Music*, more of a source book on the period than a strictly narrative
account, is the only recent study which addresses this period. Useful supplementary period studies are Blume's excellent comprehensive monographs on four historical periods, listed here in the
"Miscellaneous Sources" section.

Medieval, Renaissance

Caldwell, John. *Medieval Music.* Bloomington: Indiana
University Press, 1978.
Knighton, Tess, and David Fallows, eds. *Companion to Medieval
and Renaissance Music.* 1st American ed. New York:
Schirmer Books, 1992.
Sternfeld, F. W., ed. *Music from the Middle Ages to the
Renaissance.* London: Weidenfeld & Nicholson, 1973.
Stevens, John. *Words and Music in the Middle Ages: Song,
Narrative, Dance and Drama, 1050–1350.* Cambridge
Studies in Music. Cambridge: Cambridge University Press,
1986.
Wilson, David Fenwick. *Music of the Middle Ages: Style and
Structure.* New York: Schirmer Books, 1990.

Baroque, Classic, Romantic

Abraham, Gerald. *A Hundred Years of Music* [1830s-1930s]. 4th
ed. London: Duckworth, 1974. First published in 1938.

Klaus, Kenneth B. *The Romantic Period in Music.* Boston: Allyn
and Bacon, 1970.

Ratner, Leonard G. *Classic Music: Expression, Form, and Style.*
New York: Schirmer Books, 1980.

————. *Romantic Music: Sound and Syntax.* New York: Schirmer
Books, 1992.

Rosen, Charles. *The Classical Style: Haydn, Mozart, Beethoven.*
[Augm. ed.] New York: W. W. Norton, 1972. First
published in 1971.

Rushton, Julian. *Classical Music: A Concise History from Gluck
to Beethoven.* World of Art Series. New York: Thames and
Hudson, 1986.

Sadie, Julie Anne, comp. and ed. *Companion to Baroque Music.*
New York: Schirmer Books, 1990.

Whittall, Arnold. *Romantic Music: A Concise History from
Schubert to Sibelius.* World of Art Series. New York:
Thames and Hudson, 1987.

Twentieth Century

Antokoletz, Elliott. *Twentieth-Century Music.* Englewood Cliffs,
N.J.: Prentice Hall, 1992.

Davies, Laurence. *Paths to Modern Music: Aspects of Music from
Wagner to the Present Day.* New York: Charles Scribner's
Sons, 1971.

Griffiths, Paul. *Modern Music: A Concise History from Debussy
to Boulez.* World of Art Series. New York: Thames and
Hudson, 1985. First published in 1978 as *A Concise History
of Avant-Garde Music from Debussy to Boulez.*

Martin, William R., and Julius Drossin. *Music of the Twentieth
Century.* Englewood Cliffs, N.J.: Prentice Hall, 1980.

Simms, Bryan R. *Music of the Twentieth Century: Style and
Structure.* New York: Schirmer Books, 1986.

Sternfeld, F. W., ed. *Music in the Modern Age.* London:
Weidenfeld & Nicholson, 1973.

Stuckenschmidt, H. H. *Twentieth Century Music.* Translated by
Richard Deveson. World University Library. New York:
McGraw-Hill, 1969.

Watkins, Glenn. *Soundings: Music in the Twentieth Century.* New York: Schirmer Books, 1988.

Miscellaneous Sources

Blume, Friedrich. *Renaissance and Baroque Music: A Comprehensive Survey.* Translated by M. D. Herter Norton. New York: W. W. Norton, 1967. First published in 1949 and 1963 in *Die Musik in Geschichte und Gegenwart.*
———. *Classic and Romantic Music: A Comprehensive Survey.* Translated by M. D. Herter Norton. New York: W. W. Norton, 1970. First published in 1958 and 1963 in *Die Musik in Geschichte und Gegenwart.*

HISTORIES OF AMERICAN MUSIC

The major recent histories of music in the United States, all in English, are listed here, including some that have a specific focus as well as those that are more general or comprehensive.

Ammer, Christine. *Unsung: A History of Women in American Music.* Contributions in Women's Studies, no. 14. Westport, Conn.: Greenwood Press, 1980.
Brooks, Tilford. *America's Black Musical Heritage.* Englewood Cliffs, N.J.: Prentice Hall, 1984.
Chase, Gilbert. *America's Music from the Pilgrims to the Present.* Rev. 3rd ed. Music in American Life. Urbana: University of Illinois Press, 1987. First published in 1955.
Chase, Gilbert, et al. "United States of America." In *The New Grove Dictionary of Music and Musicians.* Vol. 19, pp. 424–52.
Davis, Ronald L. *A History of Music in American Life.* 3 vols. Huntington, N.Y.: R. E. Krieger Publishing, 1980–81.
Griffin, Clive D. *Afro-American Music.* London: Dryad Press, 1987.
Hamm, Charles. *Music in the New World.* New York: W. W. Norton, 1983.
Hitchcock, H. Wiley. *Music in the United States: A Historical Introduction.* 3rd ed. The Prentice Hall History of Music Series. Englewood, N.J.: Prentice Hall, 1988. First published in 1969.

Kingman, Daniel. *American Music: A Panorama.* 2nd ed. New York: Schirmer Books, 1990. First published in 1979.

Lowens, Irving. *Music and Musicians in Early America.* New York: W. W. Norton, 1964.

Mellers, Wilfrid. *Music in a New Found Land.* Rev. ed. New York: Oxford University Press, 1987. First published in 1964.

Porter, Lewis, and Michael Ullman, with Ed Hazell. *Jazz: From Its Origins to the Present.* Englewood Cliffs, N.J.: Prentice Hall, 1992. (Also available on CD-ROM.)

Roach, Hildred. *Black American Music: Past and Present.* 2nd ed. Malabar, Fla.: R. E. Krieger Publishing, 1992. First published in 1973.

Roberts, John S. *Black Music of Two Worlds.* New York: Praeger Publishers, 1972.

Rublowsky, John. *Black Music in America.* New York: Basic Books, 1971.

Schuller, Gunther. *The History of Jazz.* 2 vols. to date. New York: Oxford University Press, 1968–.

   1. *Early Jazz: Its Roots and Musical Development.* 1968.
   2. *The Swing Era: The Development of Jazz, 1930–1945.* 1989.

Southern, Eileen. *The Music of Black Americans: A History.* 2nd ed. New York: W. W. Norton, 1983. First published in 1971.

Tirro, Frank. *Jazz: A History.* 2nd ed. New York: W. W. Norton, 1993. First published in 1977.

ENGLISH-LANGUAGE SOURCES ON MUSICAL GENRES AND FORMS

A great many sources deal with a single category of music, often loosely termed a genre or form. The scope of such studies may be the entire history of the category or only a century, stylistic period, or other portion of its evolution, and/or a limitation by country or region may also be imposed. As might be expected, the treatment in such discussions varies from fairly concise to extremely detailed. Moreover, the approach may be oriented more to music history, literature, or theory.

In the lists that follow, divided overall into "Vocal" and "Instrumental" sections, with each subdivided by form or genre, an attempt has been made to present a good selection from more recent studies of this sort in English or English translation. Relevant volumes of the Anthology of Music (complete contents listed on pp. 185–87 below) are included here because each consists of excerpts that illustrate the form or genre in question and a preface, often extensive, in which it is discussed.

The art song, chamber music, opera, and the symphony are the subjects of four volumes in Garland Publishing's series entitled Music Research and Information Guides, a set of extensive area bibliographies, which should be consulted for further information in these categories.

A wealth of additional information on such subjects can be found in period histories and in the many published studies about specific works or genres of individual composers, too numerous to be listed here. In the field of opera, studies of individual works may be found in series such as Cambridge Opera Handbooks and English National Opera Guides.

Vocal

Solo Song

Böker-Heil, Norbert, et al. "Lied." In *The New Grove Dictionary of Music and Musicians.* Vol. 10, pp. 830–47.

Brody, Elaine, and Robert A. Fowkes. *The German Lied and Its Poetry.* New York: New York University Press, 1971.

Chew, Geoffrey. "Song." In *The New Grove Dictionary of Music and Musicians.* Vol. 17, pp. 510–21.

Fellerer, Karl Gustav. *The Monody.* Anthology of Music, vol. 31 (1968).

Lakeway, Ruth C., and Robert C. White, Jr. *Italian Art Song.* Bloomington: Indiana University Press, 1989.

Meister, Barbara. *Nineteenth-Century French Song: Fauré, Chausson, Duparc, and Debussy.* Bloomington: Indiana University Press, 1980.

Moser, Hans Joachim. *The German Solo Song and the Ballad.* Anthology of Music, vol. 14 (1958).

Noske, Frits. *French Song from Berlioz to Duparc: The Origin and Development of the Mélodie.* 2nd ed. Revised by Rita Benton and Frits Noske. Translated by Rita Benton. New York: Dover Publications, 1970. First published in 1954.

————. *The Solo Song outside German Speaking Countries.* Anthology of Music, vol. 16 (1958).

Osborne, Charles. *The Concert Song Companion: A Guide to the Classical Repertoire.* London: Victor Gollancz, 1974.
Spink, Ian. *English Song: Dowland to Purcell.* London: Batsford, 1974.
Stein, Jack M. *Poem and Music in the German Lied from Gluck to Hugo Wolf.* Cambridge: Harvard University Press, 1971.
Stevens, Denis, ed. *A History of Song.* Rev. ed. New York: W. W. Norton, 1970. First published in 1960.

CANTATA

Fortune, Nigel, et al. "Cantata." In *The New Grove Dictionary of Music and Musicians.* Vol. 3, pp. 694–718.
Jakoby, Richard. *The Cantata.* Anthology of Music, vol. 32 (1968).
Tunley, David. *The Eighteenth-Century French Cantata.* London: Dennis Dobson, 1974.
Vollen, Gene E. *The French Cantata: A Survey and Thematic Catalog.* Studies in Musicology, no. 51. Ann Arbor, Mich.: UMI Research Press, 1982. Revision of Ph.D. diss., North Texas State University, 1970.

DRAMATIC MUSIC

Surveys and General Studies

Abert, A. A. *The Opera from Its Beginnings until the Early 19th Century.* Anthology of Music, vol. 5 (1962).
Dent, Edward J. *The Rise of Romantic Opera.* Edited by Winton Dean. Cambridge: Cambridge University Press, 1976. Lectures originally delivered at Cornell University, 1937–38.
Donington, Robert. *The Rise of Opera.* New York: Charles Scribner's Sons, 1981.
Grout, Donald J., with Hermine Weigel Williams. *A Short History of Opera.* 3rd ed. New York: Columbia University Press, 1988. First published in 1947.
Headington, Christopher, et al. *Opera: A History.* 1st U.S. ed. New York: St. Martin's Press, 1987.
Kerman, Joseph. *Opera as Drama.* New and rev. ed. Berkeley: University of California Press, 1988. First published in 1956.
Mordden, Ethan. *Opera in the Twentieth Century: Sacred, Profane, Godot.* Oxford: Oxford University Press, 1978.

Orrey, Leslie. *A Concise History of Opera.* Rev. and updated ed.
by Rodney Milnes. World of Art Series. New York: Thames
and Hudson, 1987. First published in 1972.
Robinson, Michael F. *Opera before Mozart.* London: Hutchinson,
1966.
Sadie, Stanley, ed. *History of Opera.* 1st American ed. The
Norton/Grove Handbooks in Music. New York: W. W.
Norton, 1990. First published in 1989.
Sadie, Stanley, et al. "Opera." In *The New Grove Dictionary of
Music and Musicians.* Vol. 13, pp. 544–647.
Smoldon, William L. *The Music of the Medieval Church Dramas.*
Edited by Cynthia Bourgeault. London: Oxford University
Press, 1980.
Wolff, Hellmuth Christian. *The Opera: I: 17th Century; II: 18th
Century; III: 19th Century.* Anthology of Music, vols. 38
(1971), 39 (1971), 40 (1975).

Studies by Country

CZECH REPUBLIC

Tyrrell, John. *Czech Opera.* National Traditions of Opera.
Cambridge: Cambridge University Press, 1988.

ENGLAND

Dent, Edward J. *Foundations of English Opera: A Study of
Musical Drama in England during the Seventeenth Century.*
With a new introduction by Michael M. Winesanker. New
York: Da Capo Press, 1965. First published in 1928.
Fiske, Roger. *English Theatre Music in the Eighteenth Century.*
2nd ed. Oxford: Oxford University Press, 1986. First
published in 1973.
Gagey, Edmond McAdoo. *Ballad Opera.* New York: Columbia
University Press, 1937.
Lefkowitz, Murray. "Masque." In *The New Grove Dictionary of
Music and Musicians.* Vol. 11, pp. 756–69.
Price, Curtis A. *Music in the Restoration Theatre, with a
Catalogue of Instrumental Music in the Plays 1665–1713.*
Studies in Musicology, no. 4. Ann Arbor, Mich.: UMI
Research Press, 1979. Revision of Ph.D. diss., Harvard
University, 1974.
White, Eric Walter. *A History of English Opera.* London: Faber
and Faber, 1983.

FRANCE

Brown, Howard Mayer. *Music in the French Secular Theater,*
     1400–1550. Cambridge: Harvard University Press, 1963.
Crosten, William L. *French Grand Opera: An Art and a Business.*
     New York: Da Capo Press, 1972. Ph.D. diss., Columbia
     University, 1948.
Demuth, Norman. *French Opera: Its Development to the*
     Revolution. [Horsham], Sussex, England: Artemis Press,
     1963.
Fulcher, Jane F. *The Nation's Image: French Grand Opera as*
     Politics and Politicized Art. Cambridge: Cambridge
     University Press, 1987.

GERMANY AND AUSTRIA

Bauman, Thomas. *North German Opera in the Age of Goethe.*
     Cambridge: Cambridge University Press, 1985.
Brown, Bruce Alan. *Gluck and the French Theatre in Vienna.*
     Oxford: Clarendon Press, 1991.

ITALY

Kimbell, David R. B. *Italian Opera.* National Traditions of Opera.
     Cambridge: Cambridge University Press, 1991.
Pirrotta, Nino, and Elena Povoledo. *Music and Theatre from*
     Poliziano to Monteverdi. Translated by Karen Eales.
     Cambridge Studies in Music. Cambridge: Cambridge
     University Press, 1982. First published in 1969.
Robinson, Michael F. *Naples and Neapolitan Opera.* Oxford
     Monographs on Music. Oxford: Clarendon Press, 1972.
Rosand, Ellen. *Opera in Seventeenth-Century Venice: The Creation*
     of a Genre. Berkeley: University of California Press, 1991.
Rosselli, John. *The Opera Industry in Italy from Cimarosa to*
     Verdi: The Role of the Impresario. Cambridge: Cambridge
     University Press, 1984.
Troy, Charles E. *The Comic Intermezzo: A Study in the History of*
     Eighteenth-Century Italian Opera. Studies in Musicology,
     no. 9. Ann Arbor, Mich.: UMI Research Press, 1979. Ph.D.
     diss., Harvard University, 1972.
Weaver, William. *The Golden Century of Italian Opera from*
     Rossini to Puccini. New York: Thames and Hudson, 1980.
Weimer, Eric. **Opera seria** *and the Evolution of Classical Style,*
     1755–1772. Studies in Musicology, no. 78. Ann Arbor,
     Mich.: UMI Research Press, 1984. Revision of Ph.D. diss.,
     University of Chicago, 1982.

Worsthorne, Simon Towneley. *Venetian Opera in the Seventeenth Century.* Oxford: Clarendon Press, 1954.

Libretto Studies

Groos, Arthur, and Roger Parker, eds. *Reading Opera.* Princeton: Princeton University Press, 1988.

O'Grady, Deirdre. *The Last Troubadours: Poetic Drama in Italian Opera 1597–1887.* London: Routledge, 1991.

Schmidgall, Gary. *Literature as Opera.* New York: Oxford University Press, 1977.

Smith, Patrick J. *The Tenth Muse: A Historical Study of the Opera Libretto.* New York: Alfred A. Knopf, 1970.

SECULAR PART SONG

Brown, Howard Mayer, with Nigel Wilkins. "Chanson." In *The New Grove Dictionary of Music and Musicians.* Vol. 4, pp. 135–45.

Einstein, Alfred. *The Italian Madrigal.* Rev. ed. Translated by Alexander H. Krappe et al. 3 vols. Princeton: Princeton University Press, 1971. First published in 1949.

Fellowes, Edmund H. *The English Madrigal Composers.* 2nd ed. London: Oxford University Press, 1948. First published in 1921.

Fischer, Kurt von, et al. "Madrigal." In *The New Grove Dictionary of Music and Musicians.* Vol. 11, pp. 461–82.

Haar, James, ed. *Chanson and Madrigal 1480–1530: Studies in Comparison and Contrast.* A Conference at Isham Memorial Library September 13–14, 1961. Cambridge: Harvard University Press, 1964.

Kerman, Joseph. *The Elizabethan Madrigal: A Comparative Study.* Studies and Documents, no. 4. New York: American Musicological Society, 1962.

Roche, Jerome. *The Madrigal.* 2nd ed. Early Music Series, no. 11. Oxford: Oxford University Press, 1991. First published in 1972.

Werf, Hendrik van der. *The Chansons of the Troubadours and Trouvères: A Study of the Melodies and Their Relation to the Poems.* Utrecht: Oosthoek, 1972.

SACRED MUSIC

Apel, Willi. *Gregorian Chant.* Bloomington: Indiana University Press, 1958.

Blume, Friedrich, et al. *Protestant Church Music: A History.* Trans. and enl. from the 2nd ed., 1965. New York: W. W. Norton, 1974. First published in 1931.

Dearnley, Christopher. *English Church Music, 1650–1750, in Royal Chapel, Cathedral and Parish Church.* London: Oxford University Press, 1970.

Ellinwood, Leonard. *The History of American Church Music.* Rev. ed. New York: Da Capo Press, 1970. First published in 1953.

Fellerer, Karl Gustav. *The History of Catholic Church Music.* Translated by Francis A. Brunner. Baltimore: Helicon Press, 1961.

Fellowes, Edmund H. *English Cathedral Music from Edward VI to Edward VII.* 5th ed. Revised by J. A. Westrup. London: Methuen, 1969. First published in 1941.

Gatens, William J. *Victorian Cathedral Music in Theory and Practice.* Cambridge: Cambridge University Press, 1986.

Hiley, David. *Western Plainchant.* New York: Oxford University Press, 1992.

Hüschen, Heinrich. *The Motet.* Anthology of Music, vol. 47 (1975).

Hutchings, Arthur. *Church Music in the Nineteenth Century.* London: Herbert Jenkins, 1967.

Idelsohn, Abraham Z. *Jewish Music in Its Historical Development.* New York: Henry Holt, 1929.

Le Huray, Peter. *Music and the Reformation in England, 1549–1660.* 2nd ed., rev. London: Oxford University Press, 1978. First published in 1967.

Long, Kenneth R. *The Music of the English Church.* New York: St. Martin's Press, 1972.

MacIntyre, Bruce C. *The Viennese Concerted Mass of the Classic Period.* Studies in Musicology, no. 89. Ann Arbor, Mich.: UMI Research Press, 1986. Ph.D. diss., City University of New York, 1984.

Routley, Eric. *Twentieth Century Church Music.* New York: Oxford University Press, 1964.

Sanders, Ernest H., et al. "Motet." In *The New Grove Dictionary of Music and Musicians.* Vol. 12, pp. 617–47.

Schmidt-Görg, Joseph. *History of the Mass.* Anthology of Music, vol. 30 (1968).

Steiner, Ruth, et al. "Mass." In *The New Grove Dictionary of Music and Musicians.* Vol. 11, pp. 769–97.

Stevens, Denis. *Tudor Church Music.* Rev. ed. New York: W. W. Norton, 1961. First published in 1955.

Stevenson, Robert. *Spanish Cathedral Music in the Golden Age.*
    Berkeley: University of California Press, 1961.
Tack, Franz. *Gregorian Chant.* Anthology of Music, vol. 18 (1960).
Temperley, Nicholas. *The Music of the English Parish Church.* 2
    vols. Cambridge: Cambridge University Press, 1979.
Wellesz, Egon. *The Music of the Byzantine Church.* Anthology of
    Music, vol. 13 (1959).
Werner, Eric. *Hebrew Music.* Anthology of Music, vol. 20 (1961).
Werner, Eric, et al. "Jewish Music." In *The New Grove Dictionary
    of Music and Musicians.* Vol. 9, pp. 614–45.
Wienandt, Elwyn Arthur. *Choral Music of the Church.* New York:
    Free Press, 1965.
Wienandt, Elwyn Arthur, and Robert H. Young. *The Anthem in
    England and America.* New York: Free Press, 1970.

ORATORIO, PASSION, AND REQUIEM

Arnold, Denis, and Elsie Arnold. *The Oratorio in Venice.* Royal
    Musical Association Monographs, no. 2. London: Royal
    Musical Association, 1986.
Fischer, Kurt von, and Werner Braun. "Passion." In *The New
    Grove Dictionary of Music and Musicians.* Vol. 14, pp.
    276–86.
Kovalenko, Susan Chaffins. "The Twentieth-Century Requiem:
    An Emerging Concept." Ph.D. diss., Washington
    University, 1971.
Luce, Harold Talmadge. "The Requiem Mass from Its Plainsong
    Beginnings to 1600." 2 vols. Ph.D. diss., Florida State
    University, 1958.
Massenkeil, Günther. *The Oratorio.* Anthology of Music, vol. 37
    (1970).
Pahlen, Kurt, with the collaboration of Werner Pfister and
    Rosemarie König. *The World of the Oratorio: Oratorio,
    Mass, Requiem, Te Deum, Stabat Mater, and Large
    Cantatas.* Additional material for the English language
    edition by Thurston Dox. Portland, Ore.: Amadeus Press,
    1990. First published in 1985.
Pruett, James W. "Requiem Mass." In *The New Grove Dictionary
    of Music and Musicians.* Vol. 15, pp. 751–55.
Robertson, Alec. *Requiem: Music of Mourning and Consolation.*
    London: Cassell, 1967.
Smallman, Basil. *The Background of Passion Music: J. S. Bach
    and His Predecessors.* 2nd rev. and enl. ed. New York:
    Dover Publications, 1970. First published in 1957.

Smither, Howard E. *A History of the Oratorio.* 3 vols.; 4th
    announced. Chapel Hill: University of North Carolina
    Press, 1977–.
————. "Oratorio." In *The New Grove Dictionary of Music and
    Musicians.* Vol. 13, pp. 656–78.

SURVEYS OF CHORAL MUSIC

Jacobs, Arthur, ed. *Choral Music: A Symposium.* Baltimore:
    Penguin Books, 1963.
Ulrich, Homer. *A Survey of Choral Music.* The Harbrace History
    of Musical Forms. New York: Harcourt Brace Jovanovich,
    1963.
Young, Percy M. *The Choral Tradition: An Historical and
    Analytical Survey from the Sixteenth Century to the
    Present Day.* Rev. ed. New York: W. W. Norton, 1981. First
    published in 1962.

Instrumental

SYMPHONIC MUSIC

Ballantine, Christopher. *Twentieth Century Symphony.* London:
    Dennis Dobson, 1983.
Brook, Barry. "Symphonie concertante." In *The New Grove
    Dictionary of Music and Musicians.* Vol. 18, pp. 433–38.
Cuyler, Louise. *The Symphony.* The Harbrace History of Musical
    Forms. New York: Harcourt Brace Jovanovich, 1973.
Downes, Edward. *The New York Philharmonic Guide to the
    Symphony.* New York: Walker, 1976.
Engel, Hans. *The Solo Concerto.* Anthology of Music, vol. 25
    (1964).
Hausswald, Günter. *The Serenade for Orchestra.* Anthology of
    Music, vol. 34 (1970).
Hill, Ralph, ed. *The Concerto.* New York: Penguin Books, 1952.
Hoffmann-Erbrecht, Lothar. *The Symphony.* Anthology of Music,
    vol. 29 (1967).
Hutchings, Arthur. *The Baroque Concerto.* 3rd rev. ed. London:
    Faber and Faber, 1973. First published in 1959.
Hutchings, Arthur, et al. "Concerto." In *The New Grove
    Dictionary of Music and Musicians.* Vol. 4, pp. 626–40.
Kramer, Jonathan D. *Listen to the Music: A Self-Guided Tour
    through the Orchestral Repertoire.* New York: Schirmer
    Books, 1988.

LaRue, Jan, et al. "Symphony." In *The New Grove Dictionary of Music and Musicians*. Vol. 18, pp. 438–69.

Layton, Robert, ed. *A Companion to the Concerto*. London: Christopher Helm, 1988.

Macdonald, Hugh. "Symphonic Poem." In *The New Grove Dictionary of Music and Musicians*. Vol. 18, pp. 428–33.

Moore, Earl V., and Theodore E. Heger. *The Symphony and the Symphonic Poem: Analytical and Descriptive Charts of the Standard Symphonic Repertory*. 6th ed., rev. Ann Arbor, Mich.: Ulrich Books, 1974. First published in 1949.

Simpson, Robert, ed. *The Symphony*. 2 vols. Baltimore: Penguin Books, 1966–67.

Stedman, Preston. *The Symphony*. Englewood Cliffs, N.J.: Prentice Hall, 1979.

Ulrich, Homer. *Symphonic Music: Its Evolution since the Renaissance*. New York: Columbia University Press, 1952.

Veinus, Abraham. *The Concerto*. Rev. ed. New York: Dover Publications, 1964. First published in 1944.

CHAMBER MUSIC

Berger, Melvin. *Guide to Chamber Music*. New York: Dodd, Mead, 1985.

Cobbett, Walter Willson, comp. and ed., with Colin Mason, ed. *Cobbett's Cyclopedic Survey of Chamber Music*. 2nd ed. 3 vols. London: Oxford University Press, 1963. First published in 1929–30.

Griffiths, Paul. *The String Quartet: A History*. New York: Thames and Hudson, 1983.

Konold, Wulf. *The String Quartet: From Its Beginnings to Franz Schubert*. Translated by Susan Hellauer. Paperbacks in Musicology, no. 6. New York: Heinrichshofen Edition, 1983. First published in 1980.

Loft, Abram. *Violin and Keyboard: The Duo Repertoire*. 2 vols. New York: Grossman Publishers, 1973.

Meyer, Ernst H. *Early English Chamber Music: From the Middle Ages to Purcell*. 2nd, rev. ed. Edited by the author and Diana Poulton. London: Lawrence and Wishart, 1982. First published in 1946 as *English Chamber Music*.

Robertson, Alec, ed. *Chamber Music*. Baltimore: Penguin Books, 1957.

Rowen, Ruth Halle. *Early Chamber Music*. With a new preface and supplementary bibliography. Da Capo Press Music

Reprint Series. New York: Da Capo Press, 1974. First published in 1949.

Smallman, Basil. *The Piano Trio: Its History, Technique, and Repertoire.* Oxford: Clarendon Press, 1989.

Tilmouth, Michael. "String Quartet." In *The New Grove Dictionary of Music and Musicians.* Vol. 18, pp. 276–87.

Ulrich, Homer. *Chamber Music.* 2nd ed. New York: Columbia University Press, 1966. First published in 1948.

Unverricht, Hubert. *Chamber Music.* Anthology of Music, vol. 46 (1975).

KEYBOARD MUSIC

Apel, Willi. *The History of Keyboard Music to 1700.* Translated and revised by Hans Tischler. Bloomington: Indiana University Press, 1972. First published in 1967.

———. *Masters of the Keyboard: A Brief Survey of Pianoforte Music.* Cambridge: Harvard University Press, 1947.

Arnold, Corliss Richard. *Organ Literature: A Comprehensive Survey.* 2nd ed. 2 vols. Metuchen, N.J.: Scarecrow Press, 1984. First published in 1973.

Burge, David. *Twentieth-Century Piano Music.* Studies in Musical Genres and Repertories. New York: Schirmer Books, 1990.

Caldwell, John. *English Keyboard Music before the Nineteenth Century.* Blackwell's Music Series. Oxford: Basil Blackwell, 1973.

———. "Keyboard Music." In *The New Grove Dictionary of Music and Musicians.* Vol. 10, pp. 11–41.

Clark, J. Bunker. *The Dawning of American Keyboard Music.* Contributions to the Study of Music and Dance, no. 12. New York: Greenwood Press, 1988.

Dale, Kathleen. *Nineteenth-Century Piano Music: A Handbook for Pianists.* London: Oxford University Press, 1954.

Georgii, Walter. *Four Hundred Years of European Keyboard Music.* Anthology of Music, vol. 1 (1959).

Gillespie, John. *Five Centuries of Keyboard Music: An Historical Survey of Music for Harpsichord and Piano.* Belmont, Calif.: Wadsworth Publishing, 1965.

Kirby, F. E. *A Short History of Keyboard Music.* New York: Free Press, 1966.

Todd, R. Larry, ed. *Nineteenth-Century Piano Music.* Studies in Musical Genres and Repertories. New York: Schirmer Books, 1990.

Sonata

Allsop, Peter. *The Italian "Trio" Sonata: From Its Origins until Corelli.* Oxford Monographs on Music. New York: Oxford University Press, 1992.

Berger, Melvin. *Guide to Sonatas: Music for One or Two Instruments.* New York: Anchor Books/Doubleday, 1991.

Giegling, Franz. *The Solo Sonata.* Anthology of Music, vol. 15 (1960).

Hogwood, Christopher. *The Trio Sonata.* BBC Music Guides. London: British Broadcasting Corporation, 1979.

Newman, William S. *The Sonata in the Baroque Era.* 4th ed. New York: W. W. Norton, 1983. First published in 1959.

———. *The Sonata in the Classic Era.* 3rd ed. New York: W. W. Norton, 1983. First published in 1963.

———. *The Sonata since Beethoven.* 3rd ed. New York: W. W. Norton, 1983. First published in 1969.

Newman, William S., et al. "Sonata." In *The New Grove Dictionary of Music and Musicians.* Vol. 17, pp. 479–96.

Schenk, Erich. *The Italian Trio Sonata.* Anthology of Music, vol. 7 (1955).

———. *The Trio Sonata outside Italy.* Anthology of Music, vol. 35 (1970).

Shedlock, John. *The Pianoforte Sonata: Its Origin and Development.* With a new foreword by William S. Newman. Da Capo Press Reprint Series. New York: Da Capo Press, 1964. First published in 1926.

Fugue

Adrio, Adam. *The Fugue I: From the Beginnings to Johann Sebastian Bach.* Anthology of Music, vol. 19 (1961).

Bullivant, Roger. "Fugue." In *The New Grove Dictionary of Music and Musicians.* Vol. 7, pp. 9–21.

Horsley, Imogene. *Fugue: History and Practice.* New York: Free Press, 1966.

Kirkendale, Warren. *Fugue and Fugato in Rococo and Classical Chamber Music.* Rev. and exp. 2nd ed. Translated by Margaret Bent and the author. Durham, N.C.: Duke University Press, 1979. First published in 1966.

Mann, Alfred. *The Study of Fugue.* Enl. and corrected version. New York: Dover Publications, 1987. First published in 1958.

Müller-Blattau, Josef. *The Fugue II: From Handel to the Twentieth Century.* Anthology of Music, vol. 33 (1968).
Oldroyd, George. *The Technique and Spirit of Fugue: An Historical Study.* London: Oxford University Press, 1948.

MISCELLANEOUS SOURCES

Tovey, Donald Francis. *Essays in Musical Analysis.* New ed. 2 vols. London: Oxford University Press, 1981. Originally published in 6 vols., 1935–39.

1. *Symphonies and Other Orchestral Works.*
2. *Concertos and Choral Works.*

————— . *Essays in Musical Analysis: Chamber Music.* With an editor's note by Hubert J. Foss. London: Oxford University Press, 1989. First published in 1944.

CHRONOLOGIES AND OUTLINES

Treatments of music history in the form of chronological lists or outlines may be useful for study or reference. The following sources fall into three categories: "General," "Twentieth Century," and "American Music." There is a good deal of diversity within the categories, with considerable difference in scope and amount of detail. Eisler's *World Chronology* is by far the most detailed, with the Gleason/Becker outlines and Slonimsky's *Music since 1900* not far behind. The arrangement of information is either chronological by historical period, by year, by day, by composer, etc. Some sources, like Eisler and Hall, include nonmusical information; others are concerned only with music. The chronologies listed here are mostly recent, but older sources like Lahee and Schering continue to be valid.

General and Comprehensive

Cullen, Marion Elizabeth, comp. *Memorable Days in Music.* Metuchen, N.J.: Scarecrow Press, 1970.
Dufourcq, Norbert, Marcelle Benoit, and Bernard Gagnepain. *Les grandes dates de l'histoire de la musique.* 4th ed., corrected. Que sais-je? no. 1333. Paris: Presses Universitaires de France, 1991. First published in 1969.

Eisler, Paul E. *World Chronology of Music History.* Dobbs Ferry, N.Y.: Oceana Publications, 1972–. 8 to 10 vols. projected.

Gangwere, Blanche M. *Music History from the Late Roman through the Gothic Periods, 313–1425: A Documented Chronology.* Music Reference Collection, no. 6. Westport, Conn.: Greenwood Press, 1986.

————. *Music History during the Renaissance Period, 1425–1520: A Documented Chronology.* Music Reference Collection, no. 28. Westport, Conn.: Greenwood Press, 1991.

Gleason, Harold, and Warren Becker. **Music Literature Outlines.** 5 series. 2nd/3rd ed. Bloomington, Ind.: Frangipani Press, 1980–81. First published in 1949–55.

> Series 1. *Music in the Middle Ages and the Renaissance.* 3rd ed., 1981.
> Series 2. *Music in the Baroque.* 3rd ed., 1980.
> Series 3. *Early American Music from 1620 to 1920.* 2nd ed., 1981.
> Series 4. *20th-Century American Composers.* 2nd ed., 1980.
> Series 5. *Chamber Music from Haydn to Bartók.* 2nd ed., 1980.

Hall, Charles J., comp. *An Eighteenth-Century Musical Chronicle: Events 1750–1799.* Music Reference Collection, no. 25. Westport, Conn.: Greenwood Press, 1990.

————. *A Nineteenth-Century Musical Chronicle: Events 1800–1899.* Music Reference Collection, no. 21. Westport, Conn.: Greenwood Press, 1989.

————. *A Twentieth-Century Musical Chronicle: Events 1900–1988.* Music Reference Collection, no. 20. Westport, Conn.: Greenwood Press, 1989. An earlier version published in 1980 as *Hall's Musical Years, the Twentieth Century 1900–1979: A Comprehensive Year-by-Year Survey of the Fine Arts.*

Manson, Adele P. *Calendar of Music and Musicians.* Metuchen, N.J.: Scarecrow Press, 1981.

Michels, Ulrich. *DTV-Atlas zur Musik: Tafeln und Texte.* 2 vols. Kassel: Bärenreiter, 1977–85.

> 1. *Systematischer Teil; Historischer Teil [1]: Von den Anfängen bis zur Renaissance.* 1977.
> 2. *Historischer Teil [2]: Vom Barock bis zur Gegenwart.* 1985.

Miller, Hugh M. *History of Music.* Barnes and Noble Outline Series. 4th ed. New York: Barnes and Noble, 1972. First published in 1947.

Schering, Arnold. *Tabellen zur Musikgeschichte: Ein Hilfsbuch beim Studium der Musikgeschichte.* 5th ed., enlarged by Hans Joachim Moser. Wiesbaden: Breitkopf & Härtel, 1962. First published in 1914.

Wold, Milo, et al. *An Outline History of Western Music.* 7th ed. Dubuque, Iowa: Wm. C. Brown Publishers, 1990. First published in 1963.

Wörner, Karl H. *History of Music: A Book for Study and Reference.* 5th ed. Translated and supplemented by Willis Wager. New York: Free Press, 1973. First published in 1954.

Twentieth Century

Burbank, Richard. *Twentieth Century Music.* Introduction by Nicolas Slonimsky. New York: Facts on File, 1984.

Slonimsky, Nicolas. *Music since 1900.* 5th ed. New York: Schirmer Books, 1993. First published in 1937.

American

Lahee, Henry C. *Annals of Music in America: A Chronological Record of Significant Musical Events from 1640 to the Present Day, with Comments on the Various Periods into Which the Work Is Divided.* Boston: Marshall Jones, 1922.

Sablosky, Irving. *What They Heard: Music in America, 1852–1881, from the Pages of* Dwight's Journal of Music. Baton Rouge: Louisiana State University Press, 1986.

BIOGRAPHIES OF COMPOSERS IN ENGLISH

From its beginnings in the mid-18th century, the category of composer biographies has steadily grown to its present enormous size. Biographical writing has also passed through various stylistic phases; in the light of current rigorous scholarly standards, accumulated research, and availability of information, most earlier biographies must be viewed in their historical context rather than taken at face value.

The present bibliography lists reliable, serious, and for the most part recent biographies in English, or in English translation, of some of the best-known composers, listed in alphabetical order by composer. Only a few of the classic 19th-century or earlier 20th-century standards (e.g., Spitta/Bach, Thayer/Beethoven, Moser/Schütz) have been included. Those felt to be overly romanticized or popular in tone, even though still known and used, have been omitted, as have those that are essentially brief sketches or summaries. A few examples of the pictorial or documentary biography have been included.

The present list is one of the most selective in this book; for more comprehensive lists of biographies of composers and other musical figures, the section "Biographies of Musicians" in chapter 2, p. 29 above, should be consulted. The composer biographies comprising three important publishers' series are enumerated separately following the present listing. See also the periodicals devoted to individual composers, such as those listed in chapter 6 under "Musicology—Limited to a Single Composer," p. 155 below.

Ottenberg, Hans-Günter. *C. P. E. Bach.* Translated by Philip Whitmore. London: Oxford University Press, 1987. First published in 1982.

David, Hans T., and Arthur Mendel, eds. *The Bach Reader: A Life of Johann Sebastian Bach in Letters and Documents.* Rev. ed. New York: W. W. Norton, 1966. First published in 1945.

Felix, Werner. *Johann Sebastian Bach.* 1st American ed. New York: W. W. Norton, 1985. First published in 1984.

Geiringer, Karl, in collaboration with Irene Geiringer. *Johann Sebastian Bach: The Culmination of an Era.* London: Oxford University Press, 1966.

Spitta, Philipp. *Johann Sebastian Bach: His Work and Influence on the Music of Germany, 1685–1750.* Translated by Clara Bell and J. A. Fuller-Maitland. 3 vols. London: Novello, 1884–85. First published in 1873–80.

Terry, Charles Sanford. *Bach: A Biography.* 2nd ed., rev. London: Oxford University Press, 1933. First published in 1928.

Stevens, Halsey. *The Life and Music of Béla Bartók.* 3rd ed. Edited by Malcolm Gillies. London: Oxford University Press, 1993. First published in 1953.

Landon, H. C. Robbins, comp. and ed. *Beethoven: A Documentary Study.* Translated by Richard Wadleigh and Eugene Hartzell. New York: Macmillan, 1970.

Marek, George R. *Beethoven: Biography of a Genius.* New York: Funk & Wagnalls, 1969.

Solomon, Maynard. *Beethoven.* New York: Schirmer Books, 1977.

Thayer, Alexander Wheelock. *Thayer's Life of Beethoven.*
Translated by Henry Edward Krehbiel (1921). Revised and
edited by Elliot Forbes. Princeton: Princeton University
Press, 1967. First published in 1866–79 (vols. 1–3) and
1907–8 (vols. 4–5).

Carner, Mosco. *Alban Berg: The Man and the Work.* 2nd rev. ed.
New York: Holmes & Meier Publishers, 1983. First
published in 1975.
Monson, Karen. *Alban Berg.* Boston: Houghton Mifflin, 1979.
Redlich, Hans. *Alban Berg: The Man and His Music.* New York:
Abelard-Schuman, 1957.
Reich, Willi. *The Life and Work of Alban Berg.* Translated by
Cornelius Cardew. New York: Harcourt, Brace & World,
1965. First published in 1963.

Barzun, Jacques. *Berlioz and the Romantic Century.* 3rd ed. 2
vols. New York: Columbia University Press, 1969. First
published in 1950. Revised and abridged as *Berlioz and His
Century: An Introduction to the Age of Romanticism.*
Chicago: University of Chicago Press, 1982.
Cairns, David. *Berlioz 1803–1832: The Making of an Artist.*
London: André Deutsch, 1989. (Vol. 1 of a projected 2–vol.
set.)
Holoman, D. Kern. *Berlioz: A Musical Biography of the Creative
Genius of the Romantic Era.* Cambridge: Harvard
University Press, 1989.

McKay, David P., and Richard Crawford. *William Billings of
Boston: Eighteenth-Century Composer.* Princeton: Princeton
University Press, 1975.

Gál, Hans. *Johannes Brahms: His Work and Personality.* Rev. ed.
Translated by Joseph Stein. Westport, Conn.: Greenwood
Press, 1975. First published in 1961.
Geiringer, Karl, in collaboration with Irene Geiringer. *Brahms:
His Life and Work.* 3rd, enl. ed. New York: Da Capo Press,
1982. First published in 1934.
James, Burnett. *Brahms: A Critical Study.* London: J. M. Dent
and Sons, 1972.
Keys, Ivor. *Johannes Brahms.* London: Christopher Helm, 1989.
May, Florence. *The Life of Johannes Brahms.* 2nd ed. 2 vols.
London: William Reeves, Bookseller, [1948]. First published
in 1905.

White, Eric Walter. *Benjamin Britten: His Life and Operas*. 2nd ed. Edited by John Evans. Berkeley: University of California Press, 1983. First published in 1970.

Doernberg, Erwin. *The Life and Symphonies of Anton Bruckner*. London: Barrie & Rockliff, 1960.

Snyder, Kerala J. *Dieterich Buxtehude: Organist in Lübeck*. New York: Schirmer Books, 1987.

Atwood, William G. *Fryderyk Chopin: Pianist from Warsaw*. New York: Columbia University Press, 1987.
Gavoty, Bernard. *Frederic Chopin*. Translated by Martin Sokolinsky. New York: Charles Scribner's Sons, 1977. First published in 1974.
Jordan, Ruth. *Nocturne: A Life of Chopin*. New York: Taplinger Publishing, 1978.
Marek, George R., and Maria Gordon-Smith. *Chopin*. New York: Harper & Row, 1978.
Zamoyski, Adam. *Chopin: A New Biography*. 1st American ed. Garden City, N.Y.: Doubleday, 1980. First published in 1979.

Copland, Aaron, and Vivian Perlis. *Copland: 1900 through 1942*. New York: St. Martin's Press, 1984.
————. *Copland since 1943*. New York: St. Martin's Press, 1989.

Pincherle, Marc. *Corelli: His Life, His Work*. Translated by Hubert E. M. Russell. New York: W. W. Norton, 1956. First published in 1933.

Beaussant, Philippe. *François Couperin*. Translated by Alexandria Land. Portland, Ore.: Amadeus Press, 1990. First published in 1980.
Mellers, Wilfrid. *François Couperin and the French Classical Tradition*. New vers. London: Faber and Faber, 1987. First published in 1950.

Lockspeiser, Edward. *Debussy: His Life and Mind*. 2 vols. New York: Macmillan, 1962–65.

Clapham, John. *Dvořák*. 1st American ed. New York: W. W. Norton, 1979.

Hughes, Gervaise. *Dvořák: His Life and Music.* New York: Dodd, Mead, 1967.
Schönzeler, Hans-Hubert. *Dvořák.* London: Marion Boyars, 1984.

Hammond, Frederick. *Girolamo Frescobaldi.* Cambridge: Harvard University Press, 1983.

Arnold, Denis. *Giovanni Gabrieli and the Music of the Venetian High Renaissance.* London: Oxford University Press, 1979.
Kenton, Egon. *Life and Works of Giovanni Gabrieli.* Musicological Studies and Documents, no. 16. [Rome]: American Institute of Musicology, 1967.

Deutsch, Otto Erich. *Handel: A Documentary Biography.* Rev. ed. New York: W. W. Norton, 1974. First published in 1955. An updated edition based on this work with the documents in their original language, most of which are in English, is published as *Dokumente zu Leben und Schaffen: Auf der Grundlage von Otto Erich Deutsch, Handel: A Documentary Biography,* edited by the staff of the Hallischen Händel-Ausgabe (vol. 4 of *Händel-Handbuch*), Kassel: Bärenreiter, 1985.
Hogwood, Christopher. *Handel.* New York: Thames and Hudson, 1984.
Keates, Jonathan. *Handel: The Man and His Music.* New York: St. Martin's Press, 1985.
Landon, H. C. Robbins. *Handel and His World.* 1st American ed. Boston: Little, Brown, 1984.
Lang, Paul Henry. *George Frideric Handel.* Rev. ed. New York: W. W. Norton, 1977. First published in 1966.

Geiringer, Karl. *Haydn: A Creative Life in Music.* 3rd ed., rev. and enl. Berkeley: University of California Press, 1982. First published in 1946.
Landon, H. C. Robbins. *Haydn: A Documentary Study.* New York: Rizzoli, 1981.
————. *Haydn: Chronicle and Works.* 1st American ed. 5 vols. Bloomington: Indiana University Press, 1976–80.
Landon, H. C. Robbins, and David Wyn Jones. *Haydn: His Life and Music.* Bloomington: Indiana University Press, 1988.

Skelton, Geoffrey. *Paul Hindemith: The Man behind the Music: A Biography.* London: Victor Gollancz, 1975.

Burkholder, J. Peter. *Charles Ives: The Ideas behind the Music.* New Haven: Yale University Press, 1985.

Cowell, Henry, and Sidney Cowell. *Charles Ives and His Music.* 2nd ed., rev., with a new foreword, an updated list of works, bibliography, and discography. New York: Da Capo Press, 1983. First published in 1955.

Feder, Stuart. *Charles Ives, "My Father's Song": A Psychoanalytic Biography.* New Haven: Yale University Press, 1992.

Rossiter, Frank R. *Charles Ives and His America.* New York: Liveright, 1975.

Wooldridge, David. *From the Steeples and Mountains: A Study of Charles Ives.* New York: Alfred A. Knopf, 1974.

Burger, Ernst. *Franz Liszt: A Chronicle of His Life in Pictures and Documents.* Translated by Stewart Spencer. Princeton: Princeton University Press, 1989.

Perényi, Eleanor Spencer (Stone). *Liszt: The Artist as Romantic Hero.* Boston: Little, Brown, 1974.

Taylor, Ronald. *Franz Liszt: The Man and the Musician.* London: Grafton Books, 1986.

Walker, Alan. *Franz Liszt.* Rev. ed. 2 vols. Ithaca, N.Y.: Cornell University Press, 1987–89. First published in 1983.

Newman, Joyce. *Jean-Baptiste de Lully and His Tragédies lyriques.* Studies in Musicology, no. 1. Ann Arbor, Mich.: UMI Research Press, 1974.

Blaukopf, Kurt. *Gustav Mahler.* Translated by Inge Goodwin. New York: Praeger and Praeger, 1973. First published in 1969.

———, comp. and ed., with contributions by Zoltan Roman. *Mahler: A Documentary Study.* Translated by Paul Baker et al. London: Thames and Hudson, 1976.

Gartenberg, Egon. *Mahler: The Man and His Music.* New York: Schirmer Books, 1978.

La Grange, Henri-Louis de. *Mahler.* Vol. 1–. Garden City, N.Y.: Doubleday, 1973–. (Vols. 2 and 3 still only in French.) First published in 1973.

Mitchell, Donald. *Gustav Mahler: Songs and Symphonies of Life and Death: Interpretations and Annotations.* Berkeley: University of California Press, 1986.

———. *Gustav Mahler: The Early Years.* Revised and edited by Paul Banks and David Matthews. Berkeley: University of California Press, 1980.

———— . *Gustav Mahler: The Wunderhorn Years: Chronicles and Commentaries.* Boulder, Colo.: Westview Press, 1975.

Marek, George R. *Gentle Genius: The Story of Felix Mendelssohn.* New York: Funk & Wagnalls, 1972.
Werner, Eric. *Mendelssohn: A New Image of the Composer and His Age.* Translated by Dika Newlin. New York: Free Press of Glencoe, 1963. Rev. and enl. ed. in German, 1980.

Redlich, Hans. *Claudio Monteverdi: Life and Works.* Translated by Kathleen Dale. London: Oxford University Press, 1952. First published in 1949.
Schrade, Leo. *Monteverdi: Creator of Modern Music.* New York: W. W. Norton, 1950.
Tomlinson, Gary. *Monteverdi and the End of the Renaissance.* Berkeley: University of California Press, 1987.

Deutsch, Otto Erich. *Mozart: A Documentary Biography.* Rev. ed. Translated by Eric Blom et al. Stanford: Stanford University Press, 1965. First published in 1961. *New Mozart Documents: A Supplement to O.E. Deutsch's Documentary Biography.* Stanford: Stanford University Press, 1991.
Einstein, Alfred. *Mozart: His Character, His Work.* Translated by Arthur Mendel and Nathan Broder. London: Oxford University Press, 1945. Original German version published in 1947.
Hildesheimer, Wolfgang. *Mozart.* Translated by Marion Faber. New York: Farrar Straus Giroux, 1981. First published in 1977.
Hutchings, Arthur. *Mozart: The Man, the Musician.* New York: Schirmer Books, 1976.
Keys, Ivor. *Mozart: His Music in His Life.* New York: Holmes & Meier Publishers, 1979.

Leyda, Jay, and Sergei Bertensson, eds. and transls. *The Musorgsky Reader: A Life of Modeste Petrovich Musorgsky in Letters and Documents.* Rev. ed. New York: W. W. Norton, 1970. First published in 1947.
Orlova, Aleksandra. *Musorgsky's Days and Works: A Biography in Documents.* Translated and edited by Roy J. Guenther. Russian Music Studies, no. 4. Ann Arbor, Mich.: UMI Research Press, 1983. First published in 1963.
Seroff, Victor. *Modeste Moussorgsky.* New York: Funk & Wagnalls, 1968.

Schwinger, Wolfram. *Krzysztof Penderecki: His Life and Work: Encounters, Biography, and Musical Commentary*. Translated by William Mann. London: Schott, 1989. First published in 1979.

Gutman, David. *Prokofiev*. Alderman Music Makers. London: Alderman, 1987.

Robinson, Harlow. *Sergei Prokofiev: A Biography*. New York: Viking Press, 1987.

Seroff, Victor. *Sergei Prokofiev: A Soviet Tragedy: The Case of Sergei Prokofiev, His Life and Work, His Critics, and His Executioners*. New York: Funk & Wagnalls, 1968.

Zimmerman, Franklin B. *Henry Purcell, 1659–1695: His Life and Times*. 2nd, rev. ed. Philadelphia: University of Pennsylvania Press, 1983. First published in 1967.

Girdlestone, Cuthbert. *Jean-Philippe Rameau: His Life and Work*. 2nd ed., rev. and enl. New York: Dover Publications, 1969. First published in 1957.

Myers, Rollo H. *Maurice Ravel: Life and Works*. London: Gerald Duckworth, 1960.

Orenstein, Arbie. *Ravel: Man and Musician*. New York: Columbia University Press, 1975.

Weinstock, Herbert. *Rossini: A Biography*. New York: Alfred A. Knopf, 1968.

Boyd, Malcolm. *Domenico Scarlatti—Master of Music*. 1st American ed. New York: Schirmer Books, 1987. First published in 1986.

Kirkpatrick, Ralph. *Domenico Scarlatti*. 3rd ed., rev. Princeton: Princeton University Press, 1968. First published in 1953.

Reich, Willi. *Schoenberg: A Critical Biography*. Translated by Leo Black. London: Longman, 1971. First published in 1968.

Ringer, Alexander L. *Arnold Schoenberg: The Composer as Jew*. Oxford: Clarendon Press, 1990.

Stuckenschmidt, H. H. *Schoenberg: His Life, World, and Work*. 1st American ed. Translated by Humphrey Searle. New York: Schirmer Books, 1977. First published in 1974.

Brown, Maurice J. E. *Schubert: A Critical Biography*. New York: St. Martin's Press, 1958.

Deutsch, Otto Erich. *The Schubert Reader: A Life of Franz Schubert in Letters and Documents.* Rev. ed. Translated by Eric Blom. New York: W. W. Norton, 1977. First published in 1947.

Einstein, Alfred. *Schubert: A Musical Portrait.* London: Oxford University Press, 1951.

Marek, George R. *Schubert.* New York: Viking Press, 1985.

Osborne, Charles. *Schubert and His Vienna.* New York: Alfred A. Knopf, 1985.

Moser, Hans Joachim. *Heinrich Schütz: His Life and Work.* 2nd ed., rev. (1954). Translated by Carl F. Pfatteicher. St. Louis: Concordia Publishing House, 1959. First published in 1936.

Ostwald, Peter. *Schumann: The Inner Voices of a Musical Genius.* Boston: Northeastern University Press, 1985.

Taylor, Ronald. *Robert Schumann: His Life and Work.* New York: Universe Books, 1982.

MacDonald, Ian. *The New Shostakovich.* London: Fourth Estate, 1990.

Norris, Christopher, ed. *Shostakovich: The Man and His Music.* London: Lawrence and Wishart, 1982.

Tawaststjerna, Erik. *Sibelius.* Translated by Robert Layton. 3 vols. projected. Berkeley: University of California Press, 1976–. First published in 1965–67.

Del Mar, Norman. *Richard Strauss: A Critical Commentary on His Life and Works.* Corrected ed. 3 vols. London: Barrie and Jenkins, 1978. First published in 1962.

Jefferson, Alan. *The Life of Richard Strauss.* Newton Abbot, England: David & Charles, 1973.

Marek, George R. *Richard Strauss: The Life of a Non-Hero.* New York: Simon and Schuster, 1967.

Wilhelm, Kurt. *Richard Strauss: An Intimate Portrait.* Translated by Mary Whittall. London: Thames and Hudson, 1989. First published in 1984.

Boucourechliev, André. *Stravinsky.* Translated by Martin Cooper. London: Victor Gollancz, 1987. First published in 1968.

Stravinsky, Vera, and Robert Craft. *Stravinsky in Pictures and Documents.* New York: Simon and Schuster, 1978.

Tierney, Neil. *The Unknown Country: A Life of Igor Stravinsky.* London: Robert Hale, 1977.

Vlad, Roman. *Stravinsky.* 3rd ed. Translated by Frederick Fuller.
    Oxford: Oxford University Press, 1985.
White, Eric Walter. *Stravinsky: The Composer and His Works.*
    2nd ed. Berkeley: University of California Press, 1979. First
    published in 1966.

Brown, David. *Tchaikovsky.* 1st American ed. 4 vols. New York:
    W. W. Norton, 1978–92.
Kendall, Alan. *Tchaikovsky: A Biography.* London: Bodley Head,
    1988.
Orlova, Alexandra. *Tchaikovsky: A Self-Portrait.* Translated by R.
    M. Davison. Oxford: Oxford University Press, 1990.
Poznansky, Alexander. *Tchaikovsky: The Quest for the Inner
    Man.* New York: Schirmer Books, 1991.
Warrack, John. *Tchaikovsky.* New York: Charles Scribner's Sons,
    1973.

Petzoldt, Richard. *Georg Philipp Telemann.* Translated by Horace
    Fitzpatrick. New York: Oxford University Press, 1974. First
    published in 1967.

Vaughan Williams, Ursula. *R. V. W.: A Biography of Ralph
    Vaughan Williams.* London: Oxford University Press, 1964.

Kimbell, David R. B. *Verdi in the Age of Italian Romanticism.*
    Cambridge: Cambridge University Press, 1981.
Martin, George Whitney. *Verdi: His Music, Life and Times.* New
    York: Dodd, Mead, 1963.
Walker, Frank. *The Man Verdi.* Phoenix ed. With a new
    introduction by Philip Gossett. Chicago: University of
    Chicago Press, 1982. First published in 1962.
Weaver, William, comp., ed., and transl. *Verdi: A Documentary
    Study.* London: Thames and Hudson, [1977].

Kolneder, Walter. *Antonio Vivaldi: His Life and Work.* Translated
    by Bill Hopkins. Berkeley: University of California Press,
    1970. First published in 1965.
Pincherle, Marc. *Vivaldi: Genius of the Baroque.* Translated by
    Christopher Hatch. New York: W. W. Norton, 1957. First
    published in 1955.

Gregor-Dellin, Martin. *Richard Wagner: His Life, His Work, His
    Century.* Translated by J. Maxwell Brownjohn. San Diego:
    Harcourt Brace Jovanovich, 1983. First published in 1980.

Gutman, Robert W. *Richard Wagner: The Man, His Mind, and His Music.* New York: Harcourt, Brace & World, 1968.

Millington, Barry, ed. *The Wagner Compendium: A Guide to Wagner's Life and Music.* New York: Schirmer Books, 1992.

Newman, Ernest. *The Life of Richard Wagner.* 1st American ed. 4 vols. New York: Alfred A. Knopf, 1933–46.

Sabor, Rudolph. *The Real Wagner.* London: André Deutsch, 1987.

Westernhagen, Curt von. *Wagner: A Biography.* 2 vols. Translated by Mary Whittall. Cambridge: Cambridge University Press, 1978. First published in 1968.

Warrack, John. *Carl Maria von Weber.* 2nd ed. Cambridge: Cambridge University Press, 1976. First published in 1968.

Moldenhauer, Hans, and Rosaleen Moldenhauer. *Anton von Webern: A Chronicle of His Life and Works.* 1st American ed. New York: Alfred A. Knopf, 1979.

Walker, Frank. *Hugo Wolf: A Biography.* 2nd, enl. ed. New York: Alfred A. Knopf, 1968. First published in 1951.

SERIES OF COMPOSERS' BIOGRAPHIES
IN ENGLISH

As a supplement to the previous bibliography, the present one itemizes the contents of three of the best-known and most up-to-date series of composer biographies (or, in the case of some of the volumes in the New Grove series, groups of biographies) in English. The Concert Goer's Companion Series is the smallest and is apparently complete, no volumes having appeared since 1980. The other two series are comparable in breadth of coverage. The Master Musicians Series, whose initial volumes go back to the 1930s, is particularly fluid. New works have been added to the series, and also new editions of many earlier ones; some older studies have been replaced by totally new ones by other authors (in which case only the most recent work on a given composer is listed below). The New Grove Composer Biography Series, now complete, was begun in the 1980s as a means of updating composer articles in *The New Grove Dictionary* and of making them available in a practical format, but the degree of revision from dictionary to separate volume varies considerably, from comparatively little to total rewriting by other authors.

Concert Goer's Companions Series (each volume subtitled "A Biography, with a Survey of Books, Editions and Recordings"). London: Clive Bingley; Hamden, Conn.: Archon Books, Linnet Books.

> *Bach.* By Alec Robertson. 1977.
> *Beethoven.* By Rosemary Hughes. 1970.
> *Brahms.* By Kathleen Dale. 1970.
> *Chopin.* By Derek Melville. 1977.
> *Handel.* By Charles Cudworth. 1972.
> *Haydn.* By Brian Redfern. 1970.
> *Mozart.* By Alexander Hyatt King. 1970.
> *Wagner.* By Robert Anderson. 1980.

Master Musicians Series. London: J. M. Dent and Sons; New York: Octagon Books. (Schirmer Books, New York, is bringing out the 1st American ed. of selected volumes in the series. These are specified below.)

> *Bach.* By Malcolm Boyd. 1983.
> *Bartók.* By Paul Griffiths. 1984.
> *Beethoven.* By Denis Matthews. 1985.
> *Bellini.* By Leslie Orrey. 1969.
> *Berlioz.* By Hugh Macdonald. 1982.
> *Bizet.* By Winton Dean. 1965.
> *Brahms.* By Malcolm MacDonald. 1st American ed. Schirmer Books, 1990.
> *Britten.* By Michael Kennedy. 1981.
> *Bruckner.* By Derek Watson. 1975.
> *Chopin.* By Arthur Hedley. 3rd ed., rev. 1974. First published in 1947.
> *Debussy.* By Edward Lockspeiser. 5th ed. 1980. First published in 1936.
> *Delius.* By Alan Jefferson. 1972.
> *Dufay.* By David Fallows. Rev. ed. 1987. First published in 1982.
> *Dvořák.* By Alec Robertson. Rev. ed. 1974. First published in 1945.
> *Elgar.* By Ian Parrott. 1971.
> *Franck.* By Laurence Davies. 1973.
> *Grieg.* By John Horton. 1974.
> *Handel.* By Percy M. Young. Rev. ed. 1975. First published in 1947.
> *Haydn.* By Rosemary Hughes. Rev. ed. 1989. First published in 1950.

Liszt. By Derek Watson. 1st American ed. Schirmer Books, 1989.

Mahler. By Michael Kennedy. 2nd ed. 1990. First published in 1974.

Mendelssohn. By Philip Radcliffe. 3rd ed. Revised by Peter Ward Jones, 1990. First published in 1954.

Monteverdi. By Denis Arnold. 3rd. ed. Revised by Tim Carter. 1975. First published in 1963.

Mozart. By Eric Blom. Rev. ed. 1974. First published in 1935.

Mussorgsky. By M. D. Calvocoressi. Rev. ed. Completed and revised by Gerald Abraham. 1974. First published in 1946.

Puccini. By Mosco Carner. Rev. ed. 1974. First published in 1958.

Purcell. By J. A. Westrup. 8th ed. 1980. First published in 1937.

Rakhmaninov. By Geoffrey Norris. 1976.

Ravel. By Roger Nichols. 1977.

Rossini. By Richard Osborne. 1986.

Schoenberg. By Malcolm MacDonald. 1976.

Schubert. By John Reed. 1987.

Schumann. By Joan Chissell. 5th ed. 1989. First published in 1948.

Sibelius. By Robert Layton. 2nd ed. 1978. First published in 1965.

Smetana. By John Clapham. 1972.

Richard Strauss. By Michael Kennedy. Rev. ed. 1988. First published in 1976.

Stravinsky. By Francis Routh. Rev. ed. 1977. First published in 1975.

Tchaikovsky. By Edward Garden. 2nd rev. ed. 1984. First published in 1973.

Vaughan Williams. By James Day. Rev. ed. 1975. First published in 1961.

Verdi. By Julian Budden. 1985.

Vivaldi. By Michael Talbot. 1978.

Wagner. By Barry Millington. 1984.

The New Grove Composer Biography Series. London: Macmillan; New York: W. W. Norton.

Bach Family. By Christoph Wolff et al. 1983.

Beethoven. By Joseph Kerman and Alan Tyson. 1983.

Early Romantic Masters 1: Chopin, Schumann, Liszt. By Nicholas Temperley et al. 1985.

Early Romantic Masters 2: Weber, Berlioz, Mendelssohn. By John Warrack et al. 1985.

French Baroque Masters: Lully, Charpentier, Lalande, Couperin, Rameau. By James R. Anthony et al. 1986.

Gospel, Blues and Jazz: With Spiritual and Ragtime. By Paul Oliver, Max Harrison, and William Bolcom. 1986.

Handel. By Winton Dean, with Anthony Hicks. 1983.

Haydn. By Jens Peter Larsen, with Georg Feder. 1983.

High Renaissance Masters: Josquin, Palestrina, Lassus, Byrd, Victoria. By Gustave Reese et al. 1984.

Italian Baroque Masters: Monteverdi, Frescobaldi, Cavalli, Corelli, A. Scarlatti, Vivaldi, D. Scarlatti. By Denis Arnold et al. 1984.

Late Romantic Masters: Bruckner, Brahms, Dvořák, Wolf. By Deryck Cooke et al. 1985.

Masters of Italian Opera: Rossini, Donizetti, Bellini, Verdi, Puccini. By Philip Gossett et al. 1983.

Modern Masters: Bartók, Stravinsky, Hindemith. By Laszlo Somfai et al. 1984.

Mozart. By Stanley Sadie. 1983.

North European Baroque Masters: Schütz, Froberger, Buxtehude, Purcell, Telemann. By Joshua Rifkin et al. 1985.

Russian Masters 1: Glinka, Borodin, Balakirev, Musorgsky, Tchaikovsky. By David Brown et al. 1986.

Russian Masters 2: Rimsky-Korsakov, Skryabin, Rakhmaninov, Prokofiev, Shostakovich. By Gerald Abraham et al. 1986.

Schubert. By Maurice J. E. Brown, with Eric Sams. 1983.

Second Viennese School: Schoenberg, Webern, Berg. By Oliver Neighbour et al. 1983.

Turn of the Century Masters: Janáček, Mahler, Strauss, Sibelius. By John Tyrrell et al. 1985.

Twentieth-Century American Masters: Ives, Thomson, Sessions, Cowell, Gershwin, Copland, Carter, Barber, Cage, Bernstein. By William Austin et al. 1988.

Twentieth-Century English Masters: Elgar, Delius, Vaughan Williams, Holst, Walton, Tippett, Britten. By Diana McVeagh et al. 1986.

Twentieth-Century French Masters: Fauré, Debussy, Satie, Ravel, Poulenc, Messiaen, Boulez. By Jean-Michel Nectoux et al. 1986.
Wagner. By John Deathridge and Carl Dahlhaus. 1984.

COLLECTIONS OF EXCERPTS FROM PRIMARY SOURCES ON MUSIC

Strunk's *Source Readings* has long been known and used by music students and others as the source of excerpts from significant historical writings on music in English or English translation. Some of the other such anthologies of excerpts, like Strunk's, constitute a general history of writings on music (*Cambridge Readings*, Rowen, Weiss/Taruskin). Others focus on a particular aspect, either aesthetics (*Contemplating Music, Musical Aesthetics*), performance practice (MacClintock), women in music (Neuls-Bates), or black American music (Southern).

A whole category of primary sources not included here comprises compilations of twentieth-century composer interviews, of which there are numerous examples.

Cambridge Readings in the Literature of Music. John Stevens and Peter Le Huray, gen. eds. Cambridge: Cambridge University Press, 1981–.

> *Greek Musical Writings I.* Edited by Andrew Barker. 1984.
> *Music in Early Christian Literature.* Edited by James McKinnon. 1987.
> *Music and Aesthetics in the Eighteenth and Early-Nineteenth Centuries.* Edited by Peter le Huray and James Day. 1981. Abridged ed., 1988.
> *Music in European Thought, 1851–1912.* Edited by Bojan Bujić. 1988.

Contemplating Music: Source Readings in the Aesthetics of Music. Edited by Ruth Katz and Carl Dahlhaus. 4 vols. Aesthetics in Music, no. 5. Stuyvesant, N.Y.: Pendragon Press, 1987–92.

> 1. *Substance.* 1987.
> 2. *Import.* 1989.
> 3. *Essence.* 1992.
> 4. *Community of Discourse.* 1992.

MacClintock, Carol, ed., trans., and comp. *Readings in the History of Music in Performance.* Bloomington: Indiana University Press, 1979.

Musical Aesthetics: A Historical Reader. Edited by Edward A. Lippman. 3 vols. Aesthetics in Music, no. 4. Stuyvesant, N.Y.: Pendragon Press, 1986–91.

1. *From Antiquity to the 18th Century.* 1986.
2. *The Nineteenth Century.* 1988.
3. *The Twentieth Century.* 1991.

Neuls-Bates, Carol, ed. *Women in Music: An Anthology of Source Readings from the Middle Ages to the Present.* New York: Harper & Row Publishers, 1982.

Rowen, Ruth Halle, ed. *Music through Sources and Documents.* Englewood Cliffs, N.J.: Prentice Hall, 1979.

Southern, Eileen, comp. and ed. *Readings in Black American Music.* 2nd ed. New York: W. W. Norton, 1983. First published in 1971.

Strunk, Oliver, comp. *Source Readings in Music History from Classical Antiquity through the Romantic Era.* (Also published in five separate paperback volumes.) New York: W. W. Norton, 1950.

Weiss, Piero, and Richard Taruskin, comps. and annots. *Music in the Western World: A History in Documents.* New York: Schirmer Books, 1984.

HISTORIES OF MUSICAL INSTRUMENTS

The selected one-volume histories of musical instruments listed below span a fifty-year period, from Sachs's and Geiringer's classic treatments, first published in the 1940s, to Remnant's coverage of 1989. They also vary in length, geographic and historical comprehensiveness, and amount of detail (the most substantial being Sachs and Marcuse), as well as in number of illustrations (up to the profusely illustrated works by Bragard/de Hen and Remnant). Baines, Galpin, Marcuse, and Remnant are organized by category of instruments; Bragard/de Hen, Geiringer, and Sachs by historical sequence.

Books on individual instruments are not included, although there is a large literature of such sources. Other specialized studies which exist include The New Grove Musical Instruments Series, published by Macmillan, consisting of the volumes *Early Keyboard Instruments, The Organ, The Piano,* and *The Violin Family.*

Baines, Anthony, ed. *Musical Instruments through the Ages.*
    Baltimore: Penguin Books, 1961.
Bragard, Roger, and Ferdinand J. de Hen. *Musical Instruments in*
    Art and History. Translated by Bill Hopkins. New York:
    Viking Press, 1968. First published in 1967.
Galpin, Francis William. *A Textbook of European Musical*
    Instruments: Their Origin, History and Character.
    Westport, Conn.: Greenwood Press, 1976. First published
    in 1956.
Geiringer, Karl. *Instruments in the History of Western Music.* 3rd
    ed. New York: Oxford University Press, 1978. First
    published as *Musical Instruments: Their History from the*
    Stone Age to the Present Day in 1943.
Marcuse, Sibyl. *A Survey of Musical Instruments.* New York:
    Harper & Row, 1975.
Remnant, Mary. *Musical Instruments: An Illustrated History*
    from Antiquity to the Present. London: B. T. Batsford,
    1989.
Sachs, Curt. *The History of Musical Instruments.* New York:
    W. W. Norton, 1940.

PICTORIAL SOURCES ON MUSIC HISTORY

Many sources on the history of music consist primarily of pictures, including pictorial biographies, a few of which appear above
in the lists of composer biographies. Other important types of iconographical sources include catalogues of individual musical instrument collections and exhibitions. The following bibliography is a
selection of the more important comprehensive sources of this sort,
divided into works that concern music history in general and those
that concern musical instruments.

The "General" list includes the work, still in progress, that
is already the last word on the subject, *Musikgeschichte in Bil-*
dern, which consists of four multivolume series, as well as the
better-known one-volume picture histories (Kinsky, Lang, Lesure,
Pincherle). Beck and Roth is a study of historic prints with musical
subjects, and Collaer and van der Linden is a unique musical atlas
that also contains many pictures.

In the "Instruments and Ensembles" list, all the sources are
comprehensive treatments of the subject except the more specialized studies by Bowles and Winternitz (*Musical Instruments and*
Their Symbolism) and the historic works by Buonanni and Praetorius. For other discussions of the history of instruments that are not

primarily pictorial, see "Histories of Musical Instruments," p. 148 above. For further information, see Frederick Crane, *A Bibliography of the Iconography of Music* (Iowa City: University of Iowa, 1971); and Howard Mayer Brown's *New Grove* article "Iconography of Music."

General

Beck, Sydney, and Elizabeth E. Roth. *Music in Prints.* New York: New York Public Library, 1965.

Besseler, Heinrich, and Max Schneider, eds. **Musikgeschichte in Bildern.** Leipzig: Deutscher Verlag für Musik, 1961–. (Republication in English translation, Jeffery Kite-Powell et al., gen. eds., Gainesville: University Press of Florida, forthcoming.)

> Series 1. *Musikethnologie.*
> Series 2. *Musik des Altertums.*
> Series 3. *Musik des Mittelalters und der Renaissance.*
> Series 4. *Oper, Konzert, Privates Musizieren, 1600–1900.*

Collaer, Paul, and Albert van der Linden. *Historical Atlas of Music: A Comprehensive Study of the World's Music, Past and Present.* Translated by Allan Miller. Cleveland: World Publishing, 1968. First published in 1960.

Kinsky, Georg, et al., eds. *A History of Music in Pictures.* New York: Dover, 1951. First published in 1930.

Lang, Paul Henry, and Otto Bettman. *A Pictorial History of Music.* New York: W. W. Norton, 1960.

Lesure, François. *Music and Art in Society.* Translated by Denis and Sheila Stevens. University Park: Pennsylvania State University Press, 1968. First published in 1966.

Pincherle, Marc. *An Illustrated History of Music.* Rev. ed. Edited by Georges and Rosamond Bernier. Translated by Rollo Myers. New York: Reynal, 1962. First published in 1959.

Instruments and Ensembles

Baines, Anthony. *European and American Musical Instruments.* New York: Viking Press, 1966.

Bowles, Edmund A. *Musical Ensembles in Festival Books, 1500–1800: An Iconographical and Documentary Survey.*

Studies in Musicology, no. 103. Ann Arbor, Mich.: UMI
Research Press, 1989.

Bragard, Roger, and Ferdinand J. de Hen. *Musical Instruments in
Art and History.* Translated by Bill Hopkins. New York:
Viking Press, 1968. First published in 1967.

Buchner, Alexander. *Folk Music Instruments.* Translated by
Alzbeta Nováková. New York: Crown Publishers, 1972.
First published in 1968.

———. *Musical Instruments: An Illustrated History.* Translated
by Borek Vancurel. New York: Crown Publishers, 1973.
First published in 1956. An earlier translation called
Musical Instruments through the Ages was also first
published in 1956; 4th ed., 1962. There is also an enlarged
version in German: *Musikinstrumente von dem Anfängen
bis zur Gegenwart.* Translated by Otto Guth. Prague: Artia,
1972.

Buonanni, Filippo. *Descrizione degli'stromenti armonici d'ogni
genere del padre Bonanni.* [2nd ed., 1776.] First published
in 1722. Reprint of the 1776 ed.: Kassel: Bärenreiter, 1974.
The instrumental plates only are reprinted in *The
Showcase of Musical Instruments by Filippo Bonanni.* New
York: Dover Publications, 1964.

Harrison, Frank Ll., and Joan Rimmer. *European Musical
Instruments.* New York: W. W. Norton, 1964.

Montagu, Jeremy. *The World of Baroque & Classical Musical
Instruments.* Woodstock, N.Y.: Overlook Press, 1979.

———. *The World of Medieval & Renaissance Musical
Instruments.* Woodstock, N.Y.: Overlook Press, 1976.

Munrow, David. *Instruments of the Middle Ages and Renaissance.*
London: Oxford University Press, 1976.

Praetorius, Michael. *Syntagma Musicum II* [1618]: *De
Organographia, Parts I and II.* Translated and edited by
David Z. Crookes. Early Music Series, no. 7. London:
Oxford University Press, 1986.

Remnant, Mary. *Musical Instruments: An Illustrated History
from Antiquity to the Present.* London: B. T. Batsford,
1989.

Winternitz, Emanuel. *Musical Instruments and Their Symbolism
in Western Art.* 2nd ed. New Haven: Yale University Press,
1979. First published in 1967.

———. *Musical Instruments of the Western World.* London:
Thames and Hudson, 1966.

CHAPTER SIX

Current Research Journals
in Music

This chapter consists of a representative listing of scholarly research journals in music that are currently being published. The oldest is the durable *Musical Times;* among the newest are several journals (e.g., *Performance Practice Review*) that began publication in the last few years. It is in journals of this sort that new research is most likely to be reported, rather than in the host of periodicals concerned with current musical events, individual instruments, the opera scene, etc.

The list is by no means complete, but a fairly broad selection has been made. The most thorough is in the area of musicology, but other types of research journals are included, as indicated by the subdivisions of this listing. These subdivisions, however, are not rigid; e.g., a general musicological journal may carry an article of a more theoretical or ethnomusicological nature. Furthermore, among the musicology journals listed as being of a general nature, some are more so than others, in which, for example, a period or national emphasis is apparent.

The information given about each periodical specifies country of publication, frequency of appearance, first year of publication, and whether the journal is the official organ of a society or issues from a university music department or research institute. Consult the key to abbreviations preceding the list.

For other lists of music periodicals, see chapter 2 under "Periodicals," p. 23 above; for indexes of periodical articles, see under "Periodical Articles," p. 24 above.

Key to Countries: Key to Frequency of Publication:

Af   Africa   12   monthly
Au   Australia   8   eight times a year

Aus	Austria	6	six times a year
B	Belgium	4	quarterly
C	Canada	3	three times a year
E	England	2	semiannual
F	France	1	annual
G	Germany	o	occasional, irregular
Ho	Holland		
Hu	Hungary		
int	international		
Is	Israel		
I	Italy		
Sp	Spain		
Sw	Switzerland		
US	United States		

Musicology

BIBLIOGRAPHY

Fontes Artis Musicae: Review of the International Association of Music Libraries, Archives and Documentation Centres. 1954–. (int/4 from 1976)

Notes: Quarterly Journal of the Music Library Association. Nos. 1–15: 1934–42; series 2: 1943–. (US/4 [ser. 2])

HISTORICAL MUSICOLOGY

Acta Musicologica. International Musicological Society/Sociéte Internationale de Musicologie. 1928–. (int/2)

Archiv für Musikwissenschaft. 1918–26; 1952–. (G/4)

Current Musicology. Music Department, Columbia University. 1965–. (US/2)

The Journal of Musicological Research (originally *Music and Man,* 1973–79). 1979–. (E/4)

The Journal of Musicology: A Quarterly Review of Music History, Criticism, Analysis, and Performance Practice. 1982–. (US/4)

Journal of the American Musicological Society. 1948–. (US/3)

Journal of the Royal Musical Association (replaced *Proceedings of the Royal Musical Association,* 1874–1986 [E/1]). 1987–. (E/2)

Music & Letters. 1920–. (E/4)

Music Research Forum. College-Conservatory of Music, University of Cincinnati. 1986–. (US/1)

The Music Review. 1940–. (E/4)
The Musical Quarterly. 1915–. (US/4)
The Musical Times. 1844–. (E/12)
Musicology Australia: Journal of the Musicological Society of Australia (originally *Musicology,* 1964–82). 1985–. (Au/1)
Die Musikforschung. Gesellschaft für Musikforschung. 1948–. (G/4)
Nuova rivista musicale italiana. 1967–. (I/4)
Orbis Musicae. Department of Musicology, Tel-Aviv University. 1971–. (Is/o)
Recercare: rivista per lo studio e la pratica della musica antica (succeeded *Il flauto dolce,* 1971–88). Società Italiana del Flauto Dolce. 1989–. (I/1)
Repercussions: Critical and Alternative Viewpoints on Music and Scholarship. Department of Music, University of California, Berkeley. 1992–. (US/2)
Revista de musicología. Sociedad Española de Musicología. 1978–. (Sp/2)
Revue belge de musicologie/Belgisch Tijdschrift voor Muziekwetenschap. Société belge de musicologie. 1946–. (B/1)
Revue de musicologie. Société Française de Musicologie. 1917–. (F/2)
La revue musicale. 1920–. (F/o)
Rivista italiana di musicologia. Società Italiana di Musicologia. 1966–. (I/2)
Schweizerische Musikzeitung/Revue musicale suisse. 1862–. (Sw/6)
Studia Musicologica Academiae Scientiarum Hungaricae. 1961–. (Hu/2)
Studies in Music. Department of Music, University of Western Australia. 1967–. (Au/2)
Studies in Music from the University of Western Ontario. 1976–. (C/1)
Tijdschrift van de Vereniging voor Nederlandse Musiekgeschiedenis. 1882–. (Ho/2)
Yearbook of Musicology. 1993–. (US/1)

Limited to a Country and/or Period

American Music: A Quarterly Journal Devoted to All Aspects of American Music and Music in America. Sonneck Society. 1983–. (US/4)
Early Music History: Studies in Medieval and Early Modern History. 1981–. (E/1)

Musica Disciplina: A Yearbook of the History of Music. American
    Institute of Musicology. 1946–. (int/1)
19th-Century Music. 1977–. (US/3)
*Plainsong & Medieval Music: The Journal of the Plainsong and
    Medieval Music Society.* 1992–. (E/2)
"Recherches" sur la musique française classique. La vie musicale
    en France sous les rois Bourbons. 1960–. (F/1 or o)
Revue international de musique française. Société Internationale
    de Musique Française. 1980–. (int/3)

Limited to a Single Composer

*Bach: The Journal of the Riemenschneider Bach Institute in
    Affiliation with the American Chapter of the New Bach
    Society.* Baldwin-Wallace College. 1970–. (US/3)
Bach-Jahrbuch. Neue Bach-Gesellschaft. 1904–. (G/1)
Beethoven-Jahrbuch. 2nd series. Veröffentlichungen des
    Beethovenhauses in Bonn. 1953/54–. (G/1)
Händel-Jahrbuch. Georg-Friedrich-Händel-Gesellschaft. 1955–.
    (G/1)
Haydn-Studien. Joseph Haydn Institut. 1965–. (G/1)
Journal of the American Liszt Society. 1977–. (US/2)
Journal of the Arnold Schoenberg Institute. University of
    Southern California School of Music. 1976–. (US/2)
Mozart-Jahrbuch. Internationalen Stiftung Mozarteum. 1941–43,
    1950–. (Aus/1)
Schütz-Jahrbuch. Internationalen Heinrich-Schütz-Gesellschaft.
    1979–. (G/1)

Iconography

*Imago Musicae: International Yearbook of Musical
    Iconography/Internationales Jahrbuch für
    Musikikonographie/Annuaire international d'iconographie
    musicale.* Répertoire International de l'Iconographie
    Musicale/International Repertory of Musical
    Iconography/Internationales Repertorium der
    Musikikonographie. (int/1) 1984–.
RIdIM/RCMI Newsletter. Répertoire International de
    l'Iconographie Musicale/International Repertory of Musical
    Iconography/Internationales Repertorium der
    Musikikonographie. Research Center for Musical
    Iconography, City University of New York. 1971–. (int/o)

PERFORMANCE PRACTICE

Basler Jahrbuch für historische Musikpraxis: Eine Veröffentlichung
    der Schola Cantorum Basiliensis Lehr- und
    Forschungsinstitut für alte Musik an der Musik-Akademie
    der Stadt Basel. 1977–. (Sw/1)
Early Music. 1973–. (E/4)
Historical Performance: The Journal of Early Music America.
    1988–. (US/2)
The Journal of Musicology: A Quarterly Review of Music History,
    Criticism, Analysis, and Performance Practice. 1982–.
    (US/4)
Performance Practice Review. Music Department, The Claremont
    Graduate School. 1988–. (US/2) (The Fall issue includes an
    annual update of *Performance Practice, Medieval to*
    Contemporary: A Bibliographic Guide; see p. 69 above.)

Ethnomusicology

African Music: Journal of the International Library of African
    Music/Journal de la Discothèque Internationale de Musique
    Africaine. 1954–. (Af/o)
Asian Music: Journal of the Society for Asian Music. 1968–.
    (US/2)
Ethnomusicology: Journal of the Society for Ethnomusicology.
    1953–. (US/3)
Inter-American Music Review. 1978–. (US/2)
Latin American Music Review/Revista de música latino-
    americana. Institute of Latin American Studies, University
    of Texas. 1980–. (US/2)
Musica Asiatica. 1977–. (E/o)
Popular Music and Society. Department of Sociology, Bowling
    Green State University. 1971–. (US/4)
Selected Reports in Ethnomusicology. University of California.
    1966–. (US/o)
The World of Music: Journal of the International Institute for
    Traditional Music (IITM). 1957–. (int/3)
Yearbook for Inter-American Musical Research/Anuario
    interamericano de investigacion musical/Anuário
    interamericano de pesquisa musical. 1965–. (US/1)

Music Theory and New Music

Analyse musicale. Société Française d'Analyse Musicale. 1985–.
     (F/4)
Contemporary Music Review. 1984–. (E/o)
Gamut. Georgia Association of Music Theorists. 1984–. (US/1)
In Theory Only. Michigan Music Theory Society, University of
     Michigan. 1975–. (US/o)
Indiana Theory Review. Graduate Theory Association, School of
     Music, Indiana University. 1977–. (US/2)
Intégral: The Journal of Applied Musical Thought. Eastman
     Theory Association, Eastman School of Music. 1987–.
     (US/1)
Interface: Journal of New Music Research. University of Ghent,
     University of Utrecht, Royal Conservatory of the Hague.
     1972–. (Ho/4)
Journal of Music Theory. Yale School of Music. 1957–. (US/2)
Journal of Music Theory Pedagogy. Gail Boyd Stwolinski Center
     for Music Theory Pedagogy, School of Music, University of
     Oklahoma. 1987–. (US/2)
Music Analysis. 1982–. (E/3)
Music Theory Online. Society for Music Theory. 1993–. (US/6) An
     "electronic journal." Subscribers receive only the table of
     contents, then may request and receive individual articles
     via E-mail.
*Music Theory Spectrum: The Journal of the Society for Music
     Theory.* 1979–. (US/2)
Musiktheorie. 1986–. (G/3)
Perspectives of New Music. Fromm Music Foundation. 1962–.
     (US/2)
Theoria: Historical Aspects of Music Theory. School of Music,
     North Texas State University. 1985–. (US/1)
Theory and Practice. Journal of The Music Theory Society of New
     York State and The Graduate Center of the City University
     of New York. 1974–. (US/2)

Performing Instrument, Medium, or Genre

*American Choral Review: The Official Journal of the American
     Choral Foundation, Inc.* 1958–. (US/4)
Annual Review of Jazz Studies (originally *Journal of Jazz Studies,*
     1973–81). Rutgers Institute of Jazz Studies. 1982–. (US/1)

Black Music Research Journal. Center for Black Music Research,
      Columbia College, Chicago. 1981–. (US/2)
Cambridge Opera Journal. 1989–. (E/3)
Early Keyboard Journal. Journal of the Southeastern Historical
      Keyboard Society. 1982/83–. (US/1)
Galpin Society Journal. 1948–. (E/1)
Historic Brass Society Journal. 1989–. (US/1)
The Horn Call Annual. Journal of the International Horn Society.
      1989–. (int/1)
Jahrbuch für Opernforschung. 1985–. (G/1)
Journal of Band Research. American Bandmasters Association.
      1964–. (US/2)
Journal of Research in Singing and Applied Vocal Pedagogy.
      Official Publication of the International Association for
      Research in Singing. 1977–. (int/2)
Journal of the American Musical Instrument Society. 1974–.
      (US/1)
Journal of the Viola da Gamba Society of America. 1964–. (US/1)
Journal of the Violin Society of America. 1975–. (US/3)
The Opera Quarterly. 1983–. (US/4)
L'organo: rivista di cultura organaria e organistica. 1960–. (I/2)
Tibia: Magazin für Freunde alte und neuer Bläsermusik. 1976–.
      (G/4)

Music Education

Australian Journal of Music Education. Australian Society for
      Music Education. 1969–. (Au/1)
British Journal of Music Education. 1984–. (E/3)
The Bulletin of Historical Research in Music Education.
      Department of Music Education and Music Therapy,
      University of Kansas. 1980–. (US/2)
The Bulletin of Research. Pennsylvania Music Educators
      Association. 1963–. (US/1)
Bulletin of the Council for Research in Music Education. 1963–.
      (US/4)
Canadian Music Educator/Musicien educateur au Canada.
      Canadian Music Educators Association/Association
      Canadienne des Educateurs de Musique. 1959–. (C/4)
Contributions to Music Education. Ohio Music Education
      Association. 1972–. (US/1)
International Journal of Music Education. International Society of
      Music Education. 1983–. (int/2)

Journal of Research in Music Education. Society for Research in Music Education, of the Music Educators National Conference. 1953–. (US/4)

Missouri Journal of Research in Music Education. Missouri Music Educators Association. 1962–. (US/1)

Music in Early Childhood: A Research Journal. The David K. Sengstack Foundation for Childhood Enrichment. 1991–. (US/2)

The Quarterly Journal of Music Teaching and Learning. University of Northern Colorado School of Music. 1990–. (US/4)

Southeastern Journal of Music Education. University of Georgia Center for Continuing Education. 1989–. (US/1)

Update: Applications of Research in Music Education. Music Educators National Conference. 1982–. (US/2)

Other Journals

Choreography and Dance: An International Journal. 1992–. (int/o)

Computer Music Journal. 1977–. (US/4)

Computers in Music Research. Wisconsin Center for Music Technology, University of Wisconsin at Madison. 1989–. (US/1)

Criticus Musicus: A Journal of Music Criticism. 1993–. (int/3)

Dance Research. Society for Dance Research. 1983–. (E/2)

International Review of the Aesthetics and Sociology of Music. Institute of Musicology, Academy of Music, Zagreb, Yugoslovia. 1970–. (int/2)

The Journal of Aesthetic Education. University of Illinois and the Illinois Department of Public Instruction. 1966–. (US/4)

The Journal of Aesthetics and Art Criticism. American Society for Aesthetics. 1941–. (US/4)

The Journal of Music Therapy. National Association for Music Therapy. 1964–. (US/4)

Medical Problems of Performing Artists. 1986–. (US/4)

Music Perception: An Interdisciplinary Journal. 1983–. (US/4)

Open Ear: A Publication Dedicated to Sound and Music in Health and Education. 1993–. (US/4)

Psychology of Music. Society for Research in the Psychology of Music and Music Education. 1973–. (E/2)

Psychomusicology: A Journal of Research in Music Cognition. 1981–. (US/ 2 or o)

Editions of Music

This chapter opens with a list of sources of information about music notation and editing. Of the three lists of musical editions that follow, "Historical Sets and Monuments" and "Composers' Complete Works and Catalogues" are of a more scholarly nature, while the "Anthologies of Music" list is of a more practical intent. These lists vary in degree of selectivity and format, including representative publications rather than all or even most items in a particular category. For guides to the contents of these editions of music, see chapter 2 under "Music—Editions of Music," p. 40 above.

SOURCES IN ENGLISH ON MUSIC NOTATION AND EDITING

The three lists that follow are of basic sources in English that treat the notation and editing of music, and are applicable to the reproduction of music, whether the method used is handwriting, music typing, engraving, or the rapidly growing field of computer software programs. The first list is of general sources on the history and practice of notation and music printing. It includes two of the most widely respected manuals of notation and music reproduction, Read and Ross, each of which begins with a historical summary of its subject; the three standard histories of notation, Apel, Parrish, and especially Rastall; Bent's relevant article in *The New Grove Dictionary*; and Krummel and Sadie's handbook, *Music Printing and Publishing*, an update of the extensive earlier *New Grove* article on that topic.

The second list comprises important sources dealing with the specialized area of editing early music and includes general or com-

prehensive discussions, those by Broude, Brown, Caldwell, Carapetyan, Dart, Emery, and Stevens, as well as treatments of
individual aspects—authenticating sources, *musica ficta*, watermarks and paper analysis, handwriting, etc. The Festschrift edited
by Borroff is a series of transcriptions of music arranged in chronological order, each accompanied by a discussion of editorial
method, resulting in a kind of history of notation in examples.
Cudworth's article is a unique and helpful source of information
about certain matters—commonly misattributed, nicknamed, and
misnamed compositions; pseudonyms and divergent spellings of
composers' names—that are important to know when identifying
and editing works to which they pertain.

The third list brings together works from about the last twenty-
five years treating the notation of new music.

General Sources

Apel, Willi. *The Notation of Polyphonic Music 900–1600.* 5th ed.,
    rev. and with commentary. Cambridge, Mass.: Mediaeval
    Academy of America, 1953. First published in 1942.

Bent, Ian D., et al. "Notation." In *The New Grove Dictionary of
    Music and Musicians.* Vol. 13, pp. 333–420.

Krummel, D. W. *The Literature of Music Bibliography: An
    Account of the Writings on Music Printing and Publishing.*
    Fallen Leaf Reference Books in Music, no. 21. Berkeley,
    Calif.: Fallen Leaf Press, 1992.

Krummel, D. W., and Stanley Sadie, eds. *Music Printing and
    Publishing.* 1st American ed. The Norton/Grove
    Handbooks in Music. New York: W. W. Norton, 1990. First
    published in 1989.

Parrish, Carl. *The Notation of Medieval Music.* Reprint of
    corrected 1959 ed. With a new introduction by J. W.
    McKinnon. New York: W. W. Norton, 1978. First published
    in 1957.

Rastall, Richard. *The Notation of Western Music: An
    Introduction.* 1st U.S. ed. New York: St. Martin's Press,
    1982.

Read, Gardner. *Music Notation: A Manual of Modern Practice.*
    2nd ed. Boston: Crescendo Publishers, 1969. First
    published in 1964.

Ross, Ted. *The Art of Music Engraving and Processing: A
    Complete Manual, Reference and Text Book on Preparing
    Music for Reproduction and Print.* Miami: Hansen Books,
    1970.

Editing Early Music

Berger, Karol. *Musica Ficta: Theories of Accidental Inflections in Vocal Polyphony from Marchetto da Padova to Gioseffo Zarlino.* Cambridge: Cambridge University Press, 1987.

Borroff, Edith. *Notations and Editions: A Book in Honor of Louise Cuyler.* Dubuque, Iowa: Wm. C. Brown Company Publishers, 1974.

Broude, Ronald. "Editing Early Music: Some Notes on Procedure and Presentation." *The Choral Journal* 21 (January 1981): 5, 8–12.

Brown, Howard Mayer. "Editing." In *The New Grove Dictionary of Music and Musicians.* Vol. 5, pp. 839–48.

Caldwell, John. *Editing Early Music.* Early Music Series, vol. 5. Oxford: Clarendon Press, 1985.

Carapetyan, Armen. "Problems of Editing and Publishing Old Music." *Musica Disciplina* 15 (1961): 5–14.

Cudworth, Charles L. "Ye Olde Spuriosity Shoppe, or, Put It in the Anhang." *Notes* 12 (December 1954): 25–40, (September 1955): 533–53.

Dart, Thurston. *The Interpretation of Music.* 4th rev. reimpression. London: Hutchinson's University Library, 1960. Chapter 2: "The Editor's Task," pp. 18–28. First published in 1954.

Emery, Walter. *Editions and Musicians: A Survey of the Duties of Practical Musicians and Editors towards the Classics.* Reprinted with additions. London: Novello, 1958. First published in 1957.

Krummel, Donald W. "Guide for Dating Early Music: A Synopsis." *Fontes Artis Musicae* 18 (January-August 1971): 40–59.

LaRue, Jan. "Watermarks and Musicology." *Acta Musicologica* 33 (April-December 1961): 120–46.

LaRue, Jan, with J. S. G. Simmons. "Watermarks." *The New Grove Dictionary of Music and Musicians.* Vol. 20, pp. 228–31.

Routley, Nicholas. "A Practical Guide to *Musica Ficta*." *Early Music* 13 (February 1985): 59–71.

Spector, Stephen, ed. *Essays in Paper Analysis.* London: Associated University Presses, 1987.

Stevens, Denis. *Musicology: A Practical Guide.* 1st American ed. Yehudi Menuhin Music Guides. New York: Schirmer Books, 1981.

Winternitz, Emanuel. *Musical Autographs from Monteverdi to Hindemith*. Enl. and corrected ed. 2 vols. New York: Dover Publications, 1965. First published in 1955.

Wolf, Jean K., and Eugene K. Wolf. "Rastrology and Its Use in Eighteenth-Century Manuscript Studies." In Eugene K. Wolf and Edward H. Roesner, eds., *Studies in Musical Sources and Style: Essays in Honor of Jan LaRue*. Madison, Wisc.: A-R Editions, 1990. Pp. 237–91.

New Notation

Cole, Hugo. *Sounds and Signs: Aspects of Musical Notation*. London: Oxford University Press, 1974.

Cope, David. *New Music Notation*. Dubuque, Iowa: Kendall-Hunt Publishing, 1976.

Karkoschka, Erhard. *Notation in New Music: A Critical Guide to Interpretation and Realisation*. Translated by Ruth Koenig. New York: Praeger, 1972. First published in 1966.

Pooler, Frank, and Brent Pierce. *New Choral Notation: A Handbook*. New York: Walton Music, 1971.

Read, Gardner. *Modern Rhythmic Notation*. Bloomington: Indiana University Press, 1978.

————. *Source Book of Proposed Music Notation Reforms*. Music Reference Collection, no. 11. New York: Greenwood Press, 1987.

————. *20th-Century Microtonal Notation*. Contributions to the Study of Music and Dance, no. 18. New York: Greenwood Press, 1990.

Risatti, Howard A. *New Music Vocabulary: A Guide to Notational Signs for Contemporary Music*. Urbana: University of Illinois Press, 1975.

Stone, Kurt. *Music Notation in the Twentieth Century: A Practical Guidebook*. New York: W. W. Norton, 1980.

Warfield, Gerald. *Writings on Contemporary Music Notation: An Annotated Bibliography*. MLA Index and Bibliography Series, no. 16. Ann Arbor, Mich.: Music Library Association, 1976.

HISTORICAL SETS AND MONUMENTS OF MUSIC

The following selection from the many historical sets and monuments of music shows something of their diversity, as indicated by the various categories into which they fall. They also vary greatly in degree and type of scholarliness (i.e., amount of scholarly apparatus, length of preface, presence or absence of critical commentary, type of editorial method, and "user friendliness") as well as in size, ranging from a handful of volumes up to hundreds per set (e.g., *Corpus Mensurabilis Musicae, Diletto musicale*). The volumes in some sets are large, each containing many works or a single lengthy work (e.g., *Denkmäler der Tonkunst in Österreich, Musica Britannica*); at the other end of the continuum are the scholarly performing editions, such as *Nagels Musik-Archiv* and *Cantio Sacra*, most of which contain a single short work or small set of works per volume.

Some of the growing output of facsimile reprint series have been included in the list (e.g., *The Italian Cantata in the Seventeenth Century, The London Pianoforte School*), even though they are not strictly speaking *editions* of music.

In the interest of simplicity and space-saving, editorial and publication information has been abbreviated; in many of the larger sets it may change from time to time, and to attempt to give all of it would serve little purpose. For most of the items in the list complete bibliographic information may be found in Hill and Stephens; see p. 41 above.

Limited to an Era

Concentus Musicus: Veröffentlichungen der Musikgeschichtlichen Abteilung des Deutschen Historischen Instituts in Rom. Cologne: Arno Volk Verlag, etc., 1973–.

Corpus Mensurabilis Musicae [CMM]. [Rome]: American Institute of Musicology, 1947–.

The Eighteenth-Century Continuo Sonata. 10 vols. New York: Garland Publishing, 1991.

Institute of Mediaeval Music: Collected Works/Gesamtausgabe. Brooklyn, N.Y.: Institute of Mediaeval Music, 1957–.

Masters and Monuments of the Renaissance. Leeman L. Perkins, gen. ed. New York: Broude Trust, 1980–.

Monumenta Monodica Medii Aevi. Edited by Bruno Stäblein. Kassel: Bärenreiter, 1956–.

Monuments of Music and Music Literature in Facsimile. First Series—Music. New York: Broude Brothers, 1965–.

Monuments of Renaissance Music. Edward Lowinsky, gen. ed. Chicago: University of Chicago Press, 1964–.

The 19th Century/Das 19. Jahrhundert/Le 19ᵉ siècle. Kassel: Bärenreiter, 1969–.

Paléographie musicale. Solesmes: Imprimerie Saint-Pierre, etc., 1889–1958, 1969–.

Polyphonic Music of the Fourteenth Century. Kurt von Fischer, gen. ed. Monaco: Editions de l'Oiseau-Lyre, 1956–.

Publikationen älterer praktischer und theoretischer Musikwerke, vorzugsweise des XV. und XVI. Jahrhunderts. 29 vols. Leipzig: Breitkopf & Härtel, etc., 1873–1905.

Recent Researches in the Music of the Baroque Era. Christoph Wolff, gen. ed. Madison, Wis.: A-R Editions, 1964–.

Recent Researches in the Music of the Classical Era. Eugene K. Wolf, gen. ed. Madison, Wis.: A-R Editions, 1975–.

Recent Researches in the Music of the Middle Ages and Early Renaissance. Charles M. Atkinson, gen. ed. Madison, Wis.: A-R Editions, 1975–.

Recent Researches in the Music of the Nineteenth and Early Twentieth Centuries. Rufus Hallmark and D. Kern Holoman, gen. eds. Madison, Wis.: A-R Editions, 1979–.

Recent Researches in the Music of the Renaissance. James Haar, gen. ed. Madison, Wis.: A-R Editions, 1964–.

Renaissance Music in Facsimile. Edited by Howard Mayer Brown et al. 50 vols. New York: Garland Publishing, 1986–88.

Seventeenth-Century Keyboard Music. Alexander Silbiger, gen. ed. 28 vols. New York: Garland Publishing, 1987–89.

The Sixteenth-Century Chanson. Edited by Jane A. Bernstein. 30 vols. projected. New York: Garland Publishing, 1987–.

The Sixteenth-Century Motet. Edited by Richard Sherr. 30 vols. projected. New York: Garland Publishing, 1987–.

Thesauri Musici: Musik des 15., 16. und beginnenden 17. Jahrhunderts/Music of the 15th, 16th and the Beginning of the 17th Centuries. Edited by Walter Pass. Vienna: L. Doblinger, 1971–.

Three Centuries of Music in Score. Edited by Kenneth Cooper. 13 vols. New York: Garland Publishing, 1988–90.

Unbekannte Werke der Klassik und Romantik. Munich: Walter Wollenweber, [1969–].

Limited to a Region

L'arte musicale in Italia. Edited by Luigi Torchi. 7 vols. Milan: G. Ricordi, 1897–1908.

Biblioteca de Catalunya: publicacions del Departament de Música. Barcelona: Institut d'Estudis Catalans, etc., 1921–.

I classici musicali italiani. 15 vols. Milan: I Classici Musicali Italiani, 1941–43, 1956.

Denkmäler der Tonkunst in Bayern [DTB]. Denkmäler deutscher Tonkunst, ser. 2. 38 vols. Wiesbaden: Breitkopf & Härtel, etc., 1900–38. Rev. ed., 1962–. New series, 1967–.

Denkmäler der Tonkunst in Österreich [DTÖ]. Vienna: Artaria, etc., 1894–.

Denkmäler deutscher Tonkunst [DDT]. 1st series. 65 vols. Leipzig: Breitkopf & Härtel, 1892–1931. Reprint: 65 vols. + 2 suppl. vols., Wiesbaden: Breitkopf & Härtel, 1957–61.

Denkmäler rheinischer Musik. Düsseldorf, etc.: Musikverlag Schwann, 1951–.

Das Erbe deutscher Musik. Wiesbaden: Breitkopf & Härtel, etc.: 1935–.

Monumenta Musica Neerlandica. Amsterdam: Nederlandse Muziekgeschiedenis, 1959–.

Monumenta Musicae Belgicae. Berchem: "De Ring," etc., 1932–51, 1960–.

Monumentos de la música española. Barcelona: Consejo Superior de Investigaciones Científicas, etc., 1941–.

Music of the United States of America. Published for the American Musicological Society. Madison, Wis.: A-R Editions, 1993–.

Musica Antiqua Bohemica. Prague: Artia, etc., 1949–.

Musica Britannica: A National Collection of Music. London: Stainer and Bell, 1951–. (Some volumes issued in revised editions.)

Portugaliae Musica. Lisbon: Fundação Calouste Gulbenkian, 1959–.

Recent Researches in American Music. H. Wiley Hitchcock, gen. ed. Madison, Wis.: A-R Editions, 1977–.

Schweizerische Musikdenkmäler/Monuments de la musique suisse. Basel: Bärenreiter, etc., 1955–.

Limited to an Era and a Region

Early English Church Music. London: Stainer and Bell, 1963–.

The English Lute-Songs. Edited by Edmund H. Fellowes. Ser. 2, rev. ed. Revised by Thurston Dart. London: Stainer and Bell, 1959–69. First published in 1920–32 as *The English School of Lutenist Song Writers*, 2nd series.

The English Madrigalists. Edited by Edmund H. Fellowes. Rev. ed. Edited by Thurston Dart. London: Stainer and Bell, 1956–. First published in 1913–24 as *The English Madrigalist School*.

Maîtres anciens de la musique française. Paris: Heugel, etc.,
    1966–.
Les maîtres musiciens de la renaissance française. Edited by
    Henry Expert. 22 vols. Paris: Alphonse Leduc, 1894–1908.
Monuments de la musique française au temps de la renaissance.
    Edited by Henry Expert. 10 vols. Paris: Maurice Senart,
    1924–29. New series, Paris: Editions Salabert, 1958–.
The Old English Edition. Edited by G. E. P. Arkwright. 25 vols.
    London: Joseph Williams, 1899–1902.
*Polyphonies du XIIIe siècle: le manuscrit H 196 de la Faculté de
    Médecine de Montpellier.* Edited by Yvonne Rokseth. 4
    vols. Paris: Editions de l'Oiseau-Lyre, 1935–39.
*Treize livres de motets parus chez Pierre Attaingnant en 1534 et
    1535.* Edited by Albert Smijers. 14 vols. Paris: Editions de
    l'Oiseau-Lyre, 1934–36, 1960–64.
Tudor Church Music. 10 vols. + appendix. London: Oxford
    University Press, 1922–29, 1948.
*Van Ockeghem tot Sweelinck: Nederlandse Muziekgeschiedenis in
    Voorbeelden.* Edited by Albert Smijers. 7 vols. Amsterdam:
    G. Alsbach, 1949–56.

Limited to a Medium or Genre

Instrumental Ensemble

Alte Musik. Munich: F. E. C. Leuckart, 1924–.
Ars Instrumentalis: Konzertante Werke alter Meister. Hamburg:
    Musikverlag Hans Sikorski, 1953–.
Consortium: Eine Spiel- und Kammermusik-Reihe. Edited by
    Helmut Mönkemeyer. Wilhelmshaven: Heinrichshofen's
    Verlag, 1963–.
Diletto musicale: Doblingers Reihe alter Musik. Vienna: L.
    Doblinger, 1955–.
Hortus Musicus. Kassel: Bärenreiter, 1936–. (Primarily
    instrumental.)
Ludus Instrumentalis: Kammermusik alter Meister. Hamburg:
    Musikverlag Hans Sikorski, 1950–.
Musica Instrumentalis. Zurich: Musikverlag vom Pelikan, 1954–.
Nagels Musik-Archiv. Kassel: Nagels Verlag, 1927–. (Primarily
    instrumental.)
The Symphony 1720–1840. Barry S. Brook, gen. ed. 61 vols. +
    index. New York: Garland Publishing, 1979–86.

KEYBOARD

Archives des maîtres de l'orgue des XVIᵉ, XVIIᵉ, et XVIIIᵉ siècles.
Edited by Alexandre Guilmant. 10 vols. Paris: A. Durand &
Fils, Editeurs, 1898–1910.
Cantantibus Organis: Sammlung von Orgelstücken alter Meister.
Edited by Eberhard Kraus. Regensburg: Friedrich Pustet,
etc., 1958–.
Corpus of Early Keyboard Music. Willi Apel, gen. ed. [Rome]:
American Institute of Musicology, 1963–.
The International Library of Piano Music. 13 vols. New York:
University Society, 1967.
Liber Organi. Mainz: B. Schott's Söhne, 1931–38, 1954–.
Die Orgel: Ausgewählte Werke zum praktischen Gebrauch.
Lippstadt, etc., Germany: Kistner & Siegel, 1957–.
Le trésor des pianistes. Foreword by Bea Friedland. 23 vols. New
York: Da Capo Press, 1977. First published in 1861–72.

LUTE, GUITAR

*Die Tabulatur: Ausgewählte Werke in ihrer Originalnotation mit
Übertragungen für Laute (oder ein Tasteninstrument) und
Gitarre.* Edited by Helmut Mönkemeyer. Hofheim am
Taunus, Germany: Friedrich Hofmeister, 1965–.

VOCAL

Cantio Sacra: Geistliche Solokantaten. Edited by Rudolf
Ewerhart. Cologne: Edmund Bieler, 1958–.
Das Chorwerk. Edited by Friedrich Blume. Wolfenbüttel: Möseler,
1929–39, 1956–.
Early Romantic Opera. Edited by Philip Gossett and Charles
Rosen. 44 vols. New York: Garland Publishing, 1978–83.

Limited to a Medium or Genre and to a Region

Chefs d'oeuvre classiques de l'opéra français. 40 vols. Leipzig:
Breitkopf & Härtel, 1880.
The Eighteenth-Century French Cantata. Edited by David Tunley.
17 vols. projected. New York: Garland Publishing, 1990–.
*English Song 1600–1675: Facsimiles of Twenty-six Manuscripts
and an Edition of the Texts.* Edited by Elise Bickford
Jorgens. 12 vols. New York: Garland Publishing, 1986–87.

German Opera 1770–1800. Edited by Thomas Bauman. 17 vols. New York: Garland Publishing, 1985–86.

The Italian Cantata in the Seventeenth Century. Carolyn Gianturco, gen. ed. 16 vols. New York: Garland Publishing, 1985–86.

Italian Instrumental Music of the Sixteenth and Early Seventeenth Centuries. Edited by James Ladewig. 30 vols. projected. New York: Garland Publishing, 1987–.

Italian Opera 1640–1770. Edited by Howard Mayer Brown. 91 vols. New York: Garland Publishing, 1977–83.

Italian Opera 1810–1840. Edited by Philip Gossett. 25 vols. projected. New York: Garland Publishing, 1985–.

The Italian Oratorio 1650–1800: Works in a Central Baroque and Classic Tradition. Edited by Joyce L. Johnson and Howard E. Smither. 31 vols. New York: Garland Publishing, 1986–87.

Italian Secular Song 1606–1636: A Seven-Volume Reprint Collection. Edited by Gary Tomlinson. 7 vols. New York: Garland Publishing, 1986.

The London Pianoforte School 1766–1860: Clementi, Dussek, Cogan, Cramer, Field, Pinto, Sterndale Bennett, and Other Masters of the Pianoforte. Nicholas Temperley, gen. ed. 20 vols. New York: Garland Publishing, 1984–86.

Sixteenth-Century Madrigal. Edited by Jessie Ann Owens. 30 vols. projected. New York: Garland Publishing, 1987–.

Solo Motets from the Seventeenth Century: Facsimiles of Prints from the Italian Baroque. Edited by Anne Schnoebelen. 10 vols. New York: Garland Publishing, 1987–89.

Tallis to Wesley: English Organ Music . . . from the Sixteenth to the Nineteenth Centuries. London: Hinrichsen, 1956–.

Without Specific Limitations

Accademia musicale. Charles Sherman, gen. ed. Mainz, etc.: Universal Edition, 1969–.

Antiqua: Eine Sammlung alter Musik. Mainz: B. Schott's Söhne, 1966–.

Collegium Musicum. [New Haven]: Department of Music, Graduate School, Yale University, 1955–65. 2nd series: *Collegium Musicum: Yale University.* Madison, Wis.: A-R Editions, 1969–.

Harvard Publications in Music. Cambridge: Harvard University Press, 1967–.

Mitteldeutsches Musikarchiv: Veröffentlichungen des Musikwissen-
schaftlichen Seminars der Friedrich-Schiller-Universität
Jena. Leipzig: Breitkopf & Härtel, 1953–.
Music in Facsimile. New York: Garland Publishing, 1983–.
Musik alter Meister: Beiträge zur Musik- und Kulturgeschichte
Innerösterreichs. Edited by Hellmut Federhofer. Graz:
Akademische Druck- und Verlagsanstalt, 1954–.
Musikalische Denkmäler. Mainz: B. Schott's Söhne, 1955–.
Organum. Lippstadt, Germany: Kistner & Siegel, 1924–.
The Penn State Music Series. 25 vols. University Park:
Pennsylvania State University Press, 1963–71.
Publications de la Société Française de Musicologie. Ser. 1. Paris:
Heugel, 1925–.
Publikationen älterer Musik. Edited by Theodor Kroyer. 11 vols.
Leipzig: Breitkopf & Härtel, 1926–40.
Le pupitre: collection de musique ancienne. François Lesure, gen.
ed. Paris: Heugel, 1967–.
Recent Researches in the Oral Traditions of Music. Philip V.
Bohlman, gen. ed. Madison, Wis.: A-R Editions, 1993–.
Series of Early Music. Karl Geiringer, gen. ed. Bryn Mawr, Pa.:
Theodore Presser, 1968–.
Smith College Music Archives. 16 vols. Northampton, Mass.:
Smith College, 1935–72.
Thesaurus Musicus. London: Pro Musica Edition, 1979–.
The Wellesley Edition. Jan LaRue, gen. ed. Wellesley, Mass.:
Wellesley College, 1950–.

COMPOSERS' COMPLETE WORKS
AND CATALOGUES

This list, selective like the preceding one, is limited to some of
the most famous composers, listed in alphabetical order. The two
related types of sources included, complete scholarly editions and
catalogues (all but a few are thematic), have been combined in a
single list by composer to show the current state of affairs as it ap-
plies to these composers. As in the sets and monuments bibliography, editorial and publication information is abbreviated; full
citations may be found in Hill and Stephens and in Brook and
Viano (see pp. 41, 42 above).

The order of items is chronological rather than alphabetical
where there is more than one of either type of source, with editions
listed first, then catalogues. The standard older complete editions

are still useful, and for many composers' works for which there is such an older edition from the 19th or early 20th century, a new one is in progress.

Editorial methods vary, as with historical sets and monuments, but in general the modern editions are more reliable and certainly more up-to-date than their older counterparts. (It should be noted that the complete works of many composers are contained in certain sets and monuments, e.g., Machaut, Dufay, and Giovanni Gabrieli in *Corpus Mensurabilis Musicae;* and Goudimel and Cabezón in *The Institute of Medieval Music: Collected Works.*)

Carl Philipp Emanuel Bach Edition. E. Eugene Helm, coordinating ed.; Rachel Wade, gen. ed. London: Oxford University Press, 1989–.

Wotquenne, Alfred. *Thematisches Verzeichnis der Werke von Carl Philipp Emanuel Bach (1714–1788).* Leipzig: Breitkopf & Härtel, 1905.

Helm, E. Eugene. *Thematic Catalogue of the Works of Carl Philipp Emanuel Bach.* New Haven: Yale University Press, 1989.

Johann Sebastian Bach's Werke, herausgegeben von der Bach-Gesellschaft. 47 vols. Leipzig: Breitkopf & Härtel, 1851–99, 1926.

Johann Sebastian Bach: Neue Ausgabe sämtlicher Werke, herausgegeben vom Johann-Sebastian-Bach-Institut Göttingen und vom Bach-Archiv Leipzig [Neue Bach-Ausgabe]. Kassel: Bärenreiter, 1954–.

Schmieder, Wolfgang. *Thematisch-systematisches Verzeichnis der musikalischen Werke von Johann Sebastian Bach: Bach-Werke-Verzeichnis (BWV).* 2nd ed., rev. and enl. Wiesbaden: Breitkopf & Härtel, 1990.

Schulze, Hans-Joachim, and Christoph Wolff. *Bach Compendium: Analytisch bibliographisches Repertorium der Werke Johann Sebastian Bachs (BC).* Frankfurt: C. F. Peters, 1985–.

Béla Bartók: A Complete Catalogue of His Published Works/Ein vollständiges Verzeichnis seiner veröffentlichten Werke/Un catalogue complet de ses oeuvres publiées. London: Boosey & Hawkes, 1970.

Ludwig van Beethoven's Werke: Vollständige kritisch durchgesehene überall berechtigte Ausgabe. Leipzig: Breitkopf & Härtel, 1864–90. 7 suppls.: 1959–71.

Beethoven Werke, herausgegeben vom Beethoven-Archiv Bonn.
Joseph Schmidt-Görg, gen. ed. Munich: G. Henle, 1960–.
Kinsky, Georg, and Hans Halm. *Das Werk Beethovens:*
Thematisch-bibliographisches Verzeichnis seiner sämtlichen
vollendeten Kompositionen. Munich: G. Henle, 1955.

Hector Berlioz Werke. Edited by Charles Malherbe and Felix
Weingartner. 20 vols. Leipzig: Breitkopf & Härtel,
1900–1907.
Hector Berlioz: New Edition of the Complete Works. Kassel:
Bärenreiter, 1967–.
Hopkinson, Cecil. *A Bibliography of the Musical and Literary*
Works of Hector Berlioz, 1803–1869. . . . 2nd ed. Edited by
Richard Macnutt. Tunbridge Wells, England: Richard
Macnutt, 1980. First published in 1951.
Holoman, D. Kern. *Catalogue of the Works of Hector Berlioz.*
Hector Berlioz: New Edition of the Complete Works,
vol. 25. Kassel: Bärenreiter, 1987.

The Complete Works of William Billings. Edited by Hans Nathan
and Karl Kroeger; Richard Crawford, editorial consultant.
4 vols. Boston: American Musicological Society and
Colonial Society of Massachusetts, 1977–90.

Johannes Brahms Sämtliche Werke, Ausgabe der Gesellschaft der
Musikfreunde in Wien. Edited by Hans Gál and Eusebius
Mandeczewski. 16 vols. Leipzig: Breitkopf & Härtel,
[1926–27].
McCorkle, Margit L., with Donald M. McCorkle. *Johannes*
Brahms: Thematisch-bibliographisches Werkverzeichnis.
Munich: G. Henle, 1984.

Benjamin Britten: A Complete Catalogue of His Published Works.
London: Boosey & Hawkes/Faber Music, 1973.

Anton Bruckner Sämtliche Werke: Kritische Gesamtausgabe.
Edited by Robert Haas et al. 11 vols. Vienna:
Musikwissenschaftlicher Verlag, 1930–44 (incomplete).
[2nd rev. ed.], ed. Leopold Nowak, 1951–.
Grasberger, Renate. *Werkverzeichnis Anton Bruckner (WAB).*
Publikationen des Instituts für Oesterreichische
Musikdokumentation, no. 7. Tutzing: Hans Schneider, 1977.

Dietrich Buxtehudes Werke. 8 vols. Hamburg: Ugrino, 1925–37,
1958 (incomplete).

Dietrich Buxtehude: The Collected Works. Kerala J. Snyder, gen. ed. New York: Broude Brothers, 1987–.

Karstädt, Georg, ed. *Thematisch-systematisches Verzeichnis der musikalischen Werke von Dietrich Buxtehude: Buxtehude-Werke-Verzeichnis (BuxWV).* Wiesbaden: Breitkopf & Härtel, 1974.

Friedrich Chopin's Werke. 14 vols. Leipzig: Breitkopf & Härtel, 1878–80. Critical commentary and suppl.: 1878–1902.

Fryderyk Chopin: Complete Works, According to the Autographs and Original Editions, with a Critical Commentary. Edited by Ignacy J. Paderewski et al. 21 vols. Warsaw: Fryderyk Chopin Institute, 1949–62.

Brown, Maurice J. E. *Chopin: An Index of His Works in Chronological Order.* 2nd rev. ed. London: St. Martin's Press, 1972. First published in 1960.

Kobylańska, Krystyna. *Frédéric Chopin: Thematisch-bibliographisches Werkverzeichnis.* Translated into German by Helmut Stolze. Munich: G. Henle, 1979. First published in 1977.

Les oeuvres de Arcangelo Corelli. Edited by Joseph Joachim and Friedrich Chrysander. 5 vols. London: Augener, 1888–91.

Arcangelo Corelli: Historisch-kritische Gesamtausgabe der musikalischen Werke. Hans Oesch, gen. ed. Laaber, Germany: Laaber-Verlag, etc., 1976–.

Marx, Hans Joachim. *Die Überlieferung der Werke Arcangelo Corellis: Catalogue raisonné.* Arcangelo Corelli: Historisch-kritische Gesamtausgabe der musikalischen Werke, suppl. vol. Cologne: Arno Volk Verlag, 1980.

Oeuvres complètes de François Couperin. Maurice Cauchie, gen. ed. 12 vols. Paris: Edition de l'Oiseau-Lyre, 1932–33. Rev. ed., 1980–.

Cauchie, Maurice. *Thematic Index of the Works of François Couperin.* Monaco: Lyrebird Press, 1949.

Oeuvres complètes de Claude Debussy. Paris: Durand-Costallat, 1985–.

Lesure, François. *Catalogue de l'oeuvre de Claude Debussy.* Publications du Centre de Documentation Claude Debussy, no. 3. Geneva: Editions Minkoff, 1977.

Antonín Dvořák: Souborné vydání/Gesamtausgabe/Complete Edition/Edition complète. Prague: Artia, 1955–.

Burghauser, Jarmil. *Antonín Dvořák: Thematic Catalogue, Bibliography, Survey of Life and Work.* Prague: Artia, 1960.

Christoph Willibald Gluck Sämtliche Werke. Rudolf Gerber, gen. ed. Kassel: Bärenreiter, 1951–.
Wotquenne, Alfred. *Catalogue thématique des oeuvres de Chr. W. v. Gluck.* Leipzig: Breitkopf & Härtel, 1904.
Hopkinson, Cecil. *A Bibliography of the Printed Works of C. W. von Gluck, 1714–1787.* 2nd rev. and augm. ed. New York: Broude Brothers, 1967. First published in 1959.

Georg Friedrich Händels Werke. Edited by Friedrich Chrysander. 96 vols. + 6 suppl. vols. Leipzig: Breitkopf & Härtel, 1858–94, 1902.
Hallische Händel-Ausgabe: Kritische Gesamtausgabe, herausgegeben von der Georg-Friedrich-Händel-Gesellschaft. Kassel: Bärenreiter, 1955–.
Bell, A. Craig. *Handel: Chronological Thematic Catalogue.* 2nd ed. Darley, England: Grian-Aig Press, 1972. First published in 1969.
Eisen, Walter, and Margret Eisen, eds. *Händel-Handbuch: Gleichzeitig Supplement zu Hallische Händel-Ausgabe (Kritische Gesamtausgabe).* 5 vols. projected. Kassel: Bärenreiter, 1978–. (*Thematisch-systematisches Verzeichnis,* ed. Bernd Baselt, begins in vol. 1 and continues in vols. 2–3.)

Joseph Haydns Werke: Erste kritische durchgesehene Gesamtausgabe. Edited by Eusebius Mandyczewski et al. 11 vols. in 10. Leipzig: Breitkopf & Härtel, [1907–33] (incomplete).
Joseph Haydns kritische Gesamtausgabe. Georg Feder, gen. ed. 4 vols. Boston: The Haydn Society; Leipzig: Breitkopf & Härtel, 1950–51 (incomplete).
Joseph Haydns Werke, herausgegeben vom Joseph Haydn-Institut Köln. Munich: G. Henle, 1958–.
Hoboken, Anthony van. *Joseph Haydn: Thematisch-bibliographisches Werkverzeichnis.* 3 vols. Mainz: B. Schott's Söhne, 1957–78.
Bryant, Stephen C., and Gary W. Chapman. *Melodic Index to Haydn's Instrumental Music: A Thematic Locator for the Hoboken Thematisch-bibliographisches Werkverzeichnis, Volumes I and III.* New York: Pendragon Press, 1981.

*Paul Hindemith Sämtliche Werke im Auftrag der Hindemith-
    Stiftung.* Kurt von Fischer and Ludwig Finscher, gen. eds.
    Mainz: B. Schott's Söhne, 1975–.
Paul Hindemith Werkverzeichnis. Mainz: B. Schott's Söhne,
    [196?].

Werken van Josquin des Prés. Edited by Albert Smijers. 55 vols.
    Amsterdam: G. Alsbach, etc., 1922–69.
New Josquin Edition. Utrecht: Vereniging voor Nederlandse
    Muziekgeschiedenis, 1988–.

Orlando di Lassus Sämtliche Werke [old series]. Edited by Franz
    X. Haberl and Adolf Sandberger. 21 vols. Leipzig: Breitkopf
    & Härtel, [1894–1927] (incomplete).
Orlando di Lasso Sämtliche Werke, neue Reihe. Kassel:
    Bärenreiter, 1956–.
Orlando di Lasso Sämtliche Werke. 2nd ed., rev., based on the
    old series. Wiesbaden: Breitkopf & Härtel, 1968–.

*Franz Liszts musikalische Werke, herausgegeben von der Franz-
    Liszt-Stiftung.* 34 vols. Leipzig: Breitkopf & Härtel,
    1907–36.
*Franz Liszt: Neue Ausgabe Sämtlicher Werke/Ferenc Liszt:
    New Edition of the Complete Works.* Kassel: Bärenreiter,
    1970–.
*Thematisches Verzeichniss der Werke, Bearbeitungen und
    Transcriptionen von F. Liszt.* New, augm. ed. Leipzig:
    Breitkopf & Härtel, 1877. First published in 1855.

Oeuvres complètes de J.-B. Lully (1632–1687). Henry Prunières,
    gen. ed. 10 vols. Paris: Editions de la Revue Musicale, etc.,
    1930–39; reprint and suppl. vols., New York: Broude
    Brothers, 1965–71.
Jean-Baptiste Lully: The Complete Musical Works. Carl Schmidt,
    gen ed. New York: Broude Brothers, 1993–.
Schneider, Herbert. *Chronologisch-thematisches Verzeichnis
    sämtlicher Werke von Jean-Baptiste Lully (LWV).* Mainzer
    Studien zur Musikwissenschaft, vol. 14. Tutzing: Hans
    Schneider, 1981.
Gustafson, Bruce, and Matthew Lashinskie. *A Thematic Locator
    for the Works of Jean-Baptiste Lully Coordinated with
    Herbert Schneider's Chronologisch-thematisches Verzeichnis
    sämtlicher Werke von Jean-Baptiste Lully (LWV).* New
    York: Performer's Editions, 1989.

Gustav Mahler Sämtliche Werke: Kritische Gesamtausgabe,
herausgegeben von der Internationalen Gustav Mahler
Gesellschaft, Wien. Vienna: Universal Edition, etc., 1960–.

Felix Mendelssohn Bartholdy's Werke: Kritische durchgesehene
Ausgabe. Edited by Julius Rietz. 19 series. Leipzig:
Breitkopf & Härtel, 1874–77.
Leipziger Ausgabe der Werke Felix Mendelssohn Bartholdys.
Leipzig: Deutscher Verlag für Musik, 1960–.
Thematisches Verzeichniss im Druck erschienener Compositionen
von Felix Mendelssohn Bartholdy. 3rd, augm. ed. Leipzig:
[Breitkopf & Härtel], 1882. First published in 1841.

Tutte le opere di Claudio Monteverdi. . . . Edited by Gian
Francesco Malipiero. 16 vols. + suppl. Vienna: Universal
Edition, etc., 1926–42, 1968.

Wolfgang Amadeus Mozart's Werke: Kritisch durchgesehene
Gesamtausgabe. 24 series. Leipzig: Breitkopf & Härtel,
1876–1905.
Wolfgang Amadeus Mozart: Neue Ausgabe sämtlicher Werke, . . .
herausgegeben von der Internationalen Stiftung Mozarteum,
Salzburg. Kassel: Bärenreiter, 1955–.
Köchel, Ludwig Ritter von. *Chronologisch-thematisches*
Verzeichnis sämtlicher Tonwerke Wolfgang Amadé
Mozarts. . . . 6th ed. Edited by Franz Giegling et al.
Wiesbaden: Breitkopf & Härtel, 1964. First published in
1862.
Hill, George R., and Murray Gould, et al. *A Thematic Locator for*
Mozart's Works as Listed in Köchel's **Chronologisch-**
thematisches Verzeichnis, *Sixth Edition.* Music Indexes
and Bibliographies, no. 1. Hackensack, N.J.: Joseph
Boonin, 1970.

M. Mussorgsky Sämtliche Werke. Edited by Paul Lamm. 24 vols.
Moscow: State Music Publishers, 1928–34 (incomplete).

Pierluigi da Palestrina's Werke. Edited by Raffaele Casimiri.
33 vols. Leipzig: Breitkopf & Härtel, [1862–1907].
Le opere complete di Giovanni Pierluigi da Palestrina. Rome:
Fratelli Scalera, 1939–65, 1973–.

Collected Works of Sergei Prokofiev. Moscow: State Music
Publishers, 1955–.

The Works of Henry Purcell. Published by the Purcell Society.
32 vols. London: Novello, 1878–. New series of rev. and
unpub. works, 1968–.
Zimmerman, Franklin B. *Henry Purcell, 1659–1695: An Analytical
Catalogue of His Music*. London: St. Martin's Press, 1963.
————. *Henry Purcell, 1659–1695: Melodic and Intervallic
Indexes to His Complete Works*. Philadelphia:
Smith-Edwards-Dunlap, 1975.

Jean-Philippe Rameau (1683–1764): oeuvres complètes. Camille
Saint-Saëns, gen. ed. 18 vols. Paris: Durand et Fils,
1895–1913, 1924 (incomplete).
Jean-Philippe Rameau: Opera Omnia. Sylvie Bouissou, gen. ed.
38 vols. projected. Paris, 1993–.

Catalogue de l'oeuvre de Maurice Ravel. Paris: Fondation Maurice
Ravel, 1954.

Edizione critica delle opere di Gioachino Rossini. Philip Gossett
et al., gen. eds. Pesaro: Fondazione Rossini, 1979–.

Arnold Schönberg Sämtliche Werke. Joseph Rufer, gen. ed. Mainz:
B. Schott's Söhne, 1966–.
Rufer, Josef. *The Works of Arnold Schoenberg: A Catalogue of His
Compositions, Writings and Paintings*. Translated by Dika
Newlin. London: Faber and Faber, 1962. First published in
1959.

Franz Schubert's Werke: Kritisch durchgesehene Gesamtausgabe.
21 series + critical commentary/index. Leipzig: Breitkopf
& Härtel, 1884–97.
*Franz Schubert: Neue Ausgabe sämtlicher Werke, herausgegeben
von der Internationalen Schubert-Gesellschaft*. Kassel:
Bärenreiter, 1964–.
Deutsch, Otto Erich. *Franz Schubert: Thematisches Verzeichnis
seiner Werke in chronologischer Folge*. Franz Schubert:
Neue Ausgabe sämtlicher Werke, ser. 8, vol. 4. Kassel:
Bärenreiter, 1978. First published in English in 1951.

Robert Schumann's Werke. Edited by Clara Schumann. 14 series.
Leipzig: Breitkopf & Härtel, 1881–93.
*Robert Schumann: Neue Ausgabe sämtlicher Werke, herausgegeben
von der Robert-Schumann-Gesellschaft Düsseldorf/Robert
Schumann: New Edition of the Complete Works, Published*

by the Robert-Schumann-Gesellschaft Düsseldorf. Edited by
   Akio Mayeda and Klaus Wolfgang Niemöller. Mainz: B.
   Schott's Söhne, 1991–.
Hofmann, Kurt, and Siegmar Keil. *Robert Schumann:
   Thematisches Verzeichnis sämtlicher im Druck erschienenen
   musikalischen Werke mit Angabe des Jahres ihres
   Entstehens und Erscheinens.* 5th ed., rev. and enl.
   Hamburg: J. Schuberth, 1982. First published in 1860.

Heinrich Schütz's Sämtliche Werke. Edited by Philipp Spitta et al.
   18 vols. Leipzig: Breitkopf & Härtel, [1885–1927].
*Heinrich Schütz: Neue Ausgabe sämtlicher Werke, herausgegeben
   im Auftrag der Internationalen Heinrich-Schütz-
   Gesellschaft.* Kassel: Bärenreiter, 1955–.
*Stuttgarter Schütz-Ausgabe: Heinrich Schütz Sämtliche Werke
   nach den Quellen.* Edited by Günter Graulich and Paul
   Horn. Stuttgart: Hänssler-Verlag, 1971–.
Bittinger, Werner. *Schütz-Werke-Verzeichnis (SWV): Kleine
   Ausgabe, im Auftrag der Neuen Schütz-Gesellschaft.* Kassel:
   Bärenreiter, 1960.
Miller, D. Douglas, and Anne L. Highsmith, comps. *Heinrich
   Schütz: A Bibliography of the Collected Works and
   Performing Editions.* Music Reference Collection, no. 9.
   New York: Greenwood Press, 1986.

D. Shostakovich: Collected Works. Dvukh Tomakh, gen. ed. 42
   vols. Moscow: Izdatel'stvo "Muzyka," 1979–87.
MacDonald, Malcolm. *Dmitri Shostakovich: A Complete
   Catalogue.* London: Boosey & Hawkes, 1977.
Hulme, Derek C. *Dmitri Shostakovich: Catalogue, Bibliography
   & Discography.* 2nd ed. New York: Oxford University
   Press, 1991. First published in 1982.

Mueller von Asow, E. H. *Richard Strauss: Thematisches
   Verzeichnis.* 6 vols. Vienna: Verlag L. Doblinger, 1955–74.

Caesar, Clifford. *Igor Stravinsky: A Complete Catalogue.* San
   Francisco: San Francisco Press, 1982.

P. Tchaikovsky: Polnoe Sobranie Sochinenii [Complete Edition of
   Compositions]. 124 vols. Moscow: State Music Publishers,
   1940–71.
*Systematisches Verzeichnis der Werke von Pjotr Iljitsch
   Tschaikowsky: Ein Handbuch für die Musikpraxis.*
   Hamburg: Musikverlag Hans Sikorski, 1973.

Georg Philipp Telemann: Musikalische Werke, herausgegeben im Auftrag der Gesellschaft für Musikforschung. Kassel: Bärenreiter, 1950–.

Menke, Werner. *Thematisches Verzeichnis der Vokalwerke von Georg Philipp Telemann.* 2 vols. Frankfurt: Vittorio Klostermann, 1982–83.

Ruhnke, Martin. *Georg Philipp Telemann: Thematisch-systematisches Verzeichnis seiner Werke: Telemann-Werkverzeichnis (TWV).* Georg Philipp Telemann: Musikalische Werke, suppl. Kassel: Bärenreiter, 1984–.

The Works of/Le opere di Giuseppe Verdi. Philip Gossett, coordinating ed. Chicago: University of Chicago Press; Milan: G. Ricordi, 1983–.

Hopkinson, Cecil. *A Bibliography of the Works of Giuseppe Verdi, 1813–1901.* 2 vols. New York: Broude Brothers, 1973–78.

[*Antonio Vivaldi: le opere strumentali*]. Edited by Gian Francesco Malipiero. 530 vols. Rome: G. Ricordi, 1947–72.

Antonio Vivaldi: edizione critica. Edited by Paul Everett and Michael Talbot. Milan: Ricordi, 1982–.

Rinaldi, Mario. *Catalogo numerico tematico delle composizioni di Antonio Vivaldi. . . .* Rome: Editrice Cultura Moderna, [1945].

Pincherle, Marc. *Antonio Vivaldi et la musique instrumentale.* Book 2: *Inventaire thématique.* Paris: Fleury, 1948.

Coral, Lenore. *A Concordance of the Thematic Indexes to the Instrumental Works of Antonio Vivaldi.* 2nd ed. MLA Index Series, no. 4. Ann Arbor, Mich.: Music Library Association, 1972. First published in 1965.

Ohmura, Noriko. *A Reference Concordance Table of Vivaldi.* Tokyo: Kawasaki, 1972.

Ryom, Peter. *Antonio Vivaldi: table de concordances des oeuvres (RV).* Copenhagen: Engstrøm & Sødring, 1973.

———. *Verzeichnis der Werke Antonio Vivaldis (RV).* Leipzig: VEB Deutscher Verlag, 1974.

[Fanna, Antonio]. *Opere strumentali di Antonio Vivaldi (1678–1741): catalogo numerico-tematico secondo la catalogazione Fanna.* 2nd ed., rev. and enl. Milan: Ricordi, 1986. First published in 1968.

Ryom, Peter. *Répertoire des oeuvres d'Antonio Vivaldi: les compositions instrumentales [RV].* Copenhagen: Engstrøm & Sødring, 1986.

Richard Wagners musikalische Werke: Erste kritisch revidierte Gesamtausgabe. Edited by Michael Balling. 10 vols. Leipzig: Breitkopf & Härtel, 1912–ca. 1929 (incomplete).

Richard Wagner Sämtliche Werke. Edited by Carl Dahlhaus.
Mainz: B. Schott's Söhne, 1970–.
Deathridge, John, et al. *Wagner Werk-Verzeichnis (WWV):*
Verzeichnis der musikalischen Werke Richard Wagners und
ihre Quellen. Mainz: B. Schott's Söhne, 1986.

ANTHOLOGIES OF MUSIC

This category of musical editions is usually less scholarly and
more practical in intent, being geared to the student, teacher, or
performer. Most are in one or two volumes, the chief exception being the extensive multivolume Anthology of Music, whose complete contents are given in a separate list at the end. As in the case
of musical sets and monuments, the anthologies in the present list
have various delimitations by period, genre, and medium, and
have been divided into categories accordingly. Anthologies dating
from the early 20th century or before are mostly excluded in favor
of more recent American and English ones. For further information, see Hilton's *Index to Early Music in Selected Anthologies* and
Murray's *Anthologies of Music,* p. 41 above.

General

Benjamin, Thomas, et al., comps. *Music for Analysis: Examples*
from the Common Practice Period and the Twentieth
Century. 2nd ed. Boston: Houghton Mifflin, 1984. First
published in 1978.
Brandt, William, et al. **The Comprehensive Study of Music.**
1976–80.

> 1. *Anthology of Music from Plainchant through Gabrieli.*
>   New York: Harper & Row, 1980.
> 2. *Anthology of Music from Monteverdi through Mozart.*
>   New York: Harper's College Press, 1977.
> 3. *Anthology of Music from Beethoven through Wagner.*
>   New York: Harper's College Press, 1977.
> 4. *Anthology of Music from Debussy through Stockhausen.*
>   New York: Harper's College Press, 1976.

Briscoe, James R., ed. *Historical Anthology of Music by Women.*
Bloomington: Indiana University Press, 1987.

Burkhart, Charles. *Anthology for Musical Analysis.* 4th ed. New York: Holt, Rinehart, and Winston, 1986. First published in 1964.

Cohen, Albert, and John D. White. *Anthology of Music for Analysis.* New York: Appleton-Century-Crofts, 1965.

Davison, Archibald T., and Willi Apel. *Historical Anthology of Music.* 2 vols. Cambridge: Harvard University Press, 1946–50.

DeVoto, Mark, comp., ed., and annot. *Mostly Short Pieces: An Anthology for Harmonic Analysis.* New York: W. W. Norton, 1992.

Fuller, Sarah. *The European Musical Heritage 800–1750.* New York: Alfred A. Knopf, 1987.

Kamien, Roger, ed. *The Norton Scores: An Anthology for Listening.* 5th ed., in 2 vols. New York: W. W. Norton, 1990. First published in 1968.

Lerner, Edward R. *Study Scores of Musical Styles.* New York: McGraw-Hill, 1968.

Lincoln, Harry B., and Stephen Bonta. *Study Scores of Historical Styles.* 2 vols. Englewood Cliffs, N.J.: Prentice Hall, 1986–87.

Palisca, Claude V., ed. *Norton Anthology of Western Music.* 2nd ed. 2 vols. New York: W. W. Norton, 1988. First published in 1980.

Parrish, Carl, comp. and ed. *A Treasury of Early Music: An Anthology of Masterworks of the Middle Ages, the Renaissance, and the Baroque Era.* New York: W. W. Norton, 1958.

Parrish, Carl, and John F. Ohl, comps and eds. *Masterpieces of Music before 1750: An Anthology of Musical Examples from Gregorian Chant to J. S. Bach.* New York: W. W. Norton, 1951.

Schering, Arnold, comp. and ed. *Geschichte der Musik in Beispielen: Dreihundertfünfzig Tonsätze aus neun Jahrhunderten.* Leipzig: Breitkopf & Härtel, 1931.

Starr, William J., and George F. Devine. *Music Scores Omnibus.* 2nd ed. 2 vols. Englewood Cliffs, N.J.: Prentice Hall, 1974. First published in 1964.

Stein, Leon. *Anthology of Musical Forms.* Evanston, Ill.: Summy-Birchard, 1962.

Turek, Ralph, ed. *Analytical Anthology of Music.* New York: Alfred A. Knopf, 1984.

Walton, Charles W. *Music Literature for Analysis and Study.* Belmont, Calif.: Wadsworth Publishing, 1973.

Wennerstrom, Mary H. *Anthology of Musical Structure and Style.* Englewood Cliffs, N.J.: Prentice Hall, 1983.

Limited to an Era

Berry, Wallace, and Edward Chudacoff. *Eighteenth-Century Imitative Counterpoint: Music for Analysis.* New York: Appleton-Century-Crofts, 1969.

DeLio, Thomas, and Stuart Saunders Smith, eds. *Twentieth Century Music Scores.* Englewood Cliffs, N.J.: Prentice Hall, 1989.

Downs, Philip G., ed. *Anthology of Classical Music.* The Norton Introduction to Music History. New York: W. W. Norton, 1992.

Gleason, Harold, comp. and ed. *Examples of Music before 1400.* New York: Appleton-Century-Crofts, 1942.

Greenberg, Noah, and Paul Maynard, eds. *An Anthology of Early Renaissance Music.* New York: W. W. Norton, 1975.

Hoppin, Richard H., ed. *Anthology of Medieval Music.* The Norton Introduction to Music History. New York: W. W. Norton, 1978.

Kirby, F. E. *Music in the Classic Period: An Anthology with Commentary.* New York: Schirmer Books, 1979.

————. *Music in the Romantic Period: An Anthology with Commentary.* New York: Schirmer Books, 1986.

Marrocco, W. Thomas, ed. *Ars Antiqua.* Oxford: Oxford University Press, 1979.

Marrocco, W. Thomas, and Harold Gleason, comps. and eds. *Music in America: An Anthology from the Landing of the Pilgrims to the Close of the Civil War, 1620–1865.* New York: W. W. Norton, 1964.

Marrocco, W. Thomas, and Nicholas Sandon. *Medieval Music.* The Oxford Anthology of Music. London: Oxford University Press, 1977.

Morgan, Robert P., ed. *Anthology of Twentieth-Century Music.* The Norton Introduction to Music History. New York: W. W. Norton, 1992.

Plantinga, Leon, ed. *Anthology of Romantic Music.* The Norton Introduction to Music History. New York: W. W. Norton, 1984.

Simms, Bryan R. *Music of the Twentieth Century: An Anthology.* New York: Schirmer Books, 1986.

Soderlund, Gustave Fredric, and Samuel H. Scott, comps.
*Examples of Gregorian Chant and Sacred Music of the 16th
Century.* [Augm. ed.] Englewood Cliffs, N.J.: Prentice Hall,
1971. First published in 1937.

Wennerstrom, Mary H., comp. *Anthology of Twentieth-Century
Music.* 2nd ed. Englewood Cliffs, N.J.: Prentice Hall, 1988.
First published in 1969.

Wilson, David Fenwick. *Music of the Middle Ages: An Anthology
for Performance and Study.* New York: Schirmer Books,
1990.

Limited to a Medium or Genre

Brody, Elaine. *Music in Opera: A Historical Anthology.*
Englewood Cliffs, N.J.: Prentice Hall, 1970.

Christiansen, Rupert, ed. *The Grand Obsession: An Anthology of
Opera.* London: William Collins Sons, 1988.

Dunn, Thomas, ed. *The Renaissance Singer.* With an introductory
essay, "Some Notes on 16th Century Sacred Polyphony,"
by Joseph Dyer. Boston: E. C. Schirmer, 1976.

Gardner, John, and Simon Harris. *A Cappella: An Anthology of
Unaccompanied Choral Music from Seven Centuries.* New
York: Oxford University Press, 1992.

[Greenberg, Noah, et al., eds.] *New York Pro Musica Choral
Songbook: Sacred and Secular Music of Spain, England,
Germany, and the Netherlands for Mixed Voices.* New York:
Associated Music Publishers, 1966.

Jackson, Francis, et al. *Anthems for Choirs.* 4 vols. London:
Oxford University Press, 1973–76.

Jacques, Reginald, David Willcocks, and John Rutter, eds. and
arrs. *Carols for Choirs.* 4 vols. London: Oxford University
Press, 1961–80.

Lang, Paul Henry, comp. *The Concerto 1800–1900: A Norton
Music Anthology.* New York: W. W. Norton, 1969.
————. *The Symphony 1800–1900: A Norton Music Anthology.*
New York: W. W. Norton, 1969.

Le Huray, Peter, et al. *Anthems for Men's Voices.* 2 vols. Oxford:
Oxford University Press, 1965.

MacClintock, Carol, ed. *The Solo Song 1580–1730: A Norton
Music Anthology.* New York: W. W. Norton, 1973.

McGee, Timothy J. *Medieval Instrumental Dances.* Bloomington:
Indiana University Press, 1989.

Morris, Christopher, comp. *A Sixteenth-Century Anthem Book.*
6th ed., rev. London: Oxford University Press, 1988. First
published in 1960.
Robinson, Ray, ed. *Choral Music: A Norton Historical Anthology.*
New York: W. W. Norton, 1978.
Willcocks, David, and John Rutter, eds. and arrs. *100 Carols for
Choirs.* London: Oxford University Press, 1987.

Limited to a Medium or Genre and to a Region

Arnold, Denis, ed. *Ten Venetian Motets.* London: Oxford
University Press, 1980.
Dearmer, Percy, R. Vaughan Williams, and Martin Shaw. *The
Oxford Book of Carols.* London: Oxford University Press,
1928.
Dobbins, Frank, ed. *The Oxford Book of French Chansons.*
London: Oxford University Press, 1987.
Greenberg, Noah, ed. *An Anthology of Elizabethan Lute Songs,
Madrigals, and Rounds.* The Norton Library. New York:
W. W. Norton, 1955.
———. *An Anthology of English Medieval and Renaissance Vocal
Music: Part Songs for One to Six Voices.* The Norton
Library. New York: W. W. Norton, 1968.
Harman, Alec, ed. *The Oxford Book of Italian Madrigals.*
London: Oxford University Press, 1983.
Hillier, Paul, ed. *The Catch Book: 153 Catches, Including the
Complete Catches of Henry Purcell.* Oxford: Oxford
University Press, 1987.
———. *English Romantic Partsongs.* Oxford: Oxford University
Press, 1986.
Keyte, Hugh, and Andrew Parrott, eds.; Clifford Bartlett, assoc.
ed. *The New Oxford Book of Carols.* New York: Oxford
University Press, 1992.
Ledger, Philip, ed. *The Oxford Book of English Madrigals.*
London: Oxford University Press, 1978.
Le Huray, Peter, ed. *Treasury of English Church Music, 1545–1650.*
Reprint with corrections. Cambridge: Cambridge
University Press, 1982. First published in 1965.
Martens, Mason, ed. *The Bicentennial Collection of American
Choral Music (1760–1900).* Dayton, Ohio: McAfee Music,
1975.
Morris, Christopher, comp. *The Oxford Book of Tudor Anthems:
34 Anthems for Mixed Choir.* London: Oxford University
Press, 1978.

Newman, Anthony, comp. and ed. *Anthology of Early English Harpsichord Music.* New York: G. Schirmer, 1984.

Patterson, Willis C., comp. *Anthology of Art Songs by Black American Composers.* New York: E. B. Marks, 1977.

Pedrell, Felipe, comp. *Anthology of Classical Spanish Organists (16th, 17th & 18th Centuries).* 2 vols. New York: Associated Music Publishers, 1968.

Roche, Jerome, ed. *The Flower of the Italian Madrigal: For Mixed Voices.* 2 vols. Renaissance Voices. New York: Galaxy Music, 1988.

Smith, James G., comp. and ed. *The New Liberty Bell: A Bicentennial Anthology of American Choral Music.* Champaign, Ill.: Mark Foster, 1976.

Young, Percy M., ed. *The English Glee.* New York: Oxford University Press, 1990.

Comprehensive Multivolume Set

Anthology of Music: A Collection of Complete Musical Examples Illustrating the History of Music. Edited by Karl Gustav Fellerer. 48 vols. Also published as **Das Musikwerk.** Cologne: Arno Volk Verlag, 1955–76.

1. *Four Hundred Years of European Keyboard Music.* 2nd ed. By Walter Georgii. 1959. First published in 195?.
2. *Troubadours, Trouvères, Minne-, and Meistersinger.* By Friedrich Gennrich. 1960.
3. *The Sixteenth-Century Part Song in Italy, France, England and Spain.* By Hans Engel. 1961.
4. *European Folk Song: Common Forms in Characteristic Modifications.* By Walter Wiora. 1966.
5. *The Opera from Its Beginnings until the Early 19th Century.* By A. A. Abert. 1962.
6. *The Classics.* By Kurt Stephenson. 1962.
7. *The Italian Trio Sonata.* By Erich Schenk. 1955.
8. *The Character Piece.* By Willy Kahl. 1961.
9. *Medieval Polyphony.* By Heinrich Husmann. 1962.
10. *The German Part Song from the 16th Century to the Present Day.* By Helmuth Osthoff. 1955.
11. *The Variation.* By Kurt von Fischer. 1962.
12. *Improvisation in Nine Centuries of Western Music.* By Ernest T. Ferand. 1961.
13. *The Music of the Byzantine Church.* By Egon Wellesz. 1959.

14. *The German Solo Song and the Ballad.* By Hans Joachim Moser. 1958.
15. *The Solo Sonata.* By Franz Giegling. 1960.
16. *The Solo Song outside German Speaking Countries.* By Frits Noske. 1959.
17. *The Toccata.* By Erich Valentin. 1958.
18. *Gregorian Chant.* By Franz Tack. 1960.
19. *The Fugue I: From the Beginnings to J. S. Bach.* By Adam Adrio. 1961.
20. *Hebrew Music.* By Eric Werner. 1961.
21. *Romanticism in Music.* By Kurt Stephenson. 1961.
22. *The Art of the Netherlanders.* By René Bernard Lenaerts. 1964.
23. *The Concerto Grosso.* By Hans Engel. 1964.
24. *History of Instrumentation.* By Heinz Becker. 1964.
25. *The Solo Concerto.* By Hans Engel. 1964.
26. *The Suite.* By Hermann Beck. 1966.
27. *The Dance.* By Georg Reichert. 1974.
28. *Pre-Classical Polyphony.* By Karl Gustav Fellerer. 1965.
29. *The Symphony.* By Lothar Hoffmann-Erbrecht. 1967.
30. *History of the Mass.* By Joseph Schmidt-Görg. 1968.
31. *The Monody.* By Karl Gustav Fellerer. 1968.
32. *The Cantata.* By Richard Jakoby. 1968.
33. *The Fugue II: From Handel to the Twentieth Century.* By Josef Müller-Blattau. 1968.
34. *The Serenade for Orchestra.* By Günter Hausswald. 1970.
35. *The Trio Sonata outside Italy.* By Erich Schenk. 1970.
36. *Program Music.* By Wolfgang Stockmeier. 1970.
37. *The Oratorio.* By Günther Massenkeil. 1970.
38. *The Opera I: 17th Century.* By Hellmuth Christian Wolff. 1971.
39. *The Opera II: 18th Century.* By Hellmuth Christian Wolff. 1971.
40. *The Opera III: 19th Century.* By Hellmuth Christian Wolff. 1975.
41. *Original Vocal Improvisations from the 16th-18th Centuries.* By Hellmuth Christian Wolff. 1972.
42. *The Fantasia I: 16th to 18th Century.* By Peter Schluening. 1971.
43. *The Fantasia II: 18th to 20th Century.* By Peter Schluening. 1971.
44. *Non-European Folklore and Art Music.* By Marius Schneider. 1972.

45. *The Music of the Figured Bass Era.* By Günter
    Hausswald. 1974.
46. *Chamber Music.* By Hubert Unverricht. 1975.
47. *The Motet.* By Heinrich Hüschen. 1975.
48. *Survey and Index.* Karl Gustav Fellerer, ed. and comp.
    1976.

CHAPTER EIGHT

Miscellaneous Sources

This final chapter brings together two bibliographies concerning sources that are more or less complementary or peripheral to the subject of research in music, but above all *practical* in their intent. The first is a selective listing of currently available guides to aspects of research and writing in English, varying from general discussions of research techniques to manuals of style used in the humanities and other guides to proper English usage, and concluding with some representative guides to getting work published. The second list, "The Music Industry," assembles useful information pertaining to the business of music—publishing, careers, grants, competitions, etc.—especially as it is practiced in the United States.

MANUALS OF STYLE AND OTHER AIDS TO RESEARCH, WRITING, AND PUBLICATION

Some of the following lists are geared to a general readership and some to writers on music. They emphasize sources that are recent or that have demonstrated staying power. The various subdivisions and the titles of the works are for the most part self-explanatory. Particular mention should be made of the important and burgeoning field of computer applications to music research and writing (for further information, consult also the computer journals listed in chapter 6, "Current Research Journals in Music—Other Journals," p. 159 above).

The third list, "General Manuals of Style and Other Guides to English," is particularly selective, there being innumerable guides of this type in print, but it includes some of the most commonly used general manuals of style in the field—*The Chicago Manual, MLA Handbook,* and Turabian's *Manual for Writers*—as well as several other guides to English usage.

"Guides to Writing about Music" lists the best-known specialized style manuals in music, including the recent one by Wingell, and "Guides to the Publication Process" features a few representative recent guides to the often complicated venture of getting works into print.

General Aids to Research

Barzun, Jacques, and Henry F. Graff. *The Modern Researcher.* 4th ed. New York: Harcourt, Brace & World, 1985. First published in 1957.

Beasley, David. *How to Use a Research Library.* London: Oxford University Press, 1988.

Borg, Walter R., and Meredith Damien Gall. *Educational Research: An Introduction.* 4th ed. New York: Longman, 1983. First published in 1963.

Druesedow, John E., Jr. *Library Research Guide to Music: Illustrated Search Strategy and Sources.* Library Research Guides Series, no. 6. Ann Arbor, Mich.: Pierian Press, 1982.

Helm, E. Eugene, and Albert T. Luper. *Words & Music: Form and Procedure in Theses, Dissertations, Research Papers, Book Reports, Programs, Theses in Composition.* Rev. ed. Totowa, N.J.: European American Music, 1982. First published in 1971.

Madsen, David. *Successful Dissertations and Theses: A Guide to Graduate Student Research from Proposal to Completion.* San Francisco: Jossey-Bass Publishers, 1983.

Mann, Thomas. *A Guide to Library Research Methods.* New York: Oxford University Press, 1987.

Poulton, Helen J., with Marguerite S. Howland. *The Historian's Handbook: A Descriptive Guide to Reference Works.* Norman: University of Oklahoma Press, 1972.

Watanabe, Ruth T. *Introduction to Music Research.* Prentice Hall History of Music Series. Englewood Cliffs, N.J.: Prentice Hall, 1967.

Wingell, Richard J. *Writing about Music: An Introductory Guide.*
Englewood Cliffs, N.J.: Prentice Hall, 1990.

Computer Aids to Music Research

Bartle, Barton K. *Computer Software in Music and Music
Education: A Guide.* Metuchen, N.J.: Scarecrow Press,
1987.
Brinkman, Alexander R. *Pascal: Programming for Music
Research.* Chicago: University of Chicago Press, 1990.
Davis, Deta S. *Computer Applications in Music: A Bibliography.*
Computer Music and Digital Audio Series, vol. 4.
Madison, Wis.: A-R Editions, 1988.
————. *Computer Applications in Music: A Bibliography,
Supplement 1.* Computer Music and Digital Audio Series,
vol. 10. Madison, Wis.: A-R Editions, 1992.
Hammond, Ray. *The Musician and the Micro.* Poole, Dorset,
England: Blandford Press, 1983.
Harrison, David B. *Computer Applications to Music and
Musicology: A Bibliography.* Waterloo, Ont.: University of
Waterloo, 1977.
Hewlett, Walter B., and Eleanor Selfridge-Field, eds. *Computing
in Musicology: A Directory of Research.* Menlo Park,
Calif.: Center for Computer Assisted Research in the
Humanities, 1989–. (Annual publication.) Originally
entitled *Directory of Computer Assisted Research in
Musicology,* 1985–88.
Lincoln, Harry B. *Development of Computerized Techniques in
Music Research with Emphasis on the Thematic Index.*
Washington, D.C.: U.S. Office of Education, Bureau of
Research, 1968.
————, ed. *The Computer and Music.* Ithaca, N.Y.: Cornell
University Press, 1970.
Lister, Craig. *The Musical Microcomputer: A Resource Guide.*
Garland Reference Library of the Humanities, vol. 854.
New York: Garland Publishing, 1988.
Mathews, Max V., and John R. Pierce, eds. *Current Directions in
Computer Music Research.* System Development
Foundation Benchmark Series, vol. 2. Cambridge: MIT
Press, 1989.
Waters, William J., comp. *Music and the Personal Computer: An
Annotated Bibliography.* Music Reference Collection, no.
22. New York: Greenwood Press, 1989.

General Manuals of Style and Other Guides
to English

Barney, Stephen A., ed. *Annotation and Its Texts*. University of California Humanities Research Institute Series. New York: Oxford University Press, 1991.

Barzun, Jacques. *Simple & Direct: A Rhetoric for Writers*. Rev. ed. New York: Harper and Row, 1985. First published in 1975.

Bernstein, Theodore M. *The Careful Writer: A Modern Guide to English Usage*. New York: Atheneum, 1965.

Berry, Thomas Elliott. *The Craft of Writing*. New York: McGraw-Hill, 1974.

——— . *The Most Common Mistakes in English Usage*. New York: Chilton Book Company, 1961.

The Chicago Manual of Style: For Authors, Editors, and Copywriters. 13th ed., rev. and exp. Chicago: University of Chicago Press, 1982. First published in 1937.

Ehrlich, Eugene H. *The Bantam Concise Handbook of English*. Toronto: Bantam Books, 1986.

Fowler, H. W. *A Dictionary of Modern English Usage*. 2nd ed., reprinted with corrections. Revised by Ernest Gowers. Oxford: Oxford University Press, 1989. First published in 1926.

Gibaldi, Joseph, and Walter S. Achtert. *MLA Handbook for Writers of Research Papers*. 3rd ed. New York: Modern Language Association of America, 1988. First published in 1977.

Guinagh, Kevin, comp. and trans. *Dictionary of Foreign Phrases and Abbreviations*. 3rd ed. New York: H. W. Wilson, 1983. First published in 1965.

Heacock, Paul. *Which Word When? The Indispensible Dictionary of 1500 Commonly Confused Words*. New York: Dell Publishing, 1989.

Howard, V. A., and J. H. Barton. *Thinking on Paper: Refine, Express, and Actually Generate Ideas by Understanding the Processes of the Mind*. New York: William Morrow, 1986.

Kane, Thomas S. *The New Oxford Guide to Writing*. New York: Oxford University Press, 1988.

Kaye, Sanford. *Writing under Pressure: The Quick Writing Process*. New York: Oxford University Press, 1989.

Leunen, Mary-Claire van. *A Handbook for Scholars*. Rev. ed. New York: Oxford University Press, 1992. First published in 1978.

Longyear, Marie, ed. *The McGraw-Hill Style Manual: A Concise Guide for Writers and Editors.* New York: McGraw-Hill Book Co., 1983.

Maggio, Rosalie. *The Nonsexist Word Finder: A Dictionary of Gender-Free Usage.* Phoenix: Oryx Press, 1988.

Martin, Phyllis. *Word Watcher's Handbook: A Deletionary of the Most Abused and Misused Words.* 3rd ed. New York: St. Martin's Press, 1990. First published in 1977.

Nicholson, Margaret. *A Dictionary of American-English Usage: Based on Fowler's Modern English Usage.* New York: Oxford University Press, 1957.

Perrin, Porter G. *Reference Handbook of Grammar and Usage.* New York: William Morrow, 1972.

————. *Writer's Guide and Index to English.* 4th ed., rev. Revised by Karl W. Dykema and Wilma R. Ebbitt. Chicago: Scott, Foresman, 1965. First published in 1939 as *An Index to English.*

Roget's International Thesaurus. 4th ed. Revised by Robert L. Chapman. New York: Harper and Row, 1977. First published in 1911; other revisions of Roget's original classic of 1852 also available.

Strunk, William, Jr. *The Elements of Style.* 3rd ed. With revisions, introduction, and a new chapter by E. B. White. New York: Macmillan, 1979. First published in 1918.

Turabian, Kate L. *A Manual for Writers of Term Papers, Theses, and Dissertations.* 5th ed. Revised and expanded by Bonnie Birtwistle Honigsblum. Chicago: University of Chicago Press, 1982. First published in 1969.

Urdang, Laurence, ed. *The New York Times Everyday Reader's Dictionary of Misunderstood, Misused, Mispronounced Words.* [New York]: Quadrangle Books, 1972.

Webster's Standard American Style Manual. Springfield, Mass.: Merriam-Webster, 1985.

Williams, Joseph M. *Style: Toward Clarity and Grace.* Chicago: University of Chicago Press, 1990.

Words into Type. Based on Studies by Marjorie E. Skillin, Robert M. Gay, et al. Edited by Catherine B. Avery and Linda Pelstring. 3rd ed., completely rev. Englewood Cliffs, N.J.: Prentice Hall, 1974. First published in 1948.

Guides to Writing about Music

Helm, E. Eugene, and Albert T. Luper. *Words & Music: Form and Procedure in Theses, Dissertations, Research Papers, Book*

Reports, Programs, Theses in Composition. Rev. ed. Totowa, N.J.: European American Music, 1982. First published in 1971.

Holoman, D. Kern. *Writing about Music: A Style Sheet from the Editors of 19th-Century Music.* Berkeley: University of California Press, 1988.

Irvine, Demar. *Writing about Music: A Style Book for Reports and Theses.* 2nd ed., rev. and enl. Seattle: University of Washington Press, 1968. First published in 1956.

Poultney, David. "Writing about Music." Chapter 7 in *Studying Music History: Learning, Reasoning, and Writing about Music History and Literature.* Englewood Cliffs, N.J.: Prentice Hall, 1983.

Wingell, Richard J. *Writing about Music: An Introductory Guide.* Englewood Cliffs, N.J.: Prentice Hall, 1990.

Guides to the Publication Process

The Association of American University Presses Directory. New York: Association of University Presses, issued annually.

Balkin, Richard. *How to Understand and Negotiate a Book Contract or Magazine Agreement.* Cincinnati: Writer's Digest Books, 1985.

————. *A Writer's Guide to Contract Negotiations.* 2nd ed. New York: Hawthorn/Dutton, 1981. First published in 1977.

Banks, Michael A., and Ansen Dibell. *Word Processing Secrets for Writers.* Cincinnati: Writer's Digest Books, 1989.

Basart, Ann P. *Writing about Music: A Guide to Publishing Opportunities for Authors and Reviewers.* Fallen Leaf Reference Books in Music, no. 11. Berkeley, Calif.: Fallen Leaf Press, 1989.

Chicago Guide to Preparing Electronic Manuscripts for Authors and Publishers. Chicago Guides to Writing, Editing, and Publishing. Chicago: University of Chicago Press, 1987.

Directory of Publishing Opportunities in Journals and Periodicals. 5th ed. Chicago: Marquis Academic Media, 1981. First published in 1971.

International Directory of Scholarly Publishers. Paris: UNESCO, 1977–.

Luey, Beth. *Handbook for Academic Authors.* Rev. ed. Cambridge: Cambridge University Press, 1990. First published in 1987.

Parsons, Paul. *Getting Published: The Acquisition Process at University Presses.* Knoxville: University of Tennessee Press, 1989.

Powell, Walter W. *Getting into Print: The Decision-Making Process in Scholarly Publishing.* Chicago: University of Chicago Press, 1985.

Miscellaneous

Biguenet, John, and Rainer Schulte, eds. *The Craft of Translation.* Chicago Guides to Writing, Editing, and Publishing. Chicago: University of Chicago Press, 1989.

THE MUSIC INDUSTRY

The following varied lists of sources all pertain to the *business* of music, and thus may be of practical use to those desiring to enter it as much as to those who are engaged in doing research on it. It begins with general guides to the music industry and to finding careers in the field. It then addresses specific aspects: "Performing Arts, Competitions, and Festivals," "Musical Instrument Makers," "Music Publishing and Copyright," "Music Recording and Production," "Grant Support for the Arts," and "Arts Management," and concludes with a list of relevant periodicals, all American except for the British *International Arts Manager.* For further information about competitions and festivals see chapter 2 under "International Music Guides," p. 37 above.

General Sources

Baskerville, David. *Music Business Handbook and Career Guide.* 3rd ed. Los Angeles: Sherwood, 1982. First published in 1979.

Fink, Michael. *Inside the Music Business: Music in Contemporary Life.* New York: Schirmer Books, 1989.

Hale, Cecil I. *The Music Industry: A Guidebook.* 1st ed. Dubuque, Iowa: Kendall/Hunt Publishing, 1990.

Livingston, Robert Allen. *Livingston's Complete Music Business Reference.* 2 vols. Cardiff by the Sea, Calif.: La Costa Music Business Consultants, 1988.

————. *Livingston's Complete Music Industry Business and Law Reference Book.* Cardiff by the Sea, Calif.: La Costa Music Business Consultants, 1981.

Music Industry Directory. 7th ed. Chicago: Marquis Professional Publications, 1983. Formerly *The Musician's Guide: The Directory of the World of Music,* 1954–80.

Pavlakis, Christopher. *The American Music Handbook.* New York: Free Press, 1974.

Rachlin, Harvey. *The Encyclopedia of the Music Business.* New York: Harper and Row, 1981.

Shemel, Sidney, and M. William Krasilovsky. *More about This Business of Music: A Practical Guide to Four Additional Areas of the Music Industry Complex.* Rev. and enl. 4th ed. New York: Billboard Publications, 1989. First published in 1967.

————. *This Business of Music: A Practical Guide to the Music Industry for Publishers, Writers, Record Companies, Producers, Artists, Agents.* Rev. and enl. 6th ed. New York: Billboard Publications, 1990. First published in 1964.

Worrel, John William. *The Directory of the Music Industry.* Evanston, Ill.: The Instrumentalist, 1970.

Zalkind, Ronald. *Getting Ahead in the Music Business.* Zadoc Music Business Series. New York: Schirmer Books, 1979.

Careers in Music

Baskerville, David. *Music Business Handbook and Career Guide.* 4th ed. Los Angeles: Sherwood, 1985. First published in 1979.

Bessom, Malcolm E., and John T. Aquino, eds. *Careers and Music.* Reston, Va.: Music Educators National Conference, 1977.

Busnar, Gene. *Careers in Music.* New York: Julian Messner, 1982.

Cornell, Richard. *Exploring Music Careers: A Student Guidebook.* Washington: U.S. Government Printing Office, 1976.

Field, Shelly. *Career Opportunities in the Music Industry.* New York: Facts on File Publications, 1986.

Gerardi, Robert. *Opportunities in Music Careers.* 2nd ed. VGM Opportunities Series. Lincolnwood, Ill.: VGM Career Horizons, 1991.

Hammond, Ray. *Working in the Music Business.* Poole, Dorset, England: Blandford Press, 1983.

Highstein, Ellen. *Making Music in Looking Glass Land: A Guide to Survival and Business Skills for the Classical Performer*. New York: Concert Artists Guild, 1991.

Hoover, Deborah A. *Supporting Yourself as an Artist: A Practical Guide*. New York: Oxford University Press, 1985.

Jevnikar, Jana, comp. *Careers in the Arts: A Resource Guide*. New York: Center for Arts Information: Opportunity Resources for the Arts, 1981.

Papolos, Janice. *The Performing Artist's Handbook*. Cincinnati: Writer's Digest Books, 1984.

Sharp, Erica. *How to Get an Orchestra Job—and Keep It: A Practical Guide Book*. Encinitas, Calif.: Encinitas Press, 1985.

Stearns, Betty, and Clara Degen, eds. *Careers in Music*. Rev. ed. Wilmette, Ill.: American Music Conference, 1980. First published in 1966.

Summers-Dossena, Ann. *Getting It All Together: A Handbook for Performing Artists in Classical Music and Ballet*. Metuchen, N.J.: Scarecrow Press, 1985.

Usher, Nancy. *Your Own Way in Music: A Career and Resource Guide*. 1st ed. New York: St. Martin's Press, 1990.

Weissman, Dick. *Music Business: Career Opportunities and Self-Defense*. New, rev., updated ed. New York: Crown Publishers, 1990. First published in 1979.

Performing Arts, Competitions, and Festivals

Canning, Hugh, ed. *International Music and Opera Guide*. London: Tantivy Press, 1986–. Replaces *International Music Guide*, 1977–85.

Carlino, Angelo. *The Evils of Music Management, an Exposé: The Facts of Life Every Singer, Pianist and Musician Should Know about Opera and Concert Management*. New York: LaCar Publishing, 1975.

Concert Artists Guild's Guide to Competitions. New York: The Guild, 1988–. (Annual.)

Directory of Music Competitions. Desloge, Mo.: MDA Music Placement Services, 1978.

Finell, Judith Greenberg, comp. *The Contemporary Music Performance Directory: A Listing of American Performing Ensembles, Sponsoring Organizations, Performing Facilities, Concert Series, and Festivals of 20th Century Music*. New York: American Music Center, 1975.

Gottesman, Roberta, ed. *The Music Lover's Guide to Europe: A Compendium of Festivals, Concerts, and Opera.* New York: John Wiley & Sons, 1992.

Gusikoff, Lynne. *Guide to Musical America.* New York: Facts on File Publications, 1984.

Handel, Beatrice, et al., eds. *Handel's National Directory for the Performing Arts.* 4th ed. 2 vols. Dallas: NDPA, 1988–. First published in 1973.

Rabin, Carol Price. *Music Festivals in America.* Rev. and enl. Stockbridge, Mass.: Berkshire Traveller Press, 1983. First published in 1979.

———. *Music Festivals in Europe and Britain, Including Israel, Russia, Turkey and Japan.* Rev. and enl. Stockbridge, Mass.: Berkshire Traveller Press, 1984. First published in 1980.

Smith, Douglas, and Nancy Barton. *International Guide to Music Festivals.* New York: Quick Fox, 1980.

Musical Instrument Makers

Farrell, Susan Caust. *Directory of Contemporary American Musical Instrument Makers.* Columbia: University of Missouri Press, 1981.

Laskin, Grit. *The World of Musical Instrument Makers: A Guided Tour.* Oakville, Ont.: Mosaic Press, 1987.

Music Publishing and Copyright

Althouse, Jay. *Copyright: The Complete Guide for Music Educators.* East Stroudsburg, Penn.: Music in Action, 1984.

Chickering, Robert B., and Susan Hartman. *How to Register a Copyright and Protect Your Creative Work: A Basic Guide to the Copyright Law and How It Affects Anyone Who Wants to Protect Creative Work.* Updated ed. New York: Charles Scribner's Sons, 1987. First published in 1980.

Copyright Law Symposium: Nathan Burkan Memorial Competition. Sponsored by the American Society of Composers, Authors and Publishers. New York: Columbia University Press, 1939–.

Dranov, Paula. *Inside the Music Publishing Industry.* White Plains, N.Y.: Knowledge Industry Publications, 1980.

Erickson, J. Gunnar, et al. *Musician's Guide to Copyright.* Rev.
    ed. New York: Charles Scribner's Sons, 1983. First
    published in 1979.
*Final Report of the National Commission on New Technological
    Uses of Copyrighted Works, July 31, 1978.* Washington,
    D.C.: Library of Congress, 1979.
Hurst, Walter E., and Don Rico. *How to Be a Music Publisher.*
    2nd ed. Hollywood: Seven Arts Press, 1979. First
    published in 1976.
Reed, Mary Hutchings. *The Copyright Primer for Librarians and
    Educators.* Chicago: American Library Association;
    Washington, D.C.: National Education Association, 1987.
Strong, William S. *The Copyright Book: A Practical Guide.* 3rd
    ed. Cambridge: MIT Press, 1990. First published in 1981.
Wagner, Willis. *A Musician's Guide to Copyright and Publishing.*
    Brighton, Mass.: Carousel Publishing, 1975.

Music Recording and Production

Borwick, John, ed. *Sound Recording Practice for the Association
    of Professional Recording Studios.* 3rd ed. New York:
    Oxford University Press, 1987.
Cary, Tristram. *Dictionary of Musical Technology.* New York:
    Greenwood Press, 1992.
Delson, Donn, and Walter E. Hurst. *Delson's Dictionary of
    Radio and Record Industry Terms.* Thousand Oaks, Calif.:
    Bradson Press, 1986.
Hurst, Walter E. *The Record Industry Book.* 7th ed.
    Entertainment Industry Series, no. 1. Hollywood: Seven
    Arts Press, 1978. First published ca. 1960.
Moylan, William. *The Art of Recording: The Creative Resources of
    Music Production and Audio.* New York: Van Nostrand
    Reinhold, 1992.
Rapaport, Diane Sward. *How to Make and Sell Your Own Record:
    The Complete Guide to Independent Recording.* Rev. 3rd ed.
    Jerome, Ariz.: Jerome Headlands Press, 1988. First
    published in 1978.
Ryan, John. *The Production of Culture in the Music Industry: The
    ASCAP-BMI Controversy.* Lanham, Md.: University Press
    of America, 1985.
Wadhams, Wayne. *Dictionary of Music Production and
    Engineering Terminology.* New York: Schirmer Books, 1988.
────── . *The Musician's Guide to the Recording Studio.* New York:
    Schirmer Books, 1989.

————. *Sound Advice: The Musician's Guide to the Record Industry.* New York: Schirmer Books, 1990.

Grant Support for the Arts

Annual Register of Grant Support: A Directory of Funding Sources. Wilmette, Ill.: National Register Publishing, 1969–.

Conrad, Daniel Lynn, et al. *The Grants Planner: A Systems Approach to Grantsmanship.* [Rev. ed.] San Francisco: The Institute, 1979. First published in 1976.

Lefferts, Robert. *Getting a Grant in the 1980s: How to Write Successful Grant Proposals.* 2nd ed. Englewood Cliffs, N.J.: Prentice Hall, 1982.

Millsaps, Daniel, et al., eds. *The National Directory of Arts and Education Support by Business Corporations.* 2nd ed. Arts Patronage Series, no. 10. Washington, D.C.: Washington International Arts Letter, 1982. Rev. ed. of *National Directory of Arts Support by Business Corporations,* first published in 1979.

————. *The National Directory of Arts Support by Private Foundations: Volume Five.* Arts Patronage Series, no. 12. Washington, D.C.: Washington International Arts Letter, 1983. First published in 1977.

————. *The National Directory of Grants and Aid to Individuals in the Arts, International.* 7th ed. Arts Patronage Series, no. 5. Washington, D.C.: Washington International Arts Letter, 1989. First published in 1970.

Olson, Stan, et al., eds. *Foundation Grants to Individuals.* 6th ed. New York: Foundation Center, 1988. First published in 1977.

Porter, Robert A., ed. *Guide to Corporate Giving in the Arts, 4.* New York: American Council for the Arts, 1987.

————. *The Subsidized Muse: Public Support for the Arts in the United States.* Cambridge: Cambridge University Press, 1978.

White, Virginia P. *Grants for the Arts.* New York: Plenum Press, 1980.

Arts Management

Benedict, Stephen, ed. *Public Money and the Muse: Essays on Government Funding for the Arts.* New York: W. W. Norton, 1991.

Dimaggio, Paul. *Managers of the Arts: Careers and Opinions of Administrators of U.S. Resident Theaters, Art Museums,*

Symphony Orchestras, and Community Arts Agencies.
Bethesda, Md.: Seven Locks Press, 1987.

Langly, Stephen, and James Abruzzo. *Jobs in Arts and Media Management: What They Are and How to Get One!* New York: ACA Books, 1990.

Mokwa, Michael P., et al. *Marketing the Arts.* New York: Praeger, 1980.

Nakamoto, Kent, and Kathi Levin, comps. *A Selected and Annotated Bibliography on Marketing the Arts.* Updated in 1983 by H. Perry Mixter. [Madison, Wis.]: Association of College, University and Community Arts Administrators, 1983. Updated ed. of *Marketing the Arts: A Selected and Annotated Bibliography,* first published in 1978.

Nelson, Charles A., and Frederick J. Turk. *Financial Management for the Arts: A Guidebook for Arts Organizations.* New York: Associated Councils of the Arts, 1975.

Newman, Danny. *Subscribe Now! Building Arts Audiences through Dynamic Subscription Promotion.* New York: American Council for the Arts, 1977.

Orobko, William. *The Musician's Handbook: A Practical Guide to the Law and Business of Music.* 1st ed. Self Counsel Series. Vancouver: International Self-Counsel Press, 1985.

Porter, Robert, ed. *Community Arts Agencies: A Handbook and Guide.* New York: American Council for the Arts, 1978.

Rhodes, Naomi. *21 Voices: The Art of Presenting the Performing Arts.* Washington, D.C.: Association of Performing Arts Presenters, 1990.

Taubman, Joseph. *In Tune with the Music Business.* New York: Law-Arts Publishers, 1980.

———. *Performing Arts Management and Law.* 2 vols. New York: Law-Arts Publishers, 1972. Suppls., 1974 and 1981.

———. *Performing Arts Management and Law: Forms.* 4 vols. New York: Law-Arts Publishers, 1973–76.

Turk, Frederick J., and Robert P. Gallo. *Financial Management Strategies for Arts Organizations.* New York: ACA Books, 1984.

Wolf, Thomas. *The Nonprofit Organization: An Operating Manual.* Englewood Cliffs, N.J.: Prentice Hall, 1984.

Periodicals and Periodical Database

ABI/Inform. Ann Arbor, Mich.: University Microfilms International, 1989–. An index of business-related periodicals. (Exists only on CD-ROM.)

International Arts Manager. 1988–. (Bimonthly.)
International Musician. American Federation of Musicians.
    1901–. (Monthly.)
Musical America: International Directory of the Performing Arts.
    Continues *Musical America: Directory of the Performing
    Arts.* 1974–. (Annual.)

Index of Authors, Editors, Compilers, and Translators

Index of Titles

PHILLIP D. CRABTREE and DONALD H. FOSTER are both professors of musicology at the College-Conservatory of Music, University of Cincinnati. Phillip Crabtree is an active conductor and the Director of the College-Conservatory's Early Music Laboratory. He has contributed articles to *The New Grove Dictionary of Music* and *Performers' Guides to Early Music: The Renaissance*. Donald Foster is author of *Jean-Philippe Rameau: A Guide to Research* and articles on eighteenth-century French music. He has published editions of the music of L.-N. Clérambault, J.-B. Davaux, and Franz Beck.